ADVANCE PRAISE
for
Die Free: A Heroic Family Tale

"*Die Free* is a compelling American story. As Cheryl Wills traces the life of her forefathers and foremothers, she traces a critical part of American history that puts in perspective where we have come from to get to where we are. Cheryl writes with the passionate flair of a novelist that makes the book nearly impossible to put down. This is a must-read book for all members of the family, young and old alike."

~Rev. Al Sharpton, President and National Spokesman,
National Action Network

"Ancestry.com is proud that Cheryl Wills used our comprehensive website to make such an fascinating discovery. *Die Free* is a perfect example of why we do what we do! Cheryl Wills skillfully worked to uncover her family's glorious and tragic past; she learned the story of her ancestor Sandy Wills, including stunning details of his sale into slavery, his noble service in the Civil War, and how he used his newfound freedom to carve out a new beginning for generations to come. The author's deep love for her family shines through on every captivating page of *Die Free*. In the mingling of sweet and painful memories, she finds a certain freedom of her own. She reminds us that her ancestors and our ancestors did not live in vain. Their strong spirits will continue to inspire us—if we let them."

~Loretto "Lou" Dennis Szucs, Vice President, Ancestry.com,
Author, *They Became Americans;* Co-editor,
The Source: A Guidebook to American Genealogy

"*Die Free* is a testament of courage. Cheryl Wills' unselfish memoir is a history lesson for us all. She boldly goes where few authors have gone before. She gracefully shares her family's history over the last two centuries and unabashedly proclaims their victory in surviving slavery and Jim Crow in The United States of America."

~Hazel Dukes, President, NAACP NYS

"History is personal. Anyone who has difficulty making this connection should read *Die Free*, Cheryl Wills' chronicle of her ancestors' African-American journey from slavery to freedom. The stories are so deeply engaging that readers will quickly realize that in telling her personal story, Cheryl Wills is also telling ours."

~Warrington Hudlin, President, Black Filmmaker Foundation (BFF)
Award Winning Film/Television/Internet Producer and Director

"Some 200,000 black men fought in the American Civil War, yet their struggle for the right to fight and their heroic accomplishments are largely ignored. Cheryl Wills' compelling narrative clearly illustrates that sacrifice and the distance mankind will travel in pursuit of freedom."

~Frank Martin, Producer/Director,
For Love of Liberty: The Story of America's Black Patriots

"Cheryl Wills' emotions are strong and her voice is grippingly honest as she paints a portrait of the experiences of the men and women in her family. *Die Free* is thus a testimony to the legacy left by Cheryl's Great-great-great grandfather Sandy Wills and a memorable read for those who want to bear witness to a true and heartfelt rendering of the lives of African-Americans over the last 170 years."

~Dr. Brenda M. Greene, Professor of English, Executive Director,
The Center for Black Literature, Medgar Evers College, CUNY
Director, National Black Writer's Conference

"Die Free is an amazing book. Cheryl Wills' account of her ancestors' struggle for freedom over the last two centuries is a powerful reminder that the battle for liberty and equality is a constant one."

~Carmen Marc Valvo, Acclaimed Fashion Designer, and
Entertainment Industry Foundation (EIF) Ambassador

"Die Free is both confrontational and graceful. An epic family story that needed to be told. If you read *Die Free* while riding the bus or train, be prepared to miss your stop."

~Derrick Adkins, 1996 Olympic Gold Medalist & World 400 Meter Champion,
Nationally known Motivational Speaker

"Don't let the smooth and mellow news anchor delivery fool you. Get NY1 news veteran Cheryl Wills talking about the suffering and sacrifice of her enslaved African ancestors, and there's a passion unleashed that you wouldn't believe.

~Nayaba Arinde, *New York Amsterdam News*

"Die Free is a significant contribution to the body of literature that traces the experiences and family heritage of Africans in the diaspora, a journey that is all too familiar. This book is another critical milestone in exploring the cultural dimensions and necessary ties between Africans from the continent and our brethren, the African-Americans in these United States."

~Sidique Abou-Bakarr Wai, President
and National Spokesperson, United African Congress

"Finally, we get the stories through our eyes, through our interpretations and from our memories. It is indeed time for us to remember, to record, and to honor all of the people who make up the stories in our African-American narrative. They are heralding loudly today even as others call them unsung. We hear them clearly on the wings of the Sankofa and we will continue to testify. Cheryl Wills' *Die Free* most certainly is quite a testimony."

~Marva Allen, CEO, HueMan Bookstore, Harlem, N.Y.

"The discovery of Cheryl's great-great-great grandfather has been a fortuitous and unexpected find—tracking down slavery ancestry is never easy as slaves were treated as property, bought and sold, and rarely referred to by name."

~Craig Rice, Association of Professional Genealogists

This book is a mesmerizing journey traveled by Cheryl's ancestors as they endured the dehumanizing experience and brutality of slavery. The author captured the essence of the chaotic, disorganized and disruptive nature of family life after the Civil War. She tells the story with brutal frankness but with courageous grace. Unlike many authors of memoirs, Cheryl Wills didn't skirt the issues and certainly didn't sugarcoat what may be described as unpleasant truths of life in the Wills' households.

I strongly recommend this book as essential reading for those who wish to learn about the sacrifices and the successes of victims of the abhorrent debilitating system of slavery, Jim Crow laws, lack of education and religious misinterpretation of the Bible, all of which relegated Blacks to non-person status.

~Dr. Marcella Maxwell, Brooklyn College
2nd V.P. Greater New York Links

"Cheryl Wills has used her journalistic gift by taking her pen in hand to write the story of her family life and she presented it in a colorful and fascinating way; which is, indeed, the foundation for an electrifying movie. I hope that all who read this book will be inspired to put in writing their family life's journey."

~Dabney N. Montgomery, Tuskegee Airman,
Great-grandson of Joe Montgomery, United States Colored Troops

"Who would be free themselves must strike the blow.
Better even die free—than to live slaves."

~Frederick Douglass, 1863

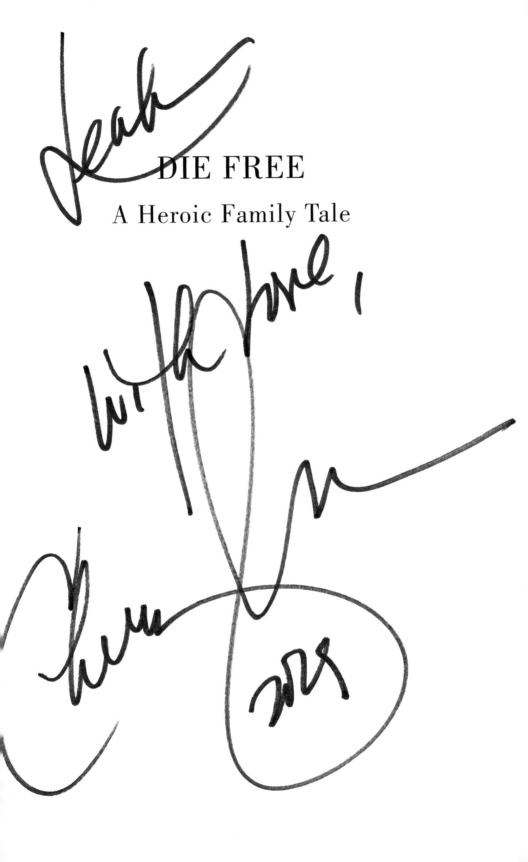

DIE FREE

A Heroic Family Tale

DIE FREE

A Heroic Family Tale

by

Cheryl Wills

Bascom Hill Publishing Group
Minneapolis, MN

BASCOM HILL
PUBLISHING GROUP

Bascom Hill Publishing Group
212 3rd Avenue North, Suite 290
Minneapolis, MN 55401
612.455.2293
www.bascomhillpublishing.com

Civil War pension applications, documents, and letters were obtained from the National Archives and Records Administration, Washington, DC

ISBN: 1-935098-40-3
ISBN: 978-1-935098-40-9
LCCN: 2010934814

Cover Design by Alan Pranke
Typeset by Sophie Chi

Printed in the United States of America

Contents

For
Clarence and Ruth
Fred and Opal
and
Sandy and Emma
You are all the wind beneath my wings.

Foreword

There really are at least eight million stories in New York City. My friend Cheryl Wills, an award-winning television anchor and reporter for *New York 1 News*, who was born and raised in this dynamic center of commerce, media, and culture, has shared thousands of them. I am pleased to count mine among the many she's covered during the last twenty years. Her journalistic coverage is a "who's who" that includes presidents, heads of state, entertainment and fashion icons, and countless others—people often at traumatic crossroads in their lives. In *Die Free*, this talented storyteller finally tells her own story.

Fortuitously, a story she did about the Internet website, www.ancestry.com, is where her journey began. Although DNA tests some years earlier showed her ancestry to be of the Bamileke people from the West African nation of Cameroon, it was on the Internet that she first encountered her Great-great-great grandfather Sandy Wills, a slave-turned-soldier fighting for freedom. Cheryl's formidable investigative skills lent well to her search through hundreds of military records and census documents, the family Bible, and a renowned genealogist to find her American story.

Cheryl's sweeping narrative takes us from the dank slave quarters and bloodstained cotton fields of Haywood County, Tennessee, during the Civil War, to the juke joints of 1930's Memphis, to the factories of Lafayette, Indiana, in the 1940s, and her grandfather's bus ride to New York City in 1950. The spirited story shares the socio-economic environs of the time, from Jim Crow to the Civil Rights movement, to the deadly streets of New York City in the 1970s, and finally to her own place in the world. The music-loving men in her life, both past and present, provide the eclectic soundtrack for the trip and spans blues, jazz, gospel, and Jimi Hendrix. The strong women provide the anchors.

While the discovery of Sandy is perhaps the soul of this journey, Cheryl's very personal one is the heart. For this is also the story of a young girl's unblemished and unbiased love for her father, Clarence Wills. Heroic in his own way, human and flawed, he was a man who was damaged by his own unmet needs and died too young. In *Die Free*, I believe Cheryl has excised her own anger at a world that enslaved Sandy, took her father too soon, and did so much damage to the generations in between. Though it has taken her more than twenty years and a dozen starts and stops for this storyteller to share her own, she has done the work. She is and we, as a whole, are better for it.

Terrie M. Williams, President and Founder of
The Terrie Williams Agency and The Stay Strong Foundation,
Author of ***Black Pain: It Just Looks Like We're Not Hurting***

Introduction

"Nobody knows the trouble I've seen…Nobody knows my
sorrow…"

~African-American Spiritual

I didn't realize my father, Clarence Wills, had suffered from depression until some thirty years after his tragic death, when I read my dear friend Terrie Williams' groundbreaking book, *Black Pain: It Just Looks Like We're Not Hurting*. Terrie opens her book with a haunting quote, "Depression is rage turned inward," and I had an epiphany. I finally understood why my sweet, handsome, and decorated father bragged about his desire to die young (which he did at thirty-eight) and begged my mother to cremate him when the inevitable happened (which she didn't).

My father had everything to live for: a beautiful wife, five young children who worshipped the ground he walked on, loving parents who idolized him, the New York City Fire Department which had promoted him, The Masons, The New York Army National Guard and, on top of all of that, he was a part-time college student, professional gospel singer, talented guitarist, and a deacon in his own father's church. He was a fearless paratrooper who mastered jumping out of moving planes, and he walked into fiery infernos in the caverns of New York City with a fire hose and snatched children from the jaws of death as they lay asleep in smoke-filled bedrooms. However, none of these accomplishments seemed to matter when my dad mounted his cherished motorcycle one fateful night in 1980 and crashed face first into a steel beam on the Williamsburg Bridge. He left us all like a thief in the night.

While goofing around on the Internet one day in 2009, I discovered Sandy Wills. He is my great-great-great grandfather and, at the height of the Civil War, he escaped from his slave master, Edmund Wills, and joined the United States Colored Troops and fought valiantly until the war's end in 1865. Had my father lived longer, he would have learned that he most likely inherited his bravery from Sandy—a lowly slave turned courageous soldier who risked his life for the freedom of his future children and grandchildren.

My "two fathers"—Sandy and Clarence—have much to say from the other side of the veil, and it is my honor to present their legacy to the world. If there is one thing they'd want me to get across to my siblings and to broken-hearted children everywhere (grown-ups included), it is this: live more abundantly and be not afraid.

Both Sandy and Clarence, the bookends for my own colorful life, walked in the shadow of death, without any guarantees about how their brilliant stories would end. Until I filled in the gaps in the accounts of their honorable lives (thanks to records from the National Archives and the United States Military), I was typically timid, somehow shy, and wanted to know the ending before I undertook any challenge or started any project. "What if I fail?" was my overriding mantra. I now know that my daredevil of a father must have spun like a top in his grave whenever he saw me retreat into my unfounded fears.

But now I can *hear* my father say, "Jump, daughter, and figure out how to land later!" Clarence and Sandy lived by that principle and, though they were separated by a century, their fearless and familiar spirits carry through the generations and pour out of my heart like water.

And then there's Sandy's wife, Emma, my great-great-great grandmother, whom I have crowned the "Mother Mary" of our family. Because she filed numerous depositions to fight for her husband's war pension after he passed away, I have hundreds of pages of her personal testimony, where she described, in stunning detail, her life from slavery (she was among the first free African-American wives and mothers after the Civil War), and later as a lionhearted widow who buried three of her nine children. Even though Emma Wills could not read or write— because slaves were strictly forbidden to do so—she saw to it that all of her children could. And while she didn't know her own birthday, she gracefully persuaded her former master's son, Joel Moore, to write down in her family Bible the day that every one of her children was born—a Bible, mind you, that she couldn't even read for herself. My Great-great-

great grandmother Emma had tremendous dignity, self-respect, and vision. She instinctively knew her life was not in vain, and here I am—some 150 years later—to prove her right.

After uncovering my family's important thread in American history, I have learned, and I hope you will also see, that few of us have anything to complain about. Our ancestors—of all races—paid a heavy price for the freedom we enjoy. The debt has already been paid. All we have to do now is follow my daddy's orders: jump—and figure out how to land later. Walk back in time with me and see for yourself.

One

Shrouded in Darkness

My dad's funeral was such a spectacle that I didn't have a moment to cry. I was thirteen years old, and the proverbial other shoe had finally dropped. This kindhearted, guitar-playing, trailblazing fireman, fearless paratrooper, decorated non-commissioned army officer, church deacon, and distinguished mason had fallen so far from grace that the three most important women in his life had secretly, though not sincerely, wished him dead: his devout Pentecostal mother, his bitter, dejected wife, and me—his firstborn.

He had disappointed, humiliated, and embarrassed each of us with such reckless abandon that we had all reached our breaking point. After my handsome sepia-toned father (who always reeked of acrid smoke after fighting fires in the heart of midtown Manhattan) outright lied to me for the final time and left me anxiously waiting in vain for the familiar sound of his tricked-out motorcycle (which he doted on more than me) to roar up to our sprawling townhouse in Rockaway Beach, New York, I unwittingly repeated the phrase I had heard my mother say throughout 1980, in a fit of unrelenting rage: "I hope he drops dead!"

Within seven hours, he did. And none of our lives were ever the same again.

On September 4, 1980, Clarence Douglas Wills was killed in the prime of his life after years of bragging to his mother and his wife that he was destined to die young. He was just thirty-eight years old. He should have been home with my mother, Ruth, to whom he had been married for almost fifteen years, and his five children: myself, my autistic brother, Clarence

Douglas Jr.; my epileptic sister, Crystal Dianne; and twin sister and brother, Celestial Daphne and Cleavon Daryl.

My mother loved my dad so much that she had given all of us names with his initials. But my dad, who had recently become alarmingly selfish and distant, preferred to be in the company of those he had fashioned as his "other" family: members of the Newcomers Motorcycle Club. Those heathens had the privilege of being the last to see my beloved daddy alive. Just before midnight, in a blaze of his own reckless glory, my dad's strong athletic body flew off his motorcycle in a collision with a car on the Williamsburg Bridge in New York City. The strap of his fancy half-helmet— he had become too cool to wear the full helmet—had dislodged and became a virtual noose around his neck, nearly decapitating him as he smashed face first into the steel beam that kept the gritty old bridge in place between Brooklyn and Manhattan. My striking, elegant, and articulate daddy was handsome no more.

Seven days later, on September 11, I sat in complete shock on the front pew of the Refuge Church of Christ on Mott Avenue in Far Rockaway, New York, for my father's funeral. The pastor of the church was Elder Leroy Joseph, whom my father had deeply respected and revered. Through the years, my dad played his guitar in Elder Joseph's church during Sunday morning worship services as a slap in the face to his own father, Fred, another pastor in Astoria, Queens, New York, with whom my father had become disgusted.

To my left on the church bench was my stunning mother. She wore her trademark big brown sunglasses. Her youngest brother, David, an army veteran, sat at her side. The siblings had both met my dad as children and they had grown up singing together in little storefront churches throughout Queens. Despite all the commotion going on at the funeral, I never saw my mom look left or right, only straight ahead, as one single tear streamed in a lone trail down her cheek—she was visibly more angry than sad.

Seated to my right were my four younger sisters and brothers; we must have been a most heart-wrenching sight, each of us dressed in our Sunday finest with our legs dangling from the seat of the long-backed bench, our feet not yet able to comfortably reach the floor. We had no idea how traumatic this single moment would be for each of us in the days, weeks, months, years, and decades to come. The adults in our presence knew that our lives had been as badly mangled as our poor father's body, which lay lifeless before us in the shiny blue casket. But, for that brief moment, we were clueless.

Various groups of uniformed people silently jockeyed for position in the front of the church to claim the ultimate authority over my dad's remains. Little did they know that I felt like he was all mine—not theirs. Dressed in their formal dark-blue uniforms, the New York City Fire Department sat in the adjoining section next to us, so many rows deep that it seemed like no one else was there except the fire department.

Red-faced Irish and Italian men fought back tears for the man they initially despised when my jovial, but cautious, proud paratrooper dad bounced through the doors of Engine 1, Ladder 24 on 142 West 31st Street just across the street from Madison Square Garden and Pennsylvania Station. He was the first black firefighter to join the oldest, and arguably most prestigious, unit in New York City, known as the "Midtown Madness." In his first couple of years in the house, the offended all-white unit gave the "nigger"—as they called him—holy hell. Long after my father quietly proved their prejudices wrong with his exceptional work ethic and quiet dignity, his brokenhearted comrades entered the church with heads bowed as they carried his remains to the front of a black Pentecostal church. They briefly glanced at his five wide-eyed children that they had once taught to slide down the pole in their firehouse. As a fireman first grade, my dad was given funeral honors, complete with an escort of twelve members of the fire department and one fire lieutenant, all wearing regulation uniform. Thousands of other members of the department attended the funeral as a mark of respect, as word spread of the "young black guy from engine 1" had tragically died on the Williamsburg Bridge. Elite members of the mighty United States Army positioned themselves up front during this funeral for the dutiful staff sergeant who earned his two stripes and paratrooper wings the old-fashioned way—with hard work, sacrifice, and fearlessness.

My dad enlisted in the service on a whim during the early Vietnam years in 1962 to spite his father, who had ticked him off one too many times. It was Clarence's only way to get out from under his father's roof and move forward with his ambitions without making a mess of his life. When he learned that he was able to take his trusty guitar with him into the service, he boarded the army bus and departed for Fort Dix military training center in New Jersey.

Also at the front of the church were the secretive but powerful masons from Mt. Lebanon Lodge 173, who tried in vain to respectfully push both the firefighters and the army out of their way as they mourned their esteemed and decorated brother and prepared to bless his remains with ancient rituals.

The church, which comfortably seated about 250 people, was packed way beyond capacity with nearly 1,000 mourners standing in rows all along the aisles, and adults tightly squeezed in pews shoulder to shoulder. Notably standing along the aisles were dozens of black-leather-vested motorcyclists who disgraced this holy sanctuary by not wearing suits in a place where both maternal and paternal members of my extended family had gathered every Sunday to dance in the spirit and speak in other tongues while enraptured in a religious fervor. The disrespectful long-haired wild things looked especially frightening to my siblings and me as they stood quietly with folded arms along the walls of the church, with a hastily cut black cloth with jagged edges plastered over the emblem on the back of their motorcycle jackets. The mere sight of them triggered such rage in my teenage soul that I strongly considered jumping from my seat and yelling to them, "Get Out! Get Out!" But I knew my grandparents, in particular, would not have approved of such an outburst (though my mother would have egged me on).

I eyeballed them with as much disgust as a thirteen-year-old girl could muster. The way I saw it, they killed my daddy and now they were desecrating my family's hallowed church with their filthy intimidating appearance. I hated them back then and I hate them now, because they showed my family no respect and encouraged my father to flip off his five children to party with them. Why my father listened to them, I will never fully understand.

The people seated quietly behind me were the most devastated of all in attendance. In the second pew was my dad's father, Grandpa Fred, who was the single reason any of us were even in New York City in the first place. He was the third generation of Wills born in Haywood County, Tennessee, and he had been desperate to be more than just a guitar-playing blues hustler, which he was in his late teens. He knew only one person in the most populated city in the nation when the Greyhound bus dropped him off at Port Authority in the 1950s. Like millions of blacks who fled the South, he hoped New York would be the answer to all of his ambitious dreams, not just for him, but for his two sons and future grandchildren. Evidently, this did not quite work out as he had hoped. He never anticipated that New York's mean streets would so ruthlessly claim the life of his oldest son.

Seated next to my grandfather was his long-suffering wife, Opal. She, too, had deep roots in Tennessee's Haywood County. She loved New York City but hated what it did to her beloved son, who now lay dead before her. Next to them was their only living son, Van, who, in the tradition of his father and brother, had mastered the guitar and cautiously followed in their footsteps, but wisely veered away from their reckless behavior.

My Uncle Van, who was drafted into the army during the war in Vietnam, loved his brother and knew him better than anyone else in that packed church. A timid fellow who had nursed a quiet depression almost all of his life, Van knew that his brother's day of reckoning had come at last. Hurt as he was, he didn't crack a single tear.

Further behind the family was a sea of brown, downcast faces who loved my dad throughout his short life. There were poor old church ladies, some dressed in black and others in white in the tradition of their African ancestors, who had delightfully danced in the spirit and sang to my father's rhythmic style of guitar playing at his father's tiny storefront church.

There were young men Clarence had trained to sing in gospel quartets, and young ladies he tutored in Sunday school. There were fellow students he met at John Jay College of Criminal Justice in Manhattan, and many neighbors from our hometown in the Rockaways in Queens, New York (where we had all lived for a decade), who thought he was a really cool guy. Then there was a host of relatives on my grandmother's side, many of whom remembered my dad as a child in Haywood County, Tennessee. None of my Grandpa Fred's people, the Wills family, were in attendance. My grandfather had deliberately severed ties with most of his brothers and sisters when they refused to follow him lockstep into his newfound Pentecostal religion with its extremist views. Slighted, he abruptly wrote them off, moved away, and did not keep in touch with them. That was such a shame because they had truly loved him, though they found his arrogance intolerable. On this terrible day, hundreds of miles away, I doubt any of them were even informed about the loss of their beloved nephew and cousin.

Also at the funeral were my mother's parents, Hardy and Sallie Ford, a dignified couple in their seventies, who had ten children and raised them in the same sanctified church along with Clarence's family. The folks seated to the right of the aisle inside this church had known each other for a very, very long time. The Fords were none too pleased to see their beautiful daughter, Ruth (who had been smitten with Clarence since she was a young girl), go through this agony and become his widow at such a young age, and be left with five fatherless children. Prior to their marriage, Ruth's father, Hardy, had cryptically warned his fiesty daughter about the "sins of the father passing to the son," but my mother paid her conservative father no mind. She believed Clarence and his father, Fred, were like night and day. In the end, she tragically discovered the father and the son were almost one in the same.

My dad's funeral seemed to go on forever. Police had shut down the roads leading to Refuge Church of Christ on Mott Avenue in Queens, New York, for hours. Police cars, fire department vehicles, army vehicles, limousines, my dad's hearse, and hundreds of elaborately decked-out motorcycles were lined in front of the church. Most people who wanted to get inside the church had to stand outside. Fortunately September 11, 1980, was a beautifully sunlit day.

As much as my father loved, played, and sang gospel music his entire life, there was nothing memorable about the songs sung during his funeral service. All the great vocalists and musicians, who sat stone-faced in the church, could not summon the courage to sing or play an instrument; they were too weak with grief. My Aunt Elaine's husband, George Williams, a talented musician in his own right, played the organ soulfully. Uncle George was as good as, if not better than, soul singer Billy Preston, who was also raised playing the organ in the church.

The adult choir from my grandparents' church, sang a song. I remember thinking how awful they sounded without their usual backup—my Grandmother Opal on the piano and my Grandpa Fred on guitar. They barely belted out the lyrics to "When We Wake Up in Glory," a soul-stirring Christian song that usually provokes church members to rise to their feet. But on this sorrowful day, no one sang along. The nine church ladies, and two men in the choir, mourned more for my Grandmother Opal, whom they loved like a mother, than for her son. Many felt their former deacon had asked for it and had deliberately thrown his precious life away.

Elder Joseph's lovely soft-spoken wife, Judy, read an abbreviated obituary—an unintentional slap in the face to my father's amazing legacy, which she did not even begin to address. (When my father's brother Van died of cancer decades later, I wrote a remarkable three-page embellished obituary for him, even though he was far-less distinguished than my dad, to make up for the lousy and inaccurate one that was mashed and thrown together for his brother.) Judy's account read:

> "Clarence Douglas Wills was born April 18, 1942, to Fred and Opal Wills in Brownsville, Tennessee. He was educated in the Cleveland, Ohio, school system and Bryant High School, New York. He was a graduate of the following colleges: International Data Processing Institute; New York City Community College, and John Jay College of Criminal Justice. He was also a 32-degree Mason of Mt. Lebanon Lodge No. 173 of New York City. Clarence's work record was as manager of the United Parcel Service in New York, and member of the Greater New York City Fire Department and the National Guard of the United States. At the time of his death he was on active duty in all of the above. His church memberships were as follows: Refuge Church of Christ, Arverne, N.Y., Elder Leroy Joseph, pastor; Light House Church of Christ, Elder Fred D. Wills, pastor; and the Life Science Church, Lynbrook, L.I., N.Y. Clarence was a loving husband, a devoted father, and a dedicated son and brother. He was a dedicated worker, kind and generous, and a friend to all who knew him. To know him was to love him. Besides his family, Clarence's love was his job fighting fires, and riding his motorcycle. Clarence departed this life on Thursday, September 4, 1980, leaving to mourn: a wife Ruth Naomi and five children: Cheryl Denise, thirteen; Clarence Douglas, twelve; Crystal Dianne, eight; Cleavon Daryl and Celestal Daphne, six-year-old twins; his mother and father, Opal Virginia Tyus Wills and Fred Douglas Wills; one brother, Van Luster; eight aunts; eleven uncles; mother-in-law and father-in-law Elder and Sister Hardy Ford; nieces, nephews, sisters-in-law, brothers-in-law, and a host of other relatives and friends."

What a crock. Not only was this astonishingly brief outline of my dad's life wildly inaccurate (he was not active with UPS at the time of his death nor was he a devoted father), but he had never stepped foot in Life Science Church in Lynbrook, Long Island. My mother says he and several other firefighters cited membership at the church for "tax purposes."

My spirited father lived an extraordinary life filled with unique music that rang constantly in his head, jumping feet first out of airplanes miles high, memorizing and mastering the ancient rituals and rites of free masonry, and rising to unchartered territory with the legendary firefighters known as New York's Bravest, and so much more. He contributed an unforgettable thread to the African-American experience by reaching great heights and regrettably, stooping to new lows. At the time of his death, he had brazenly thumbed his nose at the church that had breathed new life into him as a child, and he openly defied God and the angels that protected him, by courting the devil in a foolhardy game of "catch me if you can." Well, the devil finally caught him and, this time, he didn't give him back. But I defy anyone to judge my sweet, free-spirited daddy by his final chapter. There's a comma after that fateful night on the bridge, not a period. There was much more to his life than Clarence Wills' transgressions, spectacular though they were. His legacy proves that his errors in judgment are but a footnote in an otherwise breathtaking walk on the wild side for the thirty-eight years that he walked this earth.

Clearly, no one knew the complete story of my father. Few, if any, knew what made him take his fruitful and admirable life for granted. A man, who could have easily positioned himself to become New York City's first black fire commissioner, went on an unforgettable free-fall in spite of all of the people who loved, respected, and needed him. Why?

Thirty years later, I now have a full picture of my daddy's life. Thanks to archived historical data from the federal government, I understand the factors that likely triggered my father's catastrophic demise. I'm somewhat relieved that it's not personal, but it's still forever sad. For such a long time, I thought he loved his motorcycle and stupid biker buddies, some of whom were also staff sergeants, firemen, and police officers, more than me. Like most little girls, I loved my daddy more than anything in the entire world, and I felt safe, beautiful, and secure in his presence. When he left me for good on that awful September day, I felt insecure, ugly, and scared, and I would feel that way for a very long time.

Lucky for me, but not for my siblings, I was the child my father was most attached to and most concerned with. As his firstborn, he did everything with me in mind and was present for all of my early milestones. When I took my first steps, I fell into his arms. When I spoke my first words, he kissed me all over my face as I said, "da da." But by the time I reached my first academic milestone in the sixth grade and graduated from P.S. 225 Seaside Elementary School, he didn't bother to join me. He probably assumed he would make all of the other graduations. It's a shame he didn't celebrate with me, because he missed his only chance; he was dead by the time I graduated from ninth grade.

My father always peppered me with questions like, "What do you want to be when you grow up?" When I was in kindergarten, I said what many girls said at that time, "I want to be a nurse or a teacher." But, by the time I turned nine, I knew exactly what I wanted to be: a journalist. Of course, I didn't know what the profession was called at the time. I had a peculiar habit of reading and then cutting articles from the *New York Daily News* and adding my handwritten commentary at the bottom of the page from my loose-leaf notebook. I read my words into a tape recorder and pretended I was one of the legendary newscasters, like Roger Grimsby and Bill Beutel, on my favorite news station, WABC's Channel 7, *Eyewitness News*.

I told my dad, "I want to be like the people on TV who look into the camera and go out and do stuff."

My ever-articulate father responded, "Oh, you mean a journalist?"

I looked him in the eyes and said, "Oh, is that what it's called?"

He just smiled at me, laughed, and told me I would make a great reporter someday. He explained how he had seen just about every reporter in the city while fighting fires in midtown Manhattan, which I thought was the coolest thing, ever. That was the only time my father and I connected on a mature level. He glanced at me with hopes that I would go to college and pursue my dreams, and I returned his gaze with a look of "I'll do it for you, Daddy, just watch."

When I finally became a television reporter in Manhattan, about twenty years later on Time Warner Cable's *New York 1 News*, I used my maiden name (Wills) as a tribute to my dad and my grandpa. My father knew a zillion people, and I always hoped someone might recognize the name and wonder if that "news lady"—as I'm often called in the street—was "Clarence's daughter." My husband John was slightly offended, but I made it clear to him right away that my loyalty to my father's legacy would always supersede my loyalty to my marriage. It wasn't a nice thing to say, I know, but it was the unadulterated truth.

As a broadcast journalist, I slowly mastered the art of telling stories about people and finding out what made them tick. If there are eight million stories in this naked city, I feel like I've told almost half of them on the air over the last two decades. I reported stories of people who did notorious things and others who went above and beyond their calling. All along, I could feel my father's spirit pushing me to tell *his* story. I had started and stopped writing his biography at least a dozen times. The last one I started, I titled, **The Sins of the Firefighter,** but I stopped at the third chapter. Not until I discovered that my great-great-great grandfather was a runaway slave who fought in the Civil War—did I move full speed ahead.

Sandy Wills was born on a slave plantation in 1840 in Tipton County, Tennessee, a farming community overrun with black slaves. The frumpy town gently kissed the Mississippi River just north of Memphis. In a community where the summers were dreadfully long and wistfully hot, Sandy likely entered this world in an unsanitary, dark, and cramped shack without windows. Bloodied and soiled sheets were crumpled beneath his exhausted and forlorn slave mother, a woman history would quickly forget.

Those in attendance at Sandy's birth probably welcomed the infant with a muted joy, knowing that the child had just departed the only free world he would ever know: the womb. Sandy's dark future had already been pre-determined; he was born into a barbarous and brutal universe where he'd be forced to sing when he wanted to rest, laugh when he wanted to cry, and pray when he wanted to learn. His pregnant mother, whose name we will likely never know, may have screamed in a fit of agony not only for the excruciating and debilitating pain of childbirth; the piercing shrill that resonated throughout her body also signaled her reluctant endowment to the so-called "peculiar institution," as slavery was referred to by early colonists.

The cruelest irony was that, upon hearing of Sandy's successful delivery, the overseer and slave master were likely beside themselves with joy, certain that the newborn, which was a lucrative return on their human investment, would grow into a strong and able-bodied man. Yet, in many respects, they ruthlessly demanded that my great-great-great grandfather forever remain as he was on day one: a gurgling, dependent, illiterate child. A man child, indeed.

No one bothered to write down the exact date Sandy was born. Who cared? Slaves worked and then they died—they were not expected to be memorable or contribute anything meaningful to the world. No one wrote down the birthdates of horses, either—and like animals was exactly how slave owners viewed blacks. In a country that prided itself on literacy and record-keeping, slaves were not taught to read or write because education has always meant power, and slave owners had a vested interest in keeping slaves ignorant and powerless. However, the date of Sandy's entry into the United States of America was significant because he was among the last generation of colored children born into the wicked cycle of slavery.

What a shame that no one wrote down the day my great-great-great grandfather was born, because he did, in fact, contribute something extraordinarily meaningful to American history. Those present at his birth could not predict that, one day, this baby would summon the courage to toss a musket over his weary uniformed shoulders and point it squarely at those who not only scoffed at his freedom, but were poised to die to ensure Sandy's eternal bondage. After centuries of oppression, this baby, who was born on the fourth of forever, would soon do his part to put an end to the American stronghold of buying and selling Africans for good. On that "uneventful" day, a fearless and noble warrior had just entered the fold. Sandy Wills would take a deep breath and help blow out the candle that had kept human trafficking alive for centuries in the United States of America.

When my son John was born on New Year's Day in 1998, and when my dad died around Labor Day in 1980, not one of us had any idea that Sandy Wills had ever existed. The stark contrast between my son's life, my dad's life, and Sandy's life couldn't be more startling. John's eagerly awaited arrival on that frigid January holiday went smoothly, even though he was born by caesarian section. I was waited on around the clock by giddy hospital personnel who were still on a New Year's Day high. Everything in the hospital was sanitary and safe during my delivery; there were bright unforgiving lights above my head and a mass of thin wires glued to my exposed belly. Shortly after my baby boy was delivered, he was wrapped in the finest blue swaddling clothing that money could buy, and he was monitored by friendly and chipper nurses in pink scrubs who wanted to make sure that *this* infant got a healthy start—not so he could grow into a workhorse on a hellish plantation, but so he could have the freedom to pursue whatever opportunities he chose.

Weeks before John's twelfth birthday, we discovered Sandy's legacy, thanks to a comprehensive website called ancestry.com. I checked the site's extensive U.S. Census reports for 1870 and plugged in Haywood County, Tennessee, to find a little-known, one-horse town where my father, grandfather, and great-grandfather were born. I was stunned to see Sandy's name. *Who the heck is that?* I wondered. Sandy's name stood out because it was an odd name for a black man in the nineteenth century; most newborn boys were given biblical names like John, Matthew, or Thomas.

I instantly feared getting my hopes up about Sandy. Such a link seemed too good to be true. I wasn't the lucky type; the odds of being related to an historical figure like Sandy Wills was akin someone telling me Britain's Prince Charles was my great uncle. Before telling anyone, I hired a professional genealogist to determine if the connection was authentic. It was! Craig Rice, a genealogist based out of Michigan, was stunned that he, too, was able to make the connection so quickly. We communicated back and forth in emails and we were absolutely tickled that we found the historical needle in a haystack.

Tracing slave ancestry is no easy task for African-Americans. I found Sandy on my computer laptop during my day off from work. I wasn't on a particular mission; I was just surfing websites and killing time at home during an otherwise gray November day.

Even with a wealth of accessible information at my fingertips via the Internet, slaves were bought and sold so haphazardly in the U.S. that I *knew* it was extremely difficult to make a definitive familial link.

Additionally, while U.S. Census workers kept track of how many slaves American citizens owned, slaves were not listed by name, only by estimated ages and gender. Curiously, they were also distinguished by either "black" or "mulatto," probably because mulatto slaves fetched more money at auctions.

Furthermore, slaves did not have names to call their own. They were given the surnames of their masters, which could change with every sale of their priceless souls. For example, Sandy's wife Emma went by two surnames, West and Moore. Here's why: when Emma was born, her slave master's last name was West, and when she was sold, presumably as a preteen, her new master's surname was Moore. So, some people knew her as Emma West, while others knew her as Emma Moore. After she married Sandy, she became Emma Wills. My great-great-great grandmother possessed three surnames in one lifetime, only one of which was of her choosing—her African identity had long since been forcibly removed.

Therefore, any genealogist's attempt to track down Emma's whereabouts would be daunting, to say the least. Considering the fact that you have centuries of black slaves with the same dilemma of changing surnames and locations, you're lucky, damned lucky, when you can nail down a relative.

As a television journalist based out of New York City, I was skilled in research and I refused to give up on my quest to find out exactly who Sandy Wills was and his relation to my dad and me. But luck was on my side this time because Sandy returned to Haywood County even after slavery was abolished and the Civil War ended. For generations, Sandy's children, along with his children's children, all married legally and remained in Haywood County, and kept the Wills surname and bloodline intact. In fact, my very own father was among the last of Sandy's great-great grandchildren born in Haywood County. So census documents, coupled with military records, helped me and my genealogist bring Sandy back to life, and exhume a compelling story.

Like many African-Americans, I had always rightly assumed that I was a descendant of Africans who were held as slaves, but this was certainly the first time in my life that I had pinpointed the actual identity of a relative who was held in bondage in The United States of America. This was a humbling discovery.

When I excitedly told my son and my network of extended family and friends, jaws dropped and eyes opened wide. The irony of it all couldn't be more blatant; Sandy had spent his entire life as an illiterate slave and later as an impoverished sharecropper with no worldly possessions to speak of. But in my eyes, Sandy Wills is American royalty. He is worthy of the highest praise because, though he couldn't identify a single letter of the alphabet except an "X," he managed to spell freedom with his footsteps. I lionize his memory because he didn't take the easy way out of hell by jumping head first into the nearby Hatchie River. Sandy Wills spent a lifetime barefoot, in worn and tattered clothing, yet I stand in deference to my great-great-great grandfather because he fought under a flag bearing thirty-five stars, and he couldn't even count that high. I pay homage to

Sandy's last stand in the Union Army because he managed to dream of a bright future, while shrouded in a condition of utter darkness. And I salute this Civil War soldier because this proud African loved America and fought for her most sacred principles, even when she didn't love him back. The happiest day of my life was when I found Sandy; he really put the great in great-grandfatherdom. I only wish my dad had known about Sandy. Maybe it would have given Clarence a reason to live a long life, rather than wishing to die young.

It was time for "that" talk with my son. Not about the birds and bees, but about slavery and freedom. The dumbing down of the complicated and horrific American institution of slavery is an awkward and despicable thing to have to explain to an exuberant child who lives abundantly in a nation governed by its first black president. But for many African-American parents, this conversation is essential.

How could I explain to my Johnny boy, as I affectionately call him at times, that his Great-great-great-great grandfather Sandy was held in human bondage, forced to work without pay, and denied the opportunity to go to school?

With my dad's picture in full firefighter uniform in the background, we both laid on my king-sized bed in our cozy colonial-style home on Long Island. My son's confused expression intensified when I explained to him that when Sandy was about his age, he was sold away from his mother and father and moved to a new place to work from sun up to sun down and probably never saw his parents again. My son incredulously asked, "...and this happened in *this* country?!"

I explained to John how slavery existed not only in Tennessee but in all of the original thirteen colonies, even in our home state of New York. I made a point not to racialize or politicize the era because I do not want my son to ever resent people because of their race or their political point of view. I simply told my bright-eyed, preteen boy that whites and blacks in this country worked together to help abolish slavery and many whites died alongside blacks in the fight for emancipation.

I flipped open my computer laptop, and my son and I stared at pictures featuring slavery on the Internet. My fresh-faced son could plainly see that black people were in the fields and appeared sad, and white people were in charge and appeared mad. I instantly recognized how a child's logic is quite literally "black and white." Without proper explanation and education, youngsters can easily be taught "this type of person is good, versus, this type of person is bad." That was one ignorant line of thinking that I refused to allow my son to adopt. Although my dad was born in a hot bed of segregation, he never felt that way, either. Clarence, who had close friends of all races all of his life, never judged people based on their race. I wanted my son to be the very same way.

"I don't want you to hate anybody, Johnny," I said to him softly as his young mind struggled to conceive of a world so dramatically different from his own. His oval deep-set, chestnut eyes searched mine for consolation. My take-home message to him was that the discovery of Sandy was an historic find, and something to be deeply proud of—not only because Sandy's blood was in our veins, but because his harrowing experience is our family's legacy and a pivotal part of this nation's history. Most of all, I wanted my son to be grateful for the many sacrifices that were made for him, and I wanted him to know that his carefree happy life came with a heavy price tag. If his only prayer at night was a simple but heartfelt "Thanks," that would be good enough for me.

We stayed on my bed, my son and I, adjusting pillows and crossing and uncrossing our legs as we discussed the antebellum period prior to the start of the Civil War in 1861. My son's short attention span clearly wandered and waned; I instinctively knew that he couldn't wait until I shut up. It pained me to see his reaction.

Like any gainfully employed parent in this materialistic society, I willfully fell into the common parent's trap of giving my son just about everything his heart desired. With one week between Christmas and his New Year's Day birthday, he was firmly accustomed to an avalanche of colorfully wrapped presents with his name on them. To John from Mom. To John from Dad. To John from Aunt Crystal. To John from Uncle Cleavon. To John from Aunt Celestial. To John from Mimi. To John from Grandma Ruth, and so on and so on.

My son relished the good life. While yet in grade school, Johnny met celebrities such as Bill Cosby, and he frolicked in the halls of power at City Hall in Manhattan while I rehearsed for an annual political show with some of the most influential broadcasters in the country as part of an exclusive invitation only group called "The Inner Circle of City Hall Journalists." Before he was ten years old, John had traveled to two other continents: Europe and Asia. While in Hong Kong my son had the opportunity to attend the new Disneyland during its grand opening celebration. This kid had lived well all right but, as I adjusted my maternal focus, I saw that he had also been philosophically cheated in a most damning way.

John didn't know anything about perseverance, struggle, or sacrifice, which on the surface appeared to be a good thing; however, beneath the surface, my carefree son was unable to muster any real appreciation for the blood-stained road that got him to his current station in life. As much as I tried to make him understand my own father's legacy, he didn't get it; all he had known was that my dad was a fireman and played the guitar. My son's favorite four words were usually, "Mom, can I have..." How sad, I reasoned, for a black child, with a family legacy of slavery, to think that way. I didn't know how to explain to an eleven-year-old that he possessed infinite wonders in his very being, and that if Sandy could summon the courage to beat down the institution of slavery, then the sky was the limit for his great-great-great-great grandson.

During our talk about Sandy and slavery, I had an epiphany: While Sandy's struggle was multi-faceted, I recognized that my son's issue was more psychological. Johnny had every physical comfort a child could desire, but lacked understanding. My son was intrigued, but not moved; he was mildly interested, but not captivated. Johnny couldn't figure out how to translate Sandy's experience into his being. Where, Dear God, did I go wrong? Or, was I asking too much of a child?

Not that I had it rough as a youngster, but I had my share of childhood trauma. When my beloved father died in the prime of his life, I was left emotionally crippled and demoralized. Only thirteen years old at the time, the trajectory of my simple life had irreversibly changed course. Sure, my four sisters and brothers and I were solidly "middle class" and lived in a spacious five-bedroom apartment in Rockaway, Queens, overlooking the Atlantic Ocean, but we were forever wounded deer. Everything that sprang from our lives from then on was filtered through the prism of our dead daddy, a fireman no more. To varying degrees, we all still bear those crosses to this day.

Of course, I did not wish that my son earn his stripes by becoming a fatherless child—the way I was—nor did I ever wish for him to struggle financially or otherwise; but I had no idea how to *make* little Johnny feel grateful. As far as I knew, only heartbreak gives you such perspective. But I gave it the old "college try."

"See, Johnny, I have to plead with you to be an exceptional student and your great-great-great-great grandpa was legally prohibited from even attending school," I said with my hands waving back and forth. Johnny nodded to me dispassionately in agreement. I further took to my soapbox and passionately explained the "bridge that brought us over," which is one of my favorite sayings when I give speeches to students in and around New York City. I retreated when I saw my son's eyes drift upward at the ceiling fan. At that moment, I realized I had won a battle in tracking down Sandy, but, in this conversation, I was poised to lose the war in my attempts to educate Johnny about his legacy.

"Chillax, Mom, I get it," he snarked.

I knew the spoiled brat didn't get it, at least not at the age of eleven. I blamed myself. It was my fault; I gave him too much.

"Can I go now?" Johnny deadpanned. Despondent, I nodded. Johnny did his familiar childish gallop into the hallway leading to his bedroom and immediately fired up his PlayStation.

"Maybe he'll get it later," I muttered to myself.

Nevertheless, I was excited to tell my son about our Grandpa Sandy; how many kids in his school could actually pinpoint their slave ancestry? Probably none. But another part of me was sick to my stomach for what I did not tell my apathetic son. I didn't tell Johnny, who has never known a day of hunger in his life, how Sandy, like most slaves, ate spoiled food, had rotten teeth, and probably had worms in his stomach from eating undercooked pork. I didn't have the words to explain the trauma Sandy experienced when he looked into his mother's eyes for the last time, at about the same age as my son. I'm sure Sandy cried night after night when he realized that his mother was gone forever. As a mother, such pain was still palpable a century-and-a-half later.

When slave holder Edmund Willis Wills purchased Sandy in 1850, Sandy's new name became Sandy Willis Wills. His true surname and West African identity had long since been cleansed from his blood. He would cling to a new community of "aunts" and "uncles," as they were often referred to by the new, unrelated slave children, who had no idea where their biological parents were, or if they'd ever see them again.

On the plantation, there were Africans of all shapes and sizes, some exceedingly tall, others short, all hailing from tribes and ethnic groups of God knows where. Their skin pigments were in every hue of brown that a genetic mutation could design, from boot-lick black to cotton-ball white, and café au lait to butter pecan; it was a rainbow of colored castaways. Whatever their composition, they were all dyed-in-the-wool, red-blooded Americans, whether the constitution sanctioned them as such or not. And they stood united in their determination to instinctively endure a system that stripped them of their humanity and reduced them to human mules.

Property and slave owner, Edmund Willis Wills, was born in 1805 in the so-called mother of slavery states, Virginia. His parents had also bought and sold slaves and owned a plantation. A family business, indeed.

When Edmund came of age, he joined the westward expansion and moved his wife, children, extended family and, most importantly, his slaves, away from Virginia to Haywood County, Tennessee, where the black population easily outnumbered the whites. Throughout the 1840s and 1850s, the man widely known in the area as Master Wills proved to be adept and successful in his business of buying and selling people, becoming one of the largest slaveholders in Haywood County's enclave of Brownsville.

My Great-great-great grandfather Sandy was ten years old in 1850, when he was dressed and readied for sale in a showroom as a dreaded bell tolled for his transaction. His dark-brown skin, gleaming in the Tennessee sun, had clearly impressed Master Boss Wills. The spry youngster, who assumed his new master's middle and last name, would grow into a man that Edmund could train to do just about any job he so chose, and there was a lot to do in a county teeming with fertile crops of cotton, corn, wheat, soybeans, and fruits. Sandy had no idea, however, that there was seismic activity beneath the surface of slavery. The young lad was unaware that the 1850 Fugitive Slave Law emboldened abolitionists like Frederick Douglass and John Brown. The appalling law gave federal agents the power to recover slaves who had escaped to the North, and disregarded the rights of free blacks who were captured by slave hunters. As Edmund Wills pocketed his receipt for my great-great-great grandfather, anti-Slavery activist John Brown wrote, "The Fugitive Slave Law was to be the means of making more Abolitionists than all the lectures we have had for years." It was a firestorm in the making.

Census takers noted in 1850 that forty-five-year-old Edmund and his wife Harriet Yancey, who was born in 1814 in Virginia, had nine children named Eliza, Sarah, John, Maria, William, Hibirnia, Caledonia, Edmund, and Frances. The well-bred and privileged children all attended school and lived a life of comfort and complacency on an estate built by enslaved African men. They consumed food prepared and cooked exclusively by enslaved African women.

Personally, the most haunting aspect of Edmund's census slave schedule is that it lists only the number of Africans Edmund owned—but nothing about their identities. Gone are the names and family ties. Each slave is listed first by age, next by sex and "b" for black or "m" for mulatto, meaning of mixed race. Sandy is not explicitly named but he is one of two ten-year-old black males listed. Of the slaves owned by Edmund Wills, six were designated mulatto. Why this mattered in the life of a slave is unclear, other than to confirm what critical observers already knew but didn't talk openly about: many white masters and overseers impregnated their black female slaves. Sometimes a slave child played in the field with the master's son and the two boys were completely unaware they were half-brothers. As Frederick Douglass remarked on plantation family life in his biography, *My Bondage and My Freedom,* "The order of life is reversed here."

While the value of Edmund Willis Wills' human and real estate property was estimated at five thousand dollars in 1850, it ballooned to nearly fifty thousand dollars by 1860. He had purchased more slaves even after he bought my great-great-great grandfather. By now there were forty-eight slaves crammed into thirteen dusty and dilapidated shacks.

But Wills' net worth was small potatoes compared to his fellow slave owner, James Bond, who lived nearby in the same district. Records show that Bond had more than 220 slaves, with property estimated at $387,175, and personal or human property estimated at $409,580. It's stunning to see on paper how these God-fearing, freedom-loving, slave-owning Christians were able to strip their fellow human beings of their humanity and force them to into this horrific netherworld. It truly boggles my mind.

By 1860 (my Great-great-great grandfather Sandy was then about twenty years old), Edmund Wills did not own mulatto slaves anymore, only blacks. My genealogist, Craig Rice, believes that the mulattos were either sold or freed. In all likelihood they were probably sold because mulatto slaves were considered a hot commodity due to their lighter complexions and longer hair—they had more sex appeal, if you will.

1860 was also a year of change for the man my great-great-great grandfather called Master Wills. Edmund's wife Harriet died on August 18, 1860, at the age of forty-six. This occurred as rumors of war swept across the South when Abraham Lincoln was elected president of the United States. I wonder if she was kind or cruel to the slaves who called her Mistress. Were they glad that she died or did they weep over the loss of a woman whose children the slaves, themselves, had nursed?

My Great-great-great grandpa Sandy was probably busy in the field and toiling away with hardened fingers that were calloused and bloodied from picking cotton in a vast sea of white fluffy gold that was in international demand. My dad, as a child, would play freely in these same cotton fields, unaware of the powerful legacy hidden beneath the soil.

Meanwhile, some people had had it with slavery and were fighting back. Much of the nation was buzzing about anti-slavery activist John Brown's coordinated attack of a federal arsenal at Harper's Ferry in Virginia. In a noble bid to end slavery by violence, Brown and his followers freed a small group of slaves and took over three buildings. Within forty-eight hours, he was captured and later executed. The event led to a number of slave revolts around the country and notably created a fault line between the free North and the slave-shackled South, where abolitionists and pro-slavery factions firmly dug in their heels in a prelude to the Civil War.

As slaves grew up on the Wills plantation, Sandy hardly knew the earth was shifting beneath his feet. Slaves were conditioned and brainwashed to not only obey but to *love* their masters because the Bible admonished them to do so. On the Sabbath, preachers likely recited the third chapter of Colossians, verse 22: "Servants, obey in all things your masters according to the flesh; not with eye service, as men pleasers; but in singleness of heart, fearing God."

Many slaves, not wanting to anger God Almighty, obliged. Sandy listened to Bible stories about the blood of Jesus Christ, and ministers urged him to abandon all hope for this world and instead pray for freedom and everlasting life after he was dead.

Shameless in their mockery of the Holy Scriptures, slave masters and their ministers regularly manipulated the Holy Bible, even using the story of the curse of Ham to suggest that blacks were cursed by God to serve them for life because black people, they claimed, were descendants of Ham.

Sandy and black slaves all across the South were taught that their sole purpose in life was to labor to make profit for others but not for themselves. My great-great-great grandfather was consistently taught that his life was not his own, and all slaves were warned to ignore violent thoughts of retaliation and revenge against their masters. Whatever Sandy needed in the way of food, shelter, and medicine, would be provided for him by a "good master" whom he was instructed to view as second only to God Almighty. Like all slaves, Sandy was urged to be grateful that he was taken from, what Americans considered, a "savage" lifestyle in Africa. Slaves were prompted to count their blessings and recognize how "fortunate" they were that they were even *permitted* to live in a carefree childlike atmosphere where they did not have to worry about the "business" of the world. I can't help but be disgusted when I think that such twisted logic was successfully used to manipulate my ancestors into a life of darkness.

Slaves who ultimately could not bear the misery of their condition absorbed themselves in songs about death and the freedom that they would finally enjoy in the grave after a lifetime of forced labor. Ironically, when my father sang in gospel groups about one century after slavery ended, he unwittingly sang songs pertaining to this same misery, like "Motherless Child," "Where Could I Go But to the Lord," and "I See the Sign of the Judgment."

While the barbarous and cruel system of slavery mightily struggled to keep Sandy and millions of other slaves in check, there were some things slave owners could not do: they could not blind their slaves' eyes, they could not mute their ears, and they could not, try as they might, break their spirit.

As Sandy grew up in the slave community, he obviously sensed the injustice of it all. Other biographers have noted that many slaves gossiped about freedom, and Sandy apparently listened with eyes and ears wide open because he planned to make a run for it. He couldn't read or write, but Sandy's intelligent heart clearly must have kept perfect notes. And in the simple equation of right and wrong, Sandy judged slavery wrong. In the equation of just and unjust, Sandy deemed slavery unjust. In the equation of life and death, Sandy reasoned that life equaled freedom, and death meant slavery, for chattel slavery was hardly living at all. He didn't need a pencil and paper to write that down, for this was all written in his tortured soul.

When the winds of revolution started to whip and whistle through Sandy's bustling plantation in 1861, my great-great-great grandfather plotted his escape. He didn't need an education to know right from wrong. He would soon make a brazen move with full confidence and conviction that right *and* God were on his side. Armed with that, Sandy didn't *need* to know nothin' else.

Two

A Chink in the Armor

Although my dad lived his entire life unaware that he was a legacy of a Civil War soldier, he watched a very similar revolution unfold before his eyes during his early childhood. My father was born almost one hundred years after Sandy, in 1942—and he was like Sandy on speed. During the 1940s and '50s, my father crisscrossed American cities with his parents, Fred and Opal, who were in search of a better life far away from the very cotton and tobacco fields that his Great-great grandfather Sandy Wills once called home. The Civil War was, in essence, tragically replicated over and over in the decades that followed.

Clarence was born in the springtime in Haywood County, Tennessee, in a tiny enclave known as Brownsville, which was within a few miles of where his Great-great grandfather Sandy Wills once lived. My dad was one of the last Wills descendants born there. Shockingly, these direct descendants of Sandy had never heard of their great-great grandfather's mighty struggle for freedom in the Civil War. The new generation of Wills in the twentieth century had no time for genealogy; mere survival was tough enough. They had to tiptoe around the dangerous rules of Jim Crow, knowing that, at any moment, their lives could be snuffed out for the slightest or even imagined infraction.

Things had modestly changed for the better by the time my dad, nicknamed Sonny, was born. The first child of Fred and Opal Wills was of a deep-chocolate complexion, just like Sandy had been, and was a natural leader who trusted his fearless instincts to guide him. Clarence didn't know that the Tennessee fields that he played in were likely fertilized by the blood of men who fought mightily over whether or not he would be born a free child. Such powerful history stunningly faded into the background of their complicated and desperate lives.

Clarence idolized his father and his uncles, especially his uncle who everybody called W.D., to whom he bore a strong resemblance. "Dub," as he was known, was a skillful hunter and enjoyed his spry little nephew who always tried to do what the men did. Clarence so closely watched everything his dad and uncles did that he insisted to all the men in his family who would listen that he knew how to drive even though his tiny feet could not fully reach the gas pedal. One day when the keys were left in the unattended pick-up truck, my dad, barely four years old, started the engine and shifted the gears into drive on the dusty back road in Brownsville.

After Fred frantically rushed to stop the vehicle, the men rolled on the ground laughing as Clarence jumped out screaming, "I told ya I could do it, Dad!"

From a very early age, Clarence displayed a fearlessness and confidence that led his teenaged Uncle W.D. to declare that he would someday name his first son after his favorite nephew, Clarence Douglas Wills. About fifteen years later, he made good on that endearing promise.

Haywood County, Tennessee, slowly caught up with the rest of the industrialized nation in the mid-twentieth century. Electricity finally took the place of candles and oil lamps; horses were replaced with automobiles and snake-infested outhouses were, at long last, replaced with indoor bathrooms. Best of all, the colored folks of Haywood County had the freedom to travel as they pleased. Immediately after slavery, many blacks changed their surnames—Freeman was a common last name. Some newly freed slaves hit the road and never returned. Some searched for loved ones they had been tragically separated from, while others wanted to get as far away from their old plantation as humanly possible. But the generations of Wills 'that followed Sandy continued to call Haywood County home for nearly a century.

In the 1940s, blacks still did a lot of farming in Brownsville but, more often than not, they at least owned the land they farmed rather than sharecropping on it. Clarence's dad, Fred, nicknamed Butch, was no stranger to picking cotton during the day and belting out the Mississippi Delta blues at night in seedy juke joints. He plucked and wiggled the strings on his wooden guitar in a way that made onlookers sway and sing along. The roots of the spine-tingling, hair-raising rhythms that sprang from Memphis, Tennessee, to Vicksburg, Mississippi, and those who were blessed to have the talent to interpret the fiery music form, were held in high esteem among whites and colored folks alike.

Beads of sweat danced down my grandfather's forehead as his silky tenor voice wailed and rhymed about lost love and hard times. For a short while, he, along with his brother Tommy Wills, were the exclusive guitarists for Sonny Boy Williamson, a take-no-prisoners blues singer who was known in Memphis for jamming one end of his metal harmonica into his wide mouth and playing with no hands. Williamson was born Aleck Rice Miller to sharecropper parents in Tallahatchie County, Mississippi.

Williamson, who was known to some of his fans as The Goat and Footsie, lived hard and played even harder. When he recognized that he possessed multiple musical gifts ranging from the harmonica to the guitar, he hit the chitlin' circuit and wowed his small but faithful audiences in Southern black towns. He met my grandfather quite by chance in a juke joint outside of Memphis and, as a wandering musician without an agent or any of the formalized agreements that come with an organized band, he merely told Butch to meet him at such and such place and together they would jam.

Their casual musical arrangement on the road continued for months. They slept with loose women and spent what little money they earned on liquor and more liquor. This raffish lifestyle suited Butch and Tommy just fine until they realized they were not getting the money Sonny Boy promised to them. Such dishonesty Butch could not abide, though he certainly was no choir boy. Butch had a flair for entertainment and plunged headfirst into the boorish and corrupt lifestyle that accompanied it. My Grandfather Fred and Great Uncle Tommy, unaware that Williamson was destined for modest fame in the blues world, quit the band and decided to go it alone. The brothers would never make it to the big time, but not for lack of trying.

The only day my grandfather didn't play his guitar and sing the blues was on Sunday, out of respect for the Good Lord. Sometimes Fred brought his wife and young son along to gigs in tiny juke joints in and around Memphis. The unadorned venues were nothing to brag about, but the sounds that drifted into the Memphis air were nothing short of thrilling. Make-shift bars inside the dilapidated splintered wooden structures were a fool's paradise for lowlifes who loved to drink. Church folks didn't go, or, shall we say, were not supposed to step foot inside juke joints, but sinners couldn't get enough of the seedy dens of iniquity. Sassy teenage girls with straightened and shiny black hair sweated and swayed to live blues bands arm in arm, cheek to cheek, and breast to chest with drunk men who were two or three times their age. On the few occasions that my dad tagged along, Clarence intently watched his dad's fingers grip the neck of guitar's steely strings and zip up and down, creating melodies from the wooden box with strings that were food to the young lad's soul. Wherever his dad was, and whatever his beloved dad did, is what Clarence purposed to do, as well. The son imitated his father in all things, big and small. There was nothing timid about this darling little boy.

Juke joints were often packed beyond capacity on Friday and Saturday nights. There were no fire codes or codes of conduct. Avowed sinners relished the good times, and the good gossip that lingered after every visit. By Sunday morning, fire and brimstone preachers adamantly warned, in the most colorful language imaginable, how juke joints were the devil's workshop and those who dared enter would quickly find themselves on the road to hell. Sooner or later, most juke joint regulars, who feared dying in their sins, repented and traded the Memphis blues for the hard-charging gospel blues. There wasn't much of a difference in church really; there was also feverish dancing, passionate singing, and uncontrolled shouting, just to a different downbeat that did not have lustful lyrics. Catchy little ditties about the love of one's life metamorphosed with verses about the love of Jesus.

As sweet-sounding and intoxicating as the Mississippi Delta sound was, it couldn't pay my Grandpa Fred's bills, and there weren't many economic opportunities to be found in Brownsville. Fred even took to selling bootleg corn liquor at juke joints, which he prepared in an unsanitary tub, but he still couldn't make ends meet. Stemming from slavery times, blacks in the area were still the majority and the whites who remained in the area kept mostly to themselves. Thus, there were very few, if any, lucrative jobs to be found for blacks. The good-paying government jobs in Haywood County went exclusively to whites.

Meantime, Jim Crow was king in the South, and many colored folks were stricken with unexpressed bouts of low self-esteem as a result. Whites openly despised blacks and were avoided by blacks in public. Prominent signage that directed blacks to use separate facilities and venture to the back of buses took its toll on the collective self-image of black Americans in the twentieth century. More than a few psychologists confirmed that many black folks in fact believed the insults and lies that were perpetuated about them. Clarence, who obviously was an eyewitness to this culture, somehow refused to believe that he was stupid and unworthy. In the years to come, he repeatedly plopped himself down next to whites and took advantage of every single opportunity presented before him. He was mistreated from time to time and called horrible names but, gentleman that he was, he never lost his cool, and he continued to take a seat at the table of opportunity, even when he was clearly uninvited. Clarence never let other people's prejudices prevent him from doing what he wanted to do. If they felt uncomfortable with his cocoa-colored skin, that was their problem, he reasoned, not his. And in almost every circumstance, he won people over to his confident and self-assured side. I'm deeply proud of my daddy for never allowing institutionalized racism to cloud his vision.

Unfortunately, he was a rare breed. Some black girls, with their beautiful chocolate skins permanently kissed by God's sunshine, thought themselves appalling ugly and unworthy. Many black boys of my dad's generation considered themselves less intelligent than whites and incapable of acquiring independent wealth. My dad opened as many doors as he could, and he always encouraged folks to get an education and go for the gold.

But my dad, noble as his efforts were, couldn't change the country's racial legacy. To wit, that old "rebel yell" could still be found in the hearts of the more than a few hateful white men as they routinely and without fear of persecution, lynched, shot, or dragged a colored person to his death while tethered behind a speeding automobile. Every day was a soft martial law for blacks in Haywood County and many other parts of the nation; and as happy-go-lucky as my dad's family appeared, they were largely without sanctuary. While it was no longer the brutal slavery that Sandy endured and grew to hate, it was still such a humiliating and intimidating atmosphere that, once again, yet another Wills in Haywood County had to plot an escape to freedom.

Clarence was swept north with his parents in the mid-1940s during the so-called "great migration," when millions of humiliated and fed-up blacks in the South searched for opportunity in ubiquitous promised lands up North. At the time, Fred and Opal didn't realize that they were at the tail end of the historic north bound population shift of more than four million blacks. It was, quite simply, a no-brainer for the ambitious couple; they needed work and wanted to live without the constant threat of racial harassment.

The nomadic Wills' hoped to find greener pastures in Lafayette, Indiana, where factory work was in abundance. While the area wasn't as remote as Haywood County, the most action Lafayette saw was on the banks of the Wabash River, which is crowned by a picturesque pedestrian bridge in the heart of town. But in the mid 1940s, it was a job hunter's paradise and many employers in the area did not mind hiring blacks.

My Grandfather Fred was a loyal and dedicated worker, but he was never fond of making money for other people without getting his fair share. He was only equipped with a fourth-grade education and, though he possessed an entrepreneurial spirit and the gift for gab, Fred could never quite figure out how to execute his vision into reality. He wanted to be his own boss, but he didn't know how to crystallize it in a country that despised the very sight of him. In this respect, my dad would be the polar opposite of his father because, when he grew up, he would be able to quite easily turn his vision into reality. Of course, it was a little easier for my dad in the early sixties and seventies, because he was (mildly) better protected by federal laws banning discrimination.

After losing two children, one during childbirth and the other due to a childhood illness, Fred and Opal had another son named Van in 1945, but their four-year-old marriage was fraught with domestic violence. The couple was far from their family homestead in Haywood County, and they didn't have much of a support system in Indiana. So when marital tensions boiled over in their household, the lovebirds regularly came to blows, pecking at each other's frayed nerves. Fred, who stood about five-feet-eight-inches tall, did not hesitate to pound on his feisty, opinionated wife who stood four inches shorter than he. They cursed each other and broke their few precious belongings in front of their two young boys.

Clarence, about six years old at the time, tried to shield his little brother from the flying objects which were thrown in a fit of escalating rage; but in a tiny house, there really was no place to hide. These physical altercations between husband and wife abruptly ended when Fred grabbed a fistful of Opal's shoulder-length, black pressed hair. Game over. She loved her hair more than winning a fight with my grandfather. My father hated seeing Fred beat up on his mother—it disgusted Clarence but he was helpless to do anything about it.

On one unforgettable occasion, upon learning that her husband was in a squalid whorehouse, Opal, seething with blind rage, grabbed a rifle from the closet and stood outside the building with her son Van in tow. She told Van to wait outside with the dog as she bolted up the steps to get Fred out, dead or alive. Like a scene out of one of the family's favorite westerns, she assumed the firing position, put her finger on the trigger and told everyone within her earshot that if her husband didn't come out, she was prepared to blow away everything in her path until she found him. Within seconds, her stoned husband stumbled out of a room, pulling up his raggedy soiled trousers. Opal kept her finger on the trigger and used the barrel of the rifle to nudge him toward the door. Events like this frequently occurred between Fred and Opal. Fred would disappear and Opal went chasing after him, including the time when she set a building on fire upon learning that her husband was naked inside with another woman. These days the story makes for great fodder at the Thanksgiving dinner table, but back then it was no laughing matter. The miserable wife was tormented by her husband's philandering and abuse, and she was looking for a way out of her heartache.

One day she gazed out of her window and focused on a little wooden church with a flat roof where happy-looking black people streamed in and out just about every day of the week. They appeared plain in dress but they walked erect and expressed dignity in every step.

The sight of the church folks was appealing to my grandmother. All things considered, Opal was a lovely and sweet-natured girl and her family was well stocked with bright, talented people, but she had become a tad rough and rebellious while dealing with her wayward blues-loving husband. When she walked into that compact so-called Holiness Church, she believed in her heart that she had finally found the doorway to a peaceful God-fearing life.

The pastor was named Elder James Hope and the twenty-year-old wife and mother believed he held the keys to the kingdom of heaven. Elder Hope explained to Opal that she needed to be baptized in full immersion, specifically in the name of Jesus Christ as opposed to the "Father, Son and Holy Spirit." The pastor imparted to her that she wouldn't be truly saved from her sins until she spoke in other tongues and received what the Bible calls the "gift of the Holy Ghost." Their church community was a small-time knockoff of a religious fervor that was sweeping across the country in both white and black communities. The services were marked with feverish exhortations of the coming of Christ with strict resignation from the world, and the firm anticipation of heaven. "Will you be caught up to meet him?" was a frequent question asked of churchgoers who eagerly awaited the return of Jesus Christ in the sky. Elder Hope, a preacher like most ministers of his ilk, screamed his sermons, and beckoned Opal to read the Bible for herself, and focus specifically on Acts 2:38, which says: "Then Peter said unto them, Repent and be baptized every one of you in the name of Jesus Christ for the remission of sins, and ye shall receive the gift of the Holy Ghost."

Opal did precisely what the preacher said. She grew to love that dusty little church. She went there just about every day for one reason or another with my dad and Uncle Van in tow. There was a specific day of the week allocated for Bible study, prayer service, tarrying service, missionary service, choir rehearsal, and so on. Grandma Opal adored the saints, as they called themselves; they were broken souls who were made whole through a rigorous religious discipline. Not one among them was born saved or holy; most had seen their share of sinful days in juke joints, and more than a few had brushes with death. But they all found solace in this little sanctuary and were quite sincere in changing their anguished lives for the better. In essence, they found shelter from life's storms at the church. The gospel music stirred in their souls and gave them fuel to survive another tedious day of domestic violence and poverty. For some, this was the first time they had abided by any rules whatsoever. For others, like Opal, it satisfied an inner longing that they had always searched for. Bottom line, it was better than the wretched lifestyles they had grown accustomed to.

In a flash, she went from being Opal (or her popular nickname, Peepsie), to her new church name: Sister Wills, which she was called by the many thousands of Christians who met her for the rest of her life. Even her husband and her closest relatives called her Sister Wills. When I was a small child, I called my grandmother, Sister Wills, because that's what everyone, including my mother, called her. Only my father referred to her as Mother.

When Opal received the Holy Ghost, only then would she be "saved and sanctified." Until that day arrived, she had to conform to both inward and outward changes. She was admonished to immediately stop wearing makeup, earrings, bracelets, necklaces, and nail polish. No more v-neck or low-cut dresses, and pants for "saved" women were strictly prohibited. She couldn't go to the movies or listen to the blues. Whenever she entered the church, her head had to be covered with a modest hat, or a round or square doily, and the sleeve length of her blouses had to extend past her elbows. Her skirts and dresses had to be well past her knees; floor length was preferred though not always practical in the summertime heat. Fire-engine red and hot pink were no-no's, as well. Saved women were encouraged to adorn themselves preferably in black or white, but earthy colors like green, blue, and brown were perfectly acceptable.

These were not just random conservative rules created by the followers of this so-called apostolic doctrine. Church leaders cited the first book of Timothy, second chapter, ninth verse, which reads: "In like manner also, that women adorn themselves in modest apparel, in shamefacedness and sobriety; not with broided hair, or gold, or pearls, or costly array."

The male-dominated leadership of Holiness churches coast to coast took that verse and ran with it, stripping female members of any sense of enhancement and using that single Bible verse as a means of control over their wives' sexuality. And in the final analysis of this autocratic atmosphere, the hypocrites among the saved men looked upon at their homely and unadorned wives with scorn, and subsequently lost their sexual desire for them, opening the door wide for the mother of all sins: adultery.

There were, of course, few rules for the men to abide by, for they consistently singled out Bible stories that promoted and underscored their male dominance and superiority in all things. Men were warned that smoking and drinking alcohol was sinful and they were chastised to immediately go cold turkey if they were truly sincere about their redemption. They were also forbidden from enjoying secular entertainment and were told that the only music they should listen to was gospel even though it was sometimes indistinguishable from its close cousin, the blues.

Saved women were advised to stay with their husbands no matter how abusive, violent, hateful, or wandering they were. As in the first book of Peter, third chapter, first verse, the church ladies were conditioned to do as the verse commanded: "Likewise, ye wives, be in subjection to ye husbands..."

Women were also strictly forbidden to preach or sit in leadership in some Holiness church congregations because men cited a passage in Timothy that read, "But I suffer not a woman to teach, nor to usurp authority over the man, but to be in silence." That was a favorite among some of the more chauvinistic types.

There were, however, even stricter sects of Holiness churches than the movement Opal belonged to. In an effort to appear holy, those women were not permitted to wear nylon stockings, only leg coverings made of cotton. Nor could they straighten their curly hair, and they were only allowed to wear two colors: black and white. Even Opal thought that was a bit extreme because she loved getting her curly hair straightened with a sizzling hot comb, and she was pretty confident that Jesus didn't mind what she did with her crowning glory, either.

Much in the way that slave masters manipulated the Holy Scriptures to keep blacks in line, black men naively used the same method, twisting ancient scriptures and forcing them upon unsuspecting, truly God-fearing women to fit their dogmatic and fanatic agendas. My dear grandmother swallowed the doctrine whole, refusing even to chew on it to determine its aftertaste or appeal for her innate personality, to which, I can personally attest, was in direct contradiction to her naturally aggressive style. All in all, Sister Wills remained compliant; her philosophy was now the Bible's philosophy and she didn't dare question its relevance. As a biblical saying goes, she "rightly divided the word" and did as she was told. Whoever Opal really was inside, we would never again see in her original gilded glory.

Opal, and thousands of other Holiness women like her, both black and white, abided by these draconian rules, not because they were brainwashed; they entered into this agreement intelligently and willingly because, as far as they could see with their limited education, it was the only doorway out of their immoral lives and it provided instant relief from their spiritual heaviness. Holiness was not a cult, for members did not worship their charismatic leaders and they could reject its principles and leave the church at anytime without fear of repercussion. These upright folks were American Christians who just wanted to be good people and acceptable in the sight of God; it was really was as simple as that. Holiness, in their humble view, provided a direct route to heaven, and that's where they adamantly wanted to go after they gave up the ghost. They didn't want to make what they called an "angry" God mad at them. This was the only place in the world where they could trade mourning for joy.

My dad was baptized into this religious movement while he was yet in grade school, and one day he was stunned, upon his return from school, to find his mother on her knees hunched over on her lopsided living room couch, pleading and tarrying alone for the Holy Ghost.

Clarence witnessed her mutter the words, "Jesus, Jesus, in your name Jesus, the blood of Jesus, Fill me with your Holy Spirit, Jesus" over and over again. Dressed in her worn and faded housedress, her voice rose to bell tones then sank to a whisper until a spiritual explosion occurred. My dad witnessed his mother slip into a trance and utter unintelligible words that sounded like a foreign language that bounced rapidly off of her tongue, which is known as "speaking in tongues." To the casual observer, Opal appeared to be having an epileptic seizure. Upon seeing this trance, Clarence and Van were scared to death and tearfully pleaded for their mother to stop. When Sister Wills finally settled down, she held her sons close and breathed a sigh of relief. She firmly believed she had finally received the gift of the Holy Ghost; however, she would not rest until her husband joined her.

Initially, Fred would have none of it and thought it was ridiculous and extreme. He came from strong-willed people. His beloved mother, Lucy Oldham-Wills, had died when he was fourteen, leaving a sharp bitterness in his heart. His father, Allen, was a pleasant church-going man who always kept of flask filled with alcohol in his pocket. Sometimes, Fred's father whipped him and his brothers for being disobedient, and the lashes were always unforgettable. His father's brutality inadvertently helped create Fred's poor concept of himself despite the extraordinary talent found in him and many other members of his family. Some of his brothers played guitar, while others preferred harmonicas. But their musical gifts were not enough to help them overcome many of their personal struggles. Though Fred tried to run from poverty, it was wedded to his consciousness; the poor soul spent an entire lifetime trying to reverse course.

My Grandfather Fred, from all outward appearances, was an easygoing and friendly person with a warm and inviting smile, but he nursed an inner wrath that was devastating to anyone who set him off. He was of a light golden-mustard brown complexion with sharp facial features, extraordinarily high cheekbones, protruding brow bones, small penetrating eyes, and a wiry build. He was handsome to every girl who laid eyes on him, and he knew it. He had a smooth swagger with his limp left leg, which never set right after a childhood fall in Haywood County. His limp didn't diminish his sexual appeal one bit; hobbled as Fred was, he could always get the girl.

Ultimately, Opal was the one to nail him down. Fred was five years older than she, but the deep-cocoa-colored, sassy girl with a Coke-bottle figure and round eyes found Butch irresistible. Fred was already a chain-smoker and hard-core drinker. Opal, who neither drank nor smoked, was only fourteen years old.

While in Lafayette, my grandmother dressed my dad and Uncle Van in their Sunday best and headed out of her front door on the Sabbath, and left her drunken husband asleep, reeking of cigarette smoke, on the tattered couch. Clarence and Van were always sharp; their suits were neatly pressed and their shiny black shoes reflected the Sunday morning daylight as they walked around the corner to church.

Once inside the small neighborhood church, Sister Wills placed her boys front and center in the modest sanctuary and took her place on a tiny piano stool. As a child, my grandmother learned by ear to play negro spirituals by primarily tickling the five black keys on the piano, known by some music historians as the "slave scale." Most of the melodies intoned by African slaves are believed to have roots in the West African sorrow chant, which my grandmother unwittingly bore witness to whenever she raised her voice to sing. Her short, stubby fingers effortlessly glided across the yellowed piano keys and, as she sang, a deep, throaty wail born of the Mississippi Delta blues oozed from her soul. Her resonant alto voice was as clear as a bell and as deep as the legendary Southern river. The two dozen or so churchgoers in attendance loved to hear Sister Wills burst into song because she closed her eyes, opened her mouth wide, and let it rip. When the music and the spirit in the church reached its climax, Sister Wills would abruptly jump off that delicate piano stool and dance with her head bowed to the gospel beat in a dizzying fit of the Holy Spirit, known as shouting. It was the most joy she had ever experienced in her life, and Clarence and Van sat quietly in the rickety, lopsided wooden chairs and tapped their feet as they watched their mother rejoice. They didn't know exactly what was going on but the church music they heard was being furrowed in their little bones.

The tiny congregation sang upbeat songs like:

At the cross, at the cross
Where I first saw the light
And the burden of my heart
Rolled away ...
It was there by faith
I received my sight
And now, I am happy all the day.

Songs like that were sung from the top of their lungs and often the same stanza was repeated over and over until it came to a natural conclusion. The songs could go on for five minutes or, if the spirit was intense, it could go on for fifteen minutes, or even longer. There were no hymn books; church members just improvised as they went along. Most of the songs they sang were old Negro spirituals that once rang out from slaves on the plantation, which were spiced up with a swinging piano and a double hand clap and foot stomp. It was infectious music that fed their weary souls. The music penetrated their inner sadness and gave them the feeling of unadulterated bliss.

There was a standard part of the church program called "testimony service," where the dozen or so "saints" stood from their seats and one by one spoke passionately about whatever issue concerned them. Sister Wills loved to testify and it often started like this: "Praise the Lord, Saints. Giving honor to God, Pastor Hope, all the deacons, missionaries, and friends. Ain't God good?!"

And with her strong motherly arms waving left and right and her booming alto voice rising, she explained how she prayed in earnest for her husband to turn his life around and join the church. She relentlessly repeated this same testimony Sunday after Sunday and badgered Fred, until he finally showed up to Elder Hope's little sanctified church alongside her. The church community welcomed him with open arms and Fred, now Brother Wills, felt right at home.

Naturally, he brought along his guitar and unabashedly played the same Mississippi Delta blues riffs that he knew so well and reworked the music to fit their simple gospel songs. Not all black Christians were comfortable with that and, in the years to come, Fred was thrown out of churches for desecrating holy spirituals with what they deemed boogie-woogie music in disguise. But Elder Hope thought the sound was great. With Fred's electric guitar in the mix, the church music got a sudden jolt and the excited members stood and feverishly clapped their hands, stomped their feet, and banged the goatskin of their worn tambourines. Fred repented of his sins, vowed to quit smoking and drinking, and was baptized in a full body immersion ritual in the name of Jesus Christ (as opposed to the Father, Son, and Holy Spirit), which was of critical importance to Holiness members. Brother Wills had turned over a new leaf…or so he hoped.

The Sunday sermons, however, did not mesh well with Fred's secret visions of grandeur. He wanted to be a successful entrepreneur some day, but his pastor's philosophy was essentially that of poverty. Elder Hope, and many other ministers of this movement, frowned upon wealth by citing a legendary Bible verse in Matthew that reads, "It's easier for a camel to go through the eye of the needle, than for a rich man to enter the kingdom of God." A host of Holiness preachers, North and South, used that single metaphorical verse to demonize people who were wealthy, openly and quite blatantly suggesting that they were destined for Satan's bottomless pit because they loved money.

With that, a religious cycle of poverty gained firm traction in the black community. Once again, the Bible was wielded, however unwittingly, to disenfranchise black folks, men in particular, and encourage them to abandon all earthly goals for success in the most prosperous and advanced nation on earth, which their great-grandparents had helped build as slaves. Slave owners had famously used the Bible to encourage slaves to blind their eyes to success and independence and, tragically, blacks were now doing it to themselves, all in the name of Jesus.

There were few, if any, discussions in the church about how to prepare children for college or better jobs; most discussions centered on church rituals and functions. It was such a shame. Young industrious men, already demoralized by racism and Jim Crow laws, were further stripped of their inner ambitions, all for the sake of "holiness." Stunning and intelligent young ladies, who were perfectly capable of doing more than cleaning toilets, were exalted for their lack of moxie and persuaded to marry and have children, and nothing more. It was a most pitiful sight; a panoramic sweep of these Holiness churches in the 1940s shows members who were intelligent enough to be doctors, lawyers, engineers, poets, and so much more. But they used the Good Book to solidify their feelings of unworthiness and they proceeded to suck the life out of each other. Jesus said, "I come that you might have life, and have it more abundantly." Somehow, these good Christians, sincere and dedicated in their efforts, couldn't grasp the full meaning of that concept.

They also didn't embrace their own African selves. One of the other devastating impacts of Jim Crow was that the system not only despised blacks, it encouraged blacks to despise themselves and distance themselves from their African heritage. My grandparents, like most blacks in the 1940s, called themselves "colored people"—unaware that they were further sanitizing themselves of their true identity. They were Africans, plain and simple, and if anyone dared to call them such during this period, it was considered an insult. Jim Crow had made Africa a dirty word, and many blacks at that time believed it wholeheartedly because the only thing that they had been taught about Africa was that the continent was full of wild savages and cannibals—damnable lies. Even though I am proud to have tracked down my Great-great-great grandfather Sandy Wills, I am still disheartened that I will never know who his parents were or their original African ancestry, because there's no record of him until he was sold to Edmund Willis Wills in 1850. About three or four generations prior to this so-called sale, his great-great-great grandparents were stolen from their native homeland and put on ships and brought to America.

In 2006, I did a news report on a company called African Ancestry, where they swiped the inside of my cheek with a cotton swab and submitted it into their DNA database. Based on their results, they gave me a certificate which claimed I was partly a paternal descendant of the Bamileke people from the West African nation of Cameroon. I thought this was very interesting, but it in no way gives me a crystal clear picture of exactly who I am. During the transatlantic slave trade, Africans from all over the west coast and beyond were mixed together—the human contraband was not separated by ethnicity, tribe, or religion. So, through the ensuing years in colonial America, Nigerians mated with people from Cameroon and folks from Senegal procreated with natives from Ghana—and so on. While one thin thread of my DNA may indicate a Cameroonian link, many other holes in my ancestry remain unknown.

Unlike my grandparents, I feel honored to call myself a daughter of Africa and, had Fred and Opal been properly educated in a society that viewed them without contempt, my grandparents would have been proud of their heritage, too. When my grandmother danced in church, she was wholly unaware that the motions of her fancy footsteps were set in motion long ago in Africa. The swivel of her hips and the songs that bounced off her tongue were not indigenous to North America; they were reminiscent of a colorful and vibrant African tribe that none of us can pinpoint. Her round stunning face and deep chocolate color came from a continent that she dared not even utter its name in personal references. When she spoke in tongues while enraptured in the spell of the Holy Spirit, even I could discern the native tongue of an African chant; society tried to make her deny it—but it was right there in the fullness of her mouth. The music, her laughter, her strength, it was all from Mother Africa, and it was something of which to be proud—not ashamed.

These days, Africans from all across the continent are relocating to New York and I've had the pleasure of meeting many of them, such as Sidique Wai, who is the esteemed president of the United African Congress, which is based in New York City. He is a proud and dignified activist who was born in Sierre Leone. He is successfully bridging the gap between Africa and the Americas. I greatly admire him because he can pinpoint the home of his ancestors and return there and speak their names and sleep in their beds. I am a daughter of Africa with no place to lay my head. To Africa, I am but a visitor and a tourist—even though my bloodline is buried in its rich soil. I look at Mr. Wai and wonder if we are perhaps cousins...I also wonder how my dad would have conducted his precious life had his umbilical cord from Africa not been severed long ago.

When I was a student at Syracuse University, I joined the Student African-American Society, also known as SAS, and I proudly wore a symbolic pin that was the African continent. Sometime in 1988, my Grandpa Fred saw it and said to me, "Why are you wearing that? What's wrong with you, girl? You don't do that."

He was basically telling me—didn't you get the memo that we are supposed to be ashamed of our African roots? I defiantly said to my grandfather with fire in my eyes, "Grandpa, do you know who you are? Do you have any idea?"

He abruptly turned from me and refused to answer. I didn't follow up because I didn't want to be disrespectful to the old preacher, but I'd like to believe I severed the last thread of Jim Crow in his heart. He didn't have an answer because he already knew the answer. Africa burned in my eyes that stared into his. Nothing more needed to be said.

Despite Fred and Opal's new dedication to that old-time religion, the winds of revolution were again sweeping across just about every state in the U.S., including Indiana. In the mid-1950s, the sudden push for civil rights was picking up steam; however, this time, both Northerners and Southerners resisted full-scale integration. Times were rough everywhere as whites felt threatened by blacks who defiantly demanded equal treatment and protection under the law. And this time, the entire drama was played out on national television. Cub and seasoned reporters armed with camera crews recorded the ruthless actions of mobs backed by Southern police officers who wielded bats, clubs, and fire hoses on their fellow citizens. The world was watching.

Fred and Opal wanted nothing to do with the civil rights protests, and were content living below the racial radar. They held good wishes for emerging civil rights leaders like A. Phillip Randolph and the young Martin Luther King, but otherwise they minded their business. The apathetic couple conveniently hid behind the cross of Jesus Christ. God, they reasoned, would fight their battles in their place and they even sang popular gospel songs about being a soldier in the army of the Lord. They constantly sang a song penned by Lena Johnson McLin in 1929:

I'm a sold-ier,
in the army of the Lord,
I'm a sanctified soldier,
In the ar-my.

I am certain that these soulful church members did not sing the song the way Ms. McLin originally arranged it. Like most gospel singers, they kept the lyrics and jazzed up the melody. Sister Wills often dragged out the word "soldier" with her blessed Southern drawl that wafted through the sanctuary and bounced through the door and out into the street. These saints weren't just singing church songs, they believed what they were singing; they truly envisioned themselves in a battle against Satan's army.

As such, they prayed for people who despitefully used them, and trusted God and the winds of fate to avenge every wrong thing that happened to them. Fred and Opal didn't join their local NAACP, and they didn't quarrel with the fact that they were treated like second-class citizens. They prayed that a just God would, one day, make it right. During this time, the woman known as the Queen of Gospel, Mahalia Jackson, popularized a catchy tune that summed up some Christians' lack of involvement in the growing civil rights movement. The song is called, "If You Just Keep Still"

Sometimes I stare
With folded arms,
And the tears come
Running down.
Lord, you said you'd
You'd fight my battles,
If I just keep still.

The New Orleans-born powerhouse sang that song with such conviction that church folks everywhere sang along, but some took the lyrics to heart. "Keep Still," for some, became code for "do nothing" and let God take care of your problems. For activists, it meant: take a stand, but don't fight back. Either way, as blacks were getting their heads beaten bloody from Montgomery to Memphis during civil rights protests, my grandparents, Fred and Opal, "kept still."

But in truth, the tiny seeds of fear that were implanted in their great grandparents had blossomed in their fearful hearts. To their point, they knew that some white people had absolutely no problem, and even delighted in, murdering blacks in broad daylight who were smeared and tagged as troublemakers. Neither Fred nor Opal possessed a speck of that unrelenting courage that Sandy Wills had when he risked life and limb by joining the United States Colored Troops during the Civil War. In freedom, they were more afraid than Sandy was during slavery.

Sandy would roll over in his grave had he known that a half century after his death, his children's children would still be afraid to fight for their rights. He'd be stunned to learn that not only did his heirs not know his name, they didn't even know that he fought for their freedom in a battle that nearly divided the United States of America in half. Exhumed, my dear great-great-great grandfather would most certainly be found face down.

Brother and Sister Wills now classified themselves as saints—meaning they were literally "holier than thou." They were, as they liked to chant, "Saved, sanctified, Holy Ghost-filled and fire-baptized," meaning they lived a holy lifestyle, free of profanity, adultery, fornication, and greed. They prayed, read their Bibles, and paid tithes to the church from the little money they earned. Often, they fell prostrate on the church floor, writhing in the spirit, and sometimes foaming at the mouth, prompting the negative characterization of holy rollers. They didn't like being called names, but they were not surprised; they knew full well that they were a unique brand of Christianity.

Opal had been raised in a conservative Colored African Methodist Episcopal church, where the preacher didn't shout and the church members didn't sing too loud. They sang century-old Negro spirituals and adopted many of the traditions of the white Methodists. As a child, Fred went to the same type of church out of obedience to his adoring mother but, after she died, he couldn't be bothered with Sunday services, though he maintained a grudging respect for the Sabbath. The religious couple was aware that onlookers considered them strange and unorthodox, but they were completely convinced that they were on the fast track to heaven. They even had an air of superiority about them, firmly believing they knew a secret about God that the masses did not. They thought that, one day, they'd be "caught up" to meet Jesus in the air and, as they were whisked away that glorious day, they would peer over their sanctimonious shoulders and relish having the last laugh.

Their discipline, however, lasted for a matter of weeks. Even the Holy Ghost couldn't shield them from the wickedness of the world. They still lashed out against each other and Fred especially would "backslide," as sinning was referred to in their church, every now and again. He couldn't resist the adorned and embellished women so unlike his reformed plain-Jane wife, though he completely approved of Opal's renouncement of beautification. Floozies were drawn into Fred's deep-set eyes, and how they loved to kiss his high cheekbones and slip their tongues past his pearly white teeth. My Grandmother Opal, Holy Ghost notwithstanding, prayed that Jesus would give her the strength to resist her homicidal impulses toward her husband, who had been ordained a deacon and later a minister. But not unlike many hot-blooded Tennessee gals, Opal was prepared and equipped to stand by her man.

Disappointed with the pace of his life in Lafayette, Indiana, Fred was ready to move again. He linked up with a man at a church convention, who told him that he had a business he wanted him to manage and an apartment upstairs that in which he could reside in New York City. None of his kin from Haywood County had ever visited New York City, but they had all surely heard awesome things about the towering magnificent metropolis, where big money ruled and streets were paved of gritty gold. A couple of years before his death, I interviewed my Grandpa Fred for a black history month news segment about the great migration. He explained to me how he saw a "sketch" of New York City as a teenager and couldn't rest until he saw the sparkling city with his own eyes. My grandfather also told me that he couldn't "imagine" how people in New York City made so much money.

Unable to obtain cash for a bus ticket, Fred strapped his guitar on his back and walked to a local Greyhound bus station. As long as he had his trusty guitar and a hat, the blues-loving, down-on-his-luck, country boy could never be broke. Many times over the years, Fred had balanced his small frame on a wooden crate in Memphis and sung for his supper. Fred's sonorous voice sizzled with a Tennessee yodel that reeked of pain and joy. People of all races, ages, and persuasions stood before him as Fred lustily crooned and kept time with his right foot. Some tossed dimes and nickels into his hat and, on a good day, particularly a payday, he might get a few crumpled dollar bills.

As he crooned in front of the bus station in Lafayette, a tall, white bus driver stood before him. "Whatcha doing here, boy?"

Fred, mind you, was an adult, and not at all miffed by being called a boy. He stopped singing, but he kept playing without missing a beat. "Tryin' to git up fare to git to New York."

The driver said, "You can sho' play that thang…come on, don't worry about no ticket; just help me kill time by playin' some of that during the ride."

Fred picked up his Stetson hat, poured the change into his bony hand and put it in his pocket. He tossed his money-making guitar over his back, clumsily put his hat on his head, dumped the milk crate to the side, and boarded a bus bound for the promised lands of all promised lands: New York City.

After profusely thanking the bus driver, Fred sat in the front seat and sang his heart out. Fred's live music was much better than a radio, which the bus driver didn't have. And it certainly beat the dull buzz of the bus engine as it whirred across the American countryside. In between songs, the two strangers became fast friends. Fred struck up a conversation with the driver, who kept his eyes on the road and his hands on the large round wheel. "Where you from, boy?" the dark-haired, uniformed bus driver asked.

"Roundabout Haywood County, about fifty miles outside of Memphis," Fred replied as he raised his tenor voice a notch due to the constant hissing of the bus exhaust.

The driver briefly caught eyes with Fred and turned his attention back to the highway. "Why you goin' to New York City?"

"Got some people I wanna connect with up there," Fred said.

The long bus ride had stops throughout Indiana, Ohio, Pennsylvania, and New Jersey. Fred catnapped at night and woke up with excitement as the bus finally reached the New Jersey Turnpike.

Fred strummed his guitar again. As a "saved" man, a minister no less, Fred technically shouldn't have been singing the blues, but he bent the self-imposed Holiness rules in the same way that he bent the six guitar strings to entertain a busload of strangers.

The bus driver professed his love for country music first, and blues second. "You know Chet Atkins? He's from Tennessee, like you!"

Fred's first love was country music. "Boy, ol' Atkins is something else, I wish I could pick like him."

The driver deadpanned, "You damn close, boy, damn close."

As the bus rolled closer to the George Washington Bridge, Fred put down the guitar and waited for a glimpse of the great city of steel in the sky. It was Fred's first time to New York and the celebrated town held an air of great mystery for him. With the rectangular perimeters of the city's skyline coming into focus, Fred singled out the Empire State Building. He had arrived. What was once a childlike dream was now a reality. For the first time in his life, Fred felt powerful and free.

Fred's childhood in Haywood County was suffocating and boring; there weren't any skyscrapers or entertainment venues, just acres and acres of flat, rich land. If you wanted a piece of the action, you had to go to Memphis or Nashville. Haywood County was best for sleeping. Fred longed to be where the action was, and he found action in abundance in New York City.

The approach of the George Washington Bridge was especially thrilling because Fred had never before seen a bridge of such immense proportions. He had lived in Chicago for a short spell and even that dynamic city didn't have a bridge like this. The spectacular suspension bridge that stood majestically over the Hudson River bowled Fred over. As a youngster in the 1930s, he remembered hearing some of his uncles say it was biggest bridge in the world. Fred observed its winding cables and imposing steel beams and wondered how man created such a colossal thing, for it seemed like something only God himself could make. The bridge's towering arches were so high that Fred had to crane his neck and lean against the yellowed bus windows to see the top of it.

This gleaming bridge, which seemed to touch heaven itself, represented exactly why Fred was on the run. He wanted to be near people who did great things; perhaps, he secretly hoped, he could learn to do some great things himself. Or maybe his two sons would rub elbows with greatness. Fred wanted to build a bridge from Haywood County's barrenness and extend it to New York City's prosperity. With a trail of relatives who died in virtual anonymity in Haywood County, Fred's cause was a noble one; he wanted people to remember him when he was gone. The Big Apple contained the seeds to eternal life.

It was time to get off the bus. Fred effusively thanked his benevolent driver and navigated his way around the congested Port Authority bus depot on 42nd street that had only opened on December 15, 1950. In a matter of minutes he crossed one of the most famous bridges in the world, stepped foot in the biggest and busiest bus station in the country, and melted in the crowd. It was a no-brainer, Fred never looked back.

Needless to say, that ol' country boy felt a little out of place among the city slickers at first. His Southern drawl stood in stark contrast to the boisterous children of immigrants who had created a dialect all their own. With his wife Opal and their sons, Clarence and Van waiting, albeit impatiently, in Indiana, Fred took in the sights of the grand city and fell in love over and over again.

He made a few quick friends at Daystar Church of our Lord Jesus Christ, a Holiness church in Corona, Queens, and they told him how to get to the Statue of Liberty, where he proudly posed for a tourist picture in 1956. He was dressed to the nines in a dark suit and tie, accented with his Stetson hat delicately tilted to the side, a nod to his Southern charm. Lady

Liberty must have been impressed that the great grandson of a slave had made it safely to her base.

Fred stared up at the iconic crown that he had only seen in black-and-white photographs and dabbed his eyes. He couldn't believe that he was on New York City soil. The city was in the midst of a wave of prosperity and Fred was excited about his future. Riding the subway back to his one-room flat in Queens, he looked into the eyes of his fellow straphangers. They all appeared to have pockets full of money as they buried their heads in newspapers or gazed out the subway car's fuzzy windows, all the while keeping their perfect balance with arms raised and hands locked on the worn leather straps.

Fred desperately wanted to be somebody. For the first time in his life, he felt like a man on the verge of greatness. He faced his first disappointment when he learned that the so-called store, which he was supposed to manage, wasn't really a store at all. He had been hoodwinked. But it didn't matter. Now that he was in New York, he was going to make his own way with odd jobs and stay for a while.

Right then and there, Fred bid farewell to the Hatchie River and embraced the Hudson River. No more cotton fields, only big-city ball fields where he watched Jackie Robinson steal bases with the Brooklyn Dodgers and Mickey Mantle knock balls into the bleachers with the New York Yankees. In a seamless transition that first took place in his mind, Fred was a New Yorker. Oh, he knew full well it was a dog-eat-dog town, but he felt he had the teeth to bite and fight his way to getting a piece of the pie. And he only wanted a small piece anyway. His dream was to set up a big Holiness church and have a side business selling food. This was his simple little American dream.

Fred could not, however, avoid the sting of racism in New York City, but he was mildly comforted to learn that it wasn't really personal. Just about every New Yorker had an axe to grind against somebody. It wasn't exclusively black versus white in New York, the way it was in the South. Italians clashed with Irish, Christians clashed with Jews, blacks clashed with Latinos, and so on. But when everyone's prejudices were boiled down and shaken together, they were all transplanted New Yorkers engaged in a gritty rat race and, if you had the money to play the game, you were in. Money talked and B.S. walked in this town. The Civil War here was less racial than it was about the haves and the have-nots. And that suited Fred just fine because he was determined to side with the "haves."

As the weeks wore on, Fred settled in Long Island City, Queens. It was the largest neighborhood in the massive borough with seven zip-codes, and closest to the moneyed island of Manhattan—with its own span called the Queensboro or 59th Street Bridge, which snaked over the East River into the borough.

Fred quickly landed a job as a short order cook in a greasy restaurant situated near elevated subway tracks that melted into the 59th Street Bridge. The dive fed hungry construction workers who did ten-hour shifts in the industrial parts of the community. Fred became a regular at the junkyard in the neighborhood because he performed lots of handyman jobs to keep money in his pocket.

Meantime, back in Indiana, his sons wept for him, for they had no idea where he was or when, or even if, he was coming back. Opal kept praying that she would see her husband again someday, but it had been nearly a year. Fred didn't even bother to call. Clarence and Van were brokenhearted as they waited months on end for word from their dad. They had to leave their small home in Lafayette and move back to Tennessee, to be closer to relatives. "Mother, have you heard from Dad?" Clarence incessantly asked his mother. She didn't have an answer.

In 1956, Fred, at last, got in touch with his wife through her mother in Haywood County. He sent one bus ticket for Opal first and, weeks later, tickets for the boys, who were uprooted yet again and forced to stay with their maternal grandmother, Emma Tyus, in Tennessee.

When they stepped foot in Manhattan, Clarence and Van were enthralled with the bells and whistles of the big-time city. They had hated Tennessee but they had bonded with their favorite cousins on their mother's side like Raphael and Willie Jr. They especially adored their aunts, Laura and Mary Ruth, because they were sassy and vibrant like their mother, possessed beautiful singing voices, and played the piano. But they didn't like the negative murmurings about their father, whom some of their relatives referred to as a "no good drunken bum" that took away their beloved Sister Wills. The two boys knew better than any of them about their father's shortcomings, but they really did love him and they somehow understood why it was so difficult for their dad to settle down and fly right.

They didn't like what they saw or what he did but, in their own way, they could instinctively relate.

Feeling guilty for not seeing his children for almost a year, Fred took the boys to Coney Island Amusement Park in Brooklyn, where they had the time of their lives. It was unlike anything they had ever seen. Clarence was now about fourteen, and Van was eleven. Unable to apologize verbally, Fred just did things to show he was sorry. Had he explained to the boys why he was gone so long, they probably would have had a better understanding, and forgiven him. But the youngsters never forgot that horrible absence.

As Clarence and Van took root in Long Island City, they couldn't wait to ride the subway all over the city, especially to visit Times Square. Clarence was a quick study and, whenever he got lost underground, he asked a fellow straphanger how to find the N train back to Long Island City. As a child who had lived in both the South and the North, Clarence's dialectal tongue revealed neither region; perhaps because he had never stayed in any school long enough to plant linguistic roots. Blessed with a resonant tenor voice like his father, Clarence adamantly told his parents that he would be uprooted no more. He vowed to never leave New York City, even if it meant he remained there homeless and alone. Fred and Opal got the message. The carpetbaggers didn't really want to leave their adopted hometown anyway. In the end, they would all eventually be buried under the city and state they grew to love so much.

The transplanted New Yorkers quickly found out, however, that the bright lights of Broadway and the stunning residences along Park and Fifth Avenues were not for them. Fred's paltry salary could barely net the couple a two-room flat in a seedy rooming house whose address was 27-07 42nd Road. There was only one bathroom per floor and plenty of rodents to go around; the pests truly had the run of the joint.

Nothing was new in their shabby apartment. Everything down to the curtains was used, frayed, dented, scratched, or molded. But, it was clean. Opal was a domestic and if there was one thing she couldn't stand it was a dirty house. She couldn't control the crumbling and decrepit conditions, but she definitely had the power to keep the dishes clean, the sheets washed, and the clothing pressed. The boys kept their black Sunday shoes shined, and it took some time, but every couple of months or so Fred surprised the family with something special like a used record player from the pawn shop or a coat from a secondhand store.

When steam heat did manage to flow from the old steel radiator, it was hot enough to deliver second-degree burns if anyone dared to bump into it with exposed flesh. Clarence and Van shared one small room; Opal and Fred shared another room. The roach-infested kitchen bled into the shabby living room. They lived in a rat hole all right, but they were New Yorkers, and to their relatives who had one by one jumped ship from Haywood County, the location meant more than actual living conditions. To brag that you lived in New York was worth more than its weight in gold to country bumpkins.

Every morning, Opal rose before the sun to get first dibs on the communal bathroom, which was used by dozens of people on the crowded second floor. She took her cleaning rags, a mop, towels, washcloths, Ajax, and ammonia, and cleaned the shoddy lavatory from top to bottom. When she was done, she raced down the hall to get her boys in before the neighbors awakened, so they could bathe in a clean tub, use the freshly scrubbed toilet, and comb their hair in a mirror free of fingerprints. Fred washed up after the boys were done and Opal went last. Morning after morning for two years they lived like this.

As rinky-dink as their flat was, they introduced a dog to the mix. Skipper was a fine mixed breed with a tan coat and he was the best entertainment the boys could have. They fed the dog their dinner scraps and plopped him in front of their secondhand, black-and-white television as they watched Jackie Gleason and Red Skeleton. The family of four really loved westerns for they reminded them of home.

Fred and Opal couldn't help but reminisce about some aspects of country life in Haywood County: the fresh air, the freedom to pluck your own fruit from trees, and later relaxing on a porch on acres of family property. They also missed knowing everyone in the neighborhood; there was no such camaraderie in Queens. Strangers were always coming or going in their apartment building and all kinds of languages and accents came from the mouths of people of all colors. Fred and Opal were intrigued to hear different languages like Spanish, Greek, and Italian. They learned to talk with their hands and gesture with their eyes when they didn't understand the conversation. The sociable couple particularly enjoyed meeting black people who had also escaped many different parts of the South, stretching from Florida to the Carolinas as well as Virginia and Maryland. For a moment in time, they were all brothers and sisters, far away from overt oppression and closer than ever to their own definition of success.

On the sweltering weekends during the summer, Fred set up a little food stand just steps away from their Long Island City apartment, and enlisted his sons to help him sell hot dogs, sodas, and candy. He blithely called the make-shift operation "Wills and Sons." It was small, but it was a start.

The boys showed an entrepreneurial spirit as well. Both delivered newspapers for the *Long Island Star Journal,* which published community news from 1938–68. Clarence and Van worked Route 28 in Long Island City and dropped the rolled-up papers at the doorsteps in their neighborhood every day except Sunday. Before dawn, the industrious lads hiked over to the five-story newspaper building on 28th Street and 42nd Road. Their parents always let them keep the money and tips they earned. They used the money to purchase new gospel records, candy, soda-pop, and sometimes new sneakers.

With the little profit Fred made, he bought guitars for Clarence and Van so they could stop popping the strings on his. The guitars were used, but the boys couldn't care less, they weren't accustomed to new stuff anyway. They wanted to learn to play exactly the way dad did. Van's guitar was a wooden acoustic model, and Clarence's was a slightly more sophisticated electric guitar that could be plugged into an amplifier. Fred, who played the guitar by ear, taught the youngsters where to place their fingers for F-sharp, a standard lick for most gospel songs. He showed them the ever-important changeup from D major to G major. With that, they could pretty much play just about every song they heard in church and on gospel records. The talented and enthusiastic boys blossomed as their fingers echoed what their musical gifts whispered to them in secret.

They played gospel records on their phonograph and tried in earnest to imitate the guitar greats who played for their favorite groups, especially the Swan Silvertones, a popular quartet in the 1950s that was a favorite for black church folks everywhere. The Swan Silvertones started as an a cappella group, but when they added guitarist Linwood Hargrove, bassist Bob Cranshaw, and drummer Walter Perkins, it sounded as though angels had descended from heaven itself to cut a record. Clarence and Van imitated Hargrove's style to the letter. Their childhood fingers were not yet long enough or quick enough to perform the shuffling and swinging chords like the pros on the record, but the boys kept at it. With the album covers propped against the record player, they took turns getting up from their seats to move the needle back to the song they were practicing. They also enjoyed lead singer and famed falsetto Rev. Claude Jeter's musical interpretation of the gospel classic, "Oh, Mary Don't You Weep." It was gospel music at its finest, a perfect mix of Negro spirituals peppered with the blues and a dash of jazz. Only a scant few could not appreciate what resonated out of the mouths of those men from Tennessee. Clarence and Van were especially fond of guitarist Sterling Holloman, who played lead guitar for a Virginia-born quartet called The Harmonizing Four.

Clarence and Van were also big fans of the Swanee Quintet, The Soul Stirrers, and especially The Dixie Hummingbirds, who could really swing. The boys favorite song, which they tried in earnest to copy was a song called "Standing by the Bedside of a Neighbor." In the unique, philosophical, upbeat tune recorded on the Peacock Record label, Clarence always took lead singer Ira Tucker's part, and Van chimed in as a high tenor on the chorus. The fascinating gospel lyrics are about a person who is standing next a friend on his deathbed.

> *I was standing by the bedside of a neighbor*
> *Who was just about to cross the swelling tide,*
> *And I asked him if he would do me a favor,*
> *Kindly take this message to the other side.*

Clarence's soothing tenor voice rang out as he strummed the bass rhythms and Van copied lead guitarist Howard Carroll's solo almost perfectly. Hard as he tried, Clarence could not carbon copy Ira Tucker's vocal gymnastics. An inimitable songster, by any and all standards, Tucker used his pitch-perfect voice as an instrument that he could manipulate at will. In between catchy lyrics he rolled his r's and whooped and hollered without missing a beat. Clarence didn't even try to mimic those parts, but he could belt out a whoop or two. The brothers loved the song so much that in later years, when their voices matured, they recorded their versions of "Standing at the Bedside of a Neighbor" on a hulking reel-to-reel player that their yet to be born children and grandchildren still listen to decades later.

Many years after The Dixie Hummingbirds peaked in the gospel world, rock singer Paul Simon "discovered" the Hummingbirds and introduced them to a mainstream audience with his hit, "Loved Me Like a Rock"—where the gospel legends sang backup to Paul. On the music fringe for most of their heyday, the talented gospel pioneers from Greenville, South Carolina, were finally acknowledged by the music industry with a Grammy in 1973. But black folks knew from the time the quartet hit the scene back in 1928 that the Dixie Hummingbirds were a force of rhythmic nature. Not many black people had heard of Paul Simon and not many white people had heard of The Dixie Hummingbirds, so it was a perfect blending of musical roots, and an education for all.

When Clarence learned something new on the guitar, he taught his little brother how to copy it. The brothers took turns in call-and-response songs, where one person sang lead and the other sang the chorus. Sometimes, Fred grabbed his guitar and joined in, astounded and deeply impressed with their progress. The kids didn't have much in the way of toys so, when they returned from school, they played with the dog, engaged in a game of checkers, or practiced guitar.

Sometimes the boys begged their weary mother to join in. Opal was often exhausted after cleaning her client's bathrooms and kitchens only to return home to perform the same chores all over again. Still, she often summoned the strength to blurt out a song in their cramped apartment and her boys played as her backup. Or she clapped to their music to keep the beat. It may have sounded like noise to the neighbors but, to this family, the music was an enchanting down-home gospel opera.

The self-taught instrumentalists also picked the strings in a way that negated the need for a bass or drums. The method hearkened back to enslaved blacks in America who created the banjo, which was adapted from a number of African instruments. The snap and pop of the strings, along with lightning-fast movements with both the left and right hands, simulated the sound of a three-piece band from a one-string instrument. Pinching a pick, Clarence played a fuller sound on his electric guitar, incorporating jazzy chords and walking the classic bass lines. Van was a more flamboyant musician who love to zip up and down the neck of the guitar and dig out sounds that no one had ever heard before. The brothers complemented each other in a unique way.

Every Sunday, the foursome exhibited their skills at Daystar Church in Corona. Fred couldn't afford a car, so the family took two buses from Long Island City to the storefront church on 102nd Street and Northern Boulevard. They were a sight for sore eyes, carrying guitars and amplifiers on and off the city buses, decked out in their Sunday finery.

Inside the small church, Sister Wills took her place at the piano, and Clarence and his dad sat on chairs near the pulpit and played their hearts out as dozens of saints shook the floor while shouting to the music. Van, still too young and inexperienced to play his guitar in public, sometimes played the bongos to help keep the beat.

A black-and-white photograph from that sweet period in their marvelously simple lives shows Clarence and Van proudly holding their guitars. From the looks on their pleasant young faces, no one could tell the domestic violence they had witnessed or the poverty they had lived in, save the modest furnishings that served as a backdrop in the photograph. Each boy had one leg perched upon a table and they were all smiles, clutching two fancy boxes with strings.

At the time, the youngsters probably didn't know that the music that streamed from their heart and soul was from a long way back. When they tapped their feet and sang spirituals more than a century old, they certainly didn't know that their Great-great grandfather Sandy had contributed to the birth of that rhythm while stooped over in the cotton fields in Haywood County. Regrettably, Clarence and Van didn't know the origins of this soul-churning melody; they only knew that it burned like fire inside them and poured out like water.

The freedom that Clarence and Van enjoyed came at a heavy price, and they knew very little about it. The seniors in the family didn't really discuss the past. They didn't understand the basis for their existence in the mid-1950s; they didn't understand why some white people, even in New York, looked at them with contempt. And they certainly didn't understand why they constantly moved from state to state. With the dawn of every new day, they rose and lived in a world without context for why they were who they were. They had heard a little something about slavery and that some dead relatives were victims of it, but they didn't know the dates of the Civil War, and they didn't know that their great-great grandfather was one of the heroes that helped put an end to it. This unfortunate result is further testament of just how smothering Jim Crow was in their lives. There was no desire to glance behind them, for the road ahead of them was filled with dangerous booby-traps.

How much richer my father and grandfather's lives might have been had they known that their motherless and fatherless Great-great grandfather Sandy had bonded with his new kin, five boys in particular: Mack Wills, Richard Wills, James Wills, Andy Wills, and Dick Wills. They were all owned by Edmund Willis Wills and were not brothers by blood, but they were brothers in bondage and, on a slave plantation, bondage was thicker than blood.

Sandy was at least five years older than the other boys, so when he spoke the younger ones likely listened and obeyed. As their baby teeth fell out and their adult teeth grew in, Sandy was probably the one to organize the silly games they played and the races they ran through the wide-open fields, as they ducked around and through shoulder-high tobacco fields and crawled on their knees around the so-called big house and bee-lined over to the cotton fields.

On lazy Tennessee Sunday afternoons, Sandy, the tallest among the boys, fetched the sweetest fruit from the tallest trees for his younger hungry brothers as they lay on their backs and looked up at the expansive, blue sky and wished they could fly away into the clouds. It's a safe bet they wondered what they did to make God despise them so.

When Sandy turned twenty-one, he likely heard through the grapevine about talk of secession, as one Southern state after another left the Union. Sandy may have experienced ruthless beatings and probably witnessed his fellow slaves whipped nearly unconscious for disobedience or attempting to escape. They were always whipped out in the open, with slaves gathered around to discourage other slaves from fleeing. Sandy's broad, dark-brown back was probably scarred by the lash of the bullwhip that was used to instill dreadful fear into his heart. Somehow, Sandy emerged fearless from this sick mobocracy.

When Tennessee became the last of the Southern states to break ranks with the Union and join the Confederacy in 1861, my Great-great-great grandfather Sandy, like most slaves, reckoned that this Great War between the states was strictly about his freedom. Few whites in Tennessee or in the entire country would make that assertion, but blacks and abolitionists accepted that as fact, from the beginning of the Civil War until its bitter end.

Most whites saw the conflict as a battle over independence; Southerners were furious that the federal government, Abraham Lincoln in particular, encroached on their states rights. But one of the rights that Southern states cherished most was the freedom to profit from slavery, and the pressure was mounting to abolish it once and for all in a country that claimed to prize freedom above all else in its most sacred constitution. Hundreds of thousands of Southern men were willing to die for the cause. And they soon fell in great numbers.

In 1861, Americans started to slaughter each other in farms and cities all across Tennessee. By 1862, the slaves in the field could hear the Confederate soldiers' so-called "rebel yell," which echoed throughout countrysides as they raised their muskets against their Union brothers, now condemned as their sworn enemies. The blue-eyed soldiers in gray became known for a throaty, frightening scream that was meant to energize the Confederate troops and instill terror into the blue-suited union soldiers who were trespassing upon and desecrating Southern soil.

But as all hell broke loose in and around Memphis, the African slaves had a rebel yell of their own—a silent scream that was audible only to their fellow servants. A 232-year-old thunderous growl that was pregnant with generations of agony and humiliation. As uniformed soldiers spilled their priceless blood on Tennessee soil, the nearby slaves yelled a roar of rage that was emblazoned in their downcast eyes. As Americans pierced each other's flesh and turned open Tennessee fields into burial grounds, Sandy and other slaves bided their time; at long last, they reasoned, it was almost midnight for slaveholders.

But Sandy's vantage point from the plantation was limited. He could not see how the Yankees were destroying everything in their path as they bombarded nearby Fort Pillow, a Confederate fortification situated about forty miles north of Memphis.

It appears that Sandy's Master, Edmund Willis Wills, dug his heels into the land that he had forced slaves to cultivate for years. He had no intention of relocating his family and human property away from Haywood County, even as the Yankees destroyed railroad tracks and burned plantations to the ground. For him, it was still business as usual. My Great-great-great grandfather Sandy could not tell time but, as he heard of the raging war, he figured (as the old expression goes) that time was "winding up" for slaves everywhere.

Memphis was only about fifty miles from Sandy's plantation in Haywood County and it was a key city that federal troops wanted and needed to control. Whichever side controlled the nearby Cumberland and Tennessee Rivers, a major route for transporting supplies, would pretty much control the entire state. Union General Ulysses Grant was successful in his bid to win what was known as the Twin Rivers Campaign in February of 1862, and Memphis and Nashville fell into Union hands in a matter of months.

The "slave friendly" Yankees were now a stone's throw from Sandy's home. The scenic Hatchie River that flowed through Haywood County probably never looked so beautiful, as Sandy and his brothers contemplated their daring escape. As the oldest among them, Sandy became the boys' General Grant. Were they to steal away in the middle of the night, they would not have to venture far for safety. The resounding beat of the Union army's drummer boys was practically within earshot.

There's a strong chance that Sandy had somehow gotten wind of Abolitionist Frederick Douglass' unwavering appeal to have slaves join the Union army and fight for their own freedom. President Lincoln initially resisted the former slave's appeal, but he did not resist for long. Lincoln had long insisted that the war was not about freeing the slaves, but more about saving the Union by whatever means necessary. But as the Confederacy ranks swelled after the 1862 Southern draft, Lincoln was under immense pressure to build up his disillusioned army.

The air of emancipation was as thick as the chains that kept Africans confined in America for centuries. For slaves, the sea of blue-eyed men in deep-blue uniforms was like the army of the Living God. In mid-1862, the rebellion in all its hellish glory had all but crept up to Sandy's doorstep. Soon, enslaved souls would walk through that door of no return, one final time.

When word of the Emancipation Proclamation leaked out, my great-great-great grandpa figured he had his own passport to freedom for himself and his brothers in bondage. While Union captains and commanders mapped out their strategies to seize and cripple the South, Sandy assembled his troops: Richard, Mack, Dick, Andy, and James devised a plan to steal away from their plantation without getting caught. Emboldened by the power of their imagination, the young men envisioned themselves free and were instantly positioned to become masters of their own fate. They knew their capture would certainly mean instant execution on the spot; their brown bodies left on the war-torn countryside as fertilizer for the soil and dessert for animals in the wild. This wasn't a fear tactic. The Confederate soldiers were under strict orders to kill slaves who tried to join ranks with the Union enemy, for merely returning them to their slave masters was considered a slap on the wrist. Imagine that. Would that the men in gray knew those slaves were already prepared to die and that their internal compass was pointed at freedom and could not be shaken.

The stakes were high and it certainly wasn't as easy as walking into a Union army camp stationed fifty miles away. President Lincoln freed the slaves in two executive orders; the first order on September 22, 1862, and the second January 1, 1863. But Tennessee was exempt and not named in the orders, because Tennessee had mostly returned to Union control. So, Sandy and hundreds of thousands of slaves in Tennessee were left in limbo. They were technically still slaves in a rebel state that was controlled by the Union, but until the full surrender of the Confederacy, slaves had to stay where they were.

As Union losses piled up in other parts of the Confederacy, abolitionist Frederick Douglass finally got the ear of Abraham Lincoln. Now that the slaves were sort-of free, Douglass asserted, let them fight to secure it.

Some Americans thought that the idea of the United States Colored Troops was a most preposterous idea. The thought of slaves and free black men bearing arms clad in blue military uniforms sent chills down their spines. In truth, it was pure and unadulterated guilt. Many pro-slavery Americans feared being found out as being the perpetrators of one of the biggest cons in human history. Others feared they would wake up half dead in their beds with avenging colored soldiers, drunk with revenge, broadly smiling over them and poised to shoot or knife them to death. More than a few who lived in areas like Haywood County, where whites were and still are a minority, were terrified that they would be held as slaves by black masters. Fear ruled the day.

The storied antebellum South, with its flowery and cushy tales of sophisticated, soft-spoken women and their industrious husbands, lay in shambles. The manufactured and selective images, which this counterfeit genteel class had beamed around the world, were being exposed for what they really were: an effigy of greedy, hypocritical, mean-spirited people whose bloodthirsty inhumanity was appalling, even to the devil himself.

At long last, my Great-great-great grandfather Sandy Wills and the other 275,718 slaves in Tennessee, a state that contributed more soldiers to the Confederacy than any other, found the chink in the armor.

Three

An Ancestry of Adversity

In the mid-1950s the seeds of Clarence's destruction were firmly planted in his soul. His father's spiritual crossing over from sin to sainthood had abruptly failed. My Grandfather Fred had spent so much time focusing on his outward appearance that he had not yet grasped that his inner man was rotten to the core, and Clarence knew it all too well. There was an awful lot of posturing in these charismatic Holiness churches; in those days; saints judged each other on superficial issues. The length of a woman's skirt in church was scrutinized as much, if not more than, her understanding of the Holy Scriptures. Men were eyeballed and scrutinized in the sanctuary for signs of lust or drunkenness.

Fred had tried his hardest to stop drinking liquor, but he simply couldn't resist. He was an alcoholic and his new church family in Corona, Queens, didn't have a clue how to handle his sickness other than to tell him to "stop in the name of Jesus" and they "pleaded the blood," which meant they stood over him and prayed for demons to leave his body. It didn't work. Fred tried to curb his overpowering desire to toss the dice and woo women, but his spirituality had little influence over the power of seductiveness. Despite Fred's exposure to progressive Holiness churches like Greater Refuge Temple in Harlem, he couldn't tame the beast within. The founder of that Temple, Bishop Robert C. Lawson, was a great inspiration to Fred and Opal. Bishop Lawson was a dignified and educated man whose spirited sermons converted thousands of sinners on the spot. In the Holiness community, he was considered the real McCoy, a respected Christian leader without blemish or scandal. In 1919, Lawson organized the Church of our Lord Jesus Christ of the Apostolic Faith in his church members' private homes throughout Manhattan. As attendance swelled, he purchased a site on 133rd Street in Harlem where he held standing-room-only revivals that electrified everyone in his presence. Lawson was a strapping and handsome man of caramel-brown coloring, whose eloquence and diction was mesmerizing. His booming voice soared as he presented unwavering arguments for being baptized strictly in the "name of Jesus Christ" (as opposed to the Father, Son, and Holy Spirit), speaking in other tongues, and the incredible personal power that he believed was associated with the rituals. Baptists and Methodists sometimes ridiculed Lawson's movement as a "Jesus Only" circus, whose members acted undignified. To some conservative blacks, dancing or shouting in a holy sanctuary was considered uncouth and sacrilegious. More than a few of Harlem's famed bourgeois likened it to insanity. There's no question that Holiness Church members were not the religious norm: they were definitely outside the Christian box, even in the African-American community. The mere sight of a person writhing in a spiritual trance, and uttering words that were not discernable, was jaw-dropping to those who had never before witnessed such an act.

Bishop Lawson's Harlem congregation, however, was quite unlike the small church that Opal and Fred had grown accustomed to back in Indiana. Lawson's faithful members were not low-key rural folks who were afraid of their own shadow. These were Southern-born, fast-paced city slickers, who had fled the oppressive South during the so-called Great Migration, and prided themselves on being one of Harlem's own. Many acted as though they were born-and-bred New Yorkers, and the South no longer existed in their minds. Some were so tormented by Jim Crow that they swore they'd never again cross that Mason-Dixon line, not even for their momma's funeral.

The feisty Holiness women conformed to the same strict attire rules as Opal, but most of these urban, sanctified church ladies had a real panache about them, where onlookers hardly noticed that their joyful faces were free of makeup and their skirts were nearly down to the floor. Demure ladies who attended Lawson's Greater Refuge Temple dolled themselves up in faux furs and some even got away with wearing pearls, though it may have been frowned upon by some of the old timers. This was a big-time city church with fancy pews, polished floors, bright lights, and sparkling silver communion serviceware. Men and women alike were strongly encouraged to complete their education and get good jobs but never abandon the principles of their religion.

Within fifteen years, Lawson took his fire-and-brimstone message from Harlem to the radio airwaves, and his membership rolls exploded nationwide. Bishop Lawson was like a celebrity in Fred and Opal's eyes. The couple idolized the internationally known preacher and kept framed photos and portraits of the larger-than-life reverend in their home for the rest of their lives.

Turns out, Opal was more spiritually disciplined than her husband, and her son Clarence fully appreciated that fact. In a society that viewed her as the weaker vessel, she was, without question, the stronger of the two. Before she crawled into her lopsided bed every night, she fell to her rounded sore knees and fervently prayed, and she did the same upon rising in the morning. Before she put a morsel of food in her delicate mouth, she closed her eyes and prayed that it would nourish her body. And Opal really did pray for her enemies and was in disbelief when she learned that her minister husband was still being led astray by demons, which she called the "enemy." Interestingly, she didn't outright blame her partner for his fall from grace; she rebuked what was inside her husband, for his lapses in judgment. Opal pointed the finger at the devil, but it was a convenient out for an inconvenient truth.

My Grandfather Fred, who ventured into New York City with high hopes and big dreams, became discouraged when he recognized that his fourth-grade education was insufficient for his self-appointed mission. His reading and math comprehension skills pretty much ceased when he was nine or ten years old and, as much as he wanted to play with the big leagues, he did not possess the aptitude to do so. So, he turned to the bottle to drown out his sorrows and commenced his spectacular and sad undoing; but this time, his took his wife and two bright-eyed teenaged sons down with him.

Around 1957, Fred abruptly stopped going to church with the family, which had always been the great stabilizer of their otherwise distressing lives and, after Opal, Clarence was devastated the most. Opal, Clarence, and Van boarded the city buses and hauled their guitars without their dad. The saints at the storefront church raised their eyebrows when the trio entered Daystar Church in Corona without the head the household, and they knew something was amiss. The Ford family, who lived around the corner from the sanctuary, was especially suspicious. Hardy and Sallie Ford, who met at Lawson's Greater Refuge Temple in the 1920s and were married about a year after they met the famed preacher, knew something was terribly wrong with the Wills family they had grown to love.

Hardy was a tall, lanky reverend who was of a very serious demeanor and ruled his ten children with an iron fist, literally. His striking complexion was of the deepest brown and he walked with a confident swagger that evoked his courageous military experience in the United States Army during World War I. For years, he had sat side by side in the pulpit with Elder Wills, but there was something about him that wasn't right. Hardy was known for his keen judgment of character; he could chew you up and spit you out before you even opened your mouth. His wife, Sallie, was a real head-turner. A statuesque woman, Sister Ford, as she was known, had fair skin that was smooth like butter, and her face framed her perfectly pink lips that needed no lipstick, ever. Like Opal, she was the rock of her family, strong and convicted by her religion. Born in South Carolina, she despised the South's cruel embrace of Jim Crow and, when she was in her teens, the sassy gorgeous girl knew that she was destined to be beaten or raped at will because of her beauty, dignity, and pride. Sallie had a natural easy grace about her and walked with her head held high and was always reluctant to customarily step off the sidewalk when whites approached in her tiny South Carolina town—as the social law dictated back then. Sallie followed in the footsteps of her cousins and high-tailed it out of the suffocating South in the 1920s and relocated to New York. Hardy took one look at the teenage beauty's piercing eyes in Bishop Lawson's church and charmed her off her high-heeled shoes. As their family quickly expanded, the couple was constantly on the move in New York City. One year they lived in Harlem, and later, as more children entered their lives, they had to find larger apartments in Queens and the Bronx. Hardy was a laborer; he did construction work but he was never paid exactly what he was worth. But he was a firm believer in Holiness and he trusted God to always even the score.

Ever suspicious, Elder Ford kept a close eye on Clarence, who made eyes at Elder Ford's beloved daughter Ruth in the same manner that Hardy had once eyed his own wife. Ruth was a middle child of ten, but her father treated her like she was his one and only, which earned her the wrath of some of her siblings. My mother, Ruth, was an organic beauty who strongly resembled her mother, but with a worldly sass befitting a native smart-mouthed New Yorker. She was conceited and made no apologies for it, and many of the people around her either loved her or loathed her. Her mother (my Grandma Sallie) tried to impose the church's customary attire upon her, but Ruthie, always broke the rules and gloried in being church eye candy. The prettiest girl by far in this modest house of God, Ruth dared to adorn her sultry self in ruby red, emerald green, and hot pink, inside the homely sanctuary where most sisters wore black. Ruth defiantly hiked her skirt up just above the knee, painted her enticing full lips with clear pink gloss, and lied and claimed it was Vaseline; and, gasp, she wore short sleeves in the summertime. She was a chaste girl for her father's sake, but every boy that laid eyes on her in the church dreamed of being the first one to date her.

Ruth mercilessly teased the prepubescent boys and, when they went too far, Ruthie, ever the virtuous sex kitten, goaded her tough brothers, Aaron and Clinton, to fend them off. But Clarence was different. He wasn't aggressive, but he was confident and decisive. He loved Ruth at first sight, but he wouldn't dare tell her; he simply studied her and over time he methodically planned to marry her someday.

Ruth and Clarence were born the same year in 1942 only four months apart. Ruth couldn't hide her fascination for Clarence's musical prowess and the way his narrow eyes studied his fingers on the neck of guitar. He made beautiful music that church members enjoyed singing and dancing to. In a move that would've made Elizabeth Taylor proud, Ruth did not reveal to her young paramour how she felt, she simply played it close to the vest. Still, Ruth and Clarence's affection for each other was an open secret in Daystar Church, as was Fred's downward spiral. It was a tragic turn of events for the twenty-nine-year-old preacher who ventured into

New York's hallowed caverns with a fearless hope for the future. The ruthless city had brought the poor country boy to his knees.

The thought of Fred on his knees was an absolutely horrific sight to Clarence in particular, who had always looked up to his father. He and Van knew the first sign of trouble was when their dad stopped playing the guitar. Fred just wanted to lay in his bed in a drunken stupor and doze off and on in front of a tiny black-and-white television with his black-and-white electric guitar gathering dust in a corner. Clarence was in tenth grade in Long Island City High School, and he was so distressed by his father's breathtaking spiritual collapse that he could not focus on his homework. Fred and Opal didn't fight in front of their teenage boys anymore, but when the kids were not around, things got very violent and very ugly. The whole family hit rock bottom when Fred could no longer work, and he literally laid square in the gutter. Fred had been ordained a minister, yet nothing had changed. His inner man was still a mess.

Night after night, as Opal returned from work, she pulled an eviction notice for non-payment of rent off the door and took her boys on a miserable journey to find dad. Most of the time, Clarence couldn't bear to go. Sometimes Fred would be found wasted in the fetal position on busy Northern Blvd in a grimy corner near a liquor store surrounded by winos, his new comrades in arms.

Clarence's parents' domestic drama was more than he could stomach after being dragged all across the country due to their instability, and now the entire family had finally come unhinged. He was pushed to do something he never thought he'd do in his beloved new hometown of New York City. Not wanting to see the other shoe drop, Clarence bought himself a one-way bus ticket to his maternal grandmother's home in Cleveland the summer after he finished tenth grade. The assiduous teen also kept a wallet full of money he earned from bagging groceries at the corner store and his paper route. Clarence packed a small suitcase of clothing and his guitar and remorsefully shipped out of the center of the world.

Opal hated to see her son leave, but she knew full well the family was on the brink of homelessness and despite her fervent praying that "Jesus would make a way," without an income from her husband, they would soon be out on the street. Clarence promised his sweetheart Ruth that their paths would someday cross again, and he boarded the Greyhound bus bound for his cherished grandmother who he affectionately called "Mommy." (Both Clarence and Van called Opal "Mother.")

Within days, Opal and her youngest son, Van, had to find a new place to live as Fred roamed the streets, living miserably from pillar to post. Everyone loved Sister Wills at Daystar Church, and some of the members took turns providing shelter for her and Van. Her friendly demeanor, infectious laugh, and thunderous singing voice made her memorable and lovable to all who met her. No one was happy to see this prayer warrior's family fall to pieces in full view of the congregation.

Sometimes Opal was able to track down her husband and bring him to the room she temporarily flopped in; other times he was nowhere to be found. Van, about thirteen years old at the time, became something of a recluse and tried to insulate himself from the madness around him. During this period, he lost interest in school and soon stopped going to class altogether. His guitar became his best friend and it pained him deeply that his brother was not there to play alongside him. These two gifted brothers, Clarence and Van, bore the brunt of their father's transgressions, and much of the emotional damage their tender vessels sustained would never be undone in the decades that followed. They were eyewitnesses to the sins of their ecclesiastic father, the progenitor of their new music. The sad spectacle proved to be a watershed moment in their fragile lives. The boys, who publicly showed their father the respect he was due, swallowed their pain which, in turn, punctured their souls in the worst way. The gifted youngsters, who together dreamed ambitious plans to conquer the world with their fanciful music, took one look at their father and reconsidered their aspirations. It was a simple math; if their fire-baptized Holy Ghost-filled dad got knocked down by demons, the sophomoric sons didn't stand a chance.

Opal, though she had been down this road many times before with her troubled husband, was shattered as well. She had rigorously trained herself to blame an abstract devil for his woes, but she knew that her petulant sweetheart was, at last, losing his grip. And finally, Fred, barely able to glimpse himself in the mirror, judged himself a failure in the eyes of God and man. In his mind, he truly believed in the power of Jesus Christ, but his heart revealed otherwise. Turns out, his subtle acceptance of his perceived inferiority was stronger than the cross and the religious symbols he tried to embrace. A pathetic little voice in his head, which had whispered vulgarities to the tiniest cells in his DNA for centuries, once again convinced Fred that he was unworthy, and that he was stupid to even try to prove otherwise. The emotional story of Lazarus being raised from the dead could not reverse Fred's contempt for his own image. Poetic verses detailing Job's rise and fall in the Old Testament did little to persuade the young minister that he, too, could leap, bound and gagged, from his self-imposed grave. The enterprising Southerner, who ventured into the America's grandest city on a song and a prayer, awestruck by its imposing bridges and structure, was suddenly eyeballing the swine of the megalopolis.

Fred was acting like his own father, now. Allen Wills, born in Brownsville, Haywood County, in 1896, was a drinker, too. Allen didn't really know his father, Alex Wills, but he apparently adored his mother, Rennie. No one knows what happened to Alex; he disappeared when Allen and his two sisters, Emma (named after his beloved mother) and Lyn, were young children. Perhaps that drove Allen to drink in later years. His mom, Rennie, widowed by 1910, tried to be both mother and father to her three kids, but it certainly wasn't easy. When Allen filled out his draft card for World War I, he acknowledged his mother was named "Rennie Wills" but, for his father, the officer wrote Allen's reply, "I don't know." For reasons unknown, Allen didn't even know his father's name, though there is a marriage certificate in the State of Tennessee, uniting Alex Wills and Rennie Burton. Hard as I tried, I couldn't find a record of death for Alex Wills in Tennessee. He could have been lynched or murdered, or maybe he just abandoned his family and they assumed he was dead. Whatever the case, Alex's disappearance left his oldest son, Allen, a somewhat broken man. Allen returned the favor to Fred and, not to be outdone, Fred donated his inherited heartbreak to Clarence and Van. An ancestry of adversity, the devil's own luck was reaping ghastly dividends, again. This was probably not the kind of freedom that Sandy Wills fought for.

DIE FREE

As Fred danced with spirits inside bottles of alcohol, Opal remained steadfast and prayerful, and stood by her troubled husband. One might say she loved Fred too much. Night after night, she dragged him out of the gutter and plopped him into a bathtub, in a noble attempt to scrub his scarlet sins away and prove her unyielding devotion to her wedding vows. Opal was a sentimental country gal who fiercely relished being in love. A vibrant middle child of twelve siblings, she outright disobeyed and defied her parents, Earnest and Emma Tyus, and sneaked around with Fred in the dark during her prepubescent years and got herself pregnant as soon as her ovaries were ripened. Unlike her studious sisters close to her age, Katherine, Lynn, and Lillian, Opal obsessed about love and romance. She was always trying to match up some of her brothers, Squire and Harry, with her girlfriends. To make matters worse, she ran away with Fred and eloped in Mississippi in 1941. It was the only state in the South that would marry a girl that young. Fred was already eighteen and could do as he pleased. But Opal was barely in the eighth grade and her parents hoped that their talented thirteen-year-old daughter, who sang and played the piano, would graduate from high school, and not run around with that ruffian known as Butch. It was not to be. Opal sent a message loud and clear that she was a rule-breaker and meekly returned to her homestead in Brownsville as a married girl with a baby on the way. She had a number of older sisters and brothers, but her child was the first in line to usher in the new generation. Clarence's unlikely arrival made him the first grandchild for both the Tyus and the Wills families. Game. Set. Match.

Clarence spent the summer after tenth grade depressed and on his own at his grandmother's house in Cleveland. He missed his best friend, Frankie, a white teen that he had really bonded with. Frankie and Clarence canvassed the five boroughs in the mid-1950s. They regularly visited Times Square and took novelty pictures, including one in a mock metal cell where the duo posed behind bars with a sign that emblazoned "Times Square Jail" and beneath them a small pennant read "New York City." Both teens, dressed in winter jackets, were aglow with smiles and Clarence had his arm draped around Frankie's shoulder.

Ruth was also a source of heartache for Clarence. She was a great catch and Clarence secretly feared that, while the cat was away, Ruth would play. And that's exactly what happened, but Clarence wrote her love letters to keep the fires burning. "My Darling Ruth," his letters began. After explaining his activities in Cleveland, he professed his undying love for her, in a very consistent cursive handwriting where he looped his L's and W's with a distinctive flair. Ruth always wrote back with updated pictures of herself cloaked in fake pearls and other counterfeit finery.

Worst of all, Clarence missed his mother's laugh; oh, he loved his mother so and hated what she had to put up with. His secret dream was to one day buy his mother a new house and fill it with the latest appliances and a new piano. Everything Opal had was either used or hand-me-downs. Clarence really hated that and believed that he could be a better provider than his dad. But he knew his mother was a strong woman and, if Opal was with you, she was with you all the way. He missed his mother's tender hugs and kisses; she always looked upon her sons with genuine adoration. Because of that, Clarence couldn't bear to imagine the nightmare his mother and brother were enduring from his abusive father back in Queens.

After spending a few months in Cleveland, Clarence moved again to Michigan, where his mother's younger sister, Laura, lived in a spacious house on 1167 East Alma Avenue. Clarence and Laura were close in age and, although she was his aunt, they romped around in Brownsville like sister and brother. Best of all, the piano was to Laura what the guitar was to Clarence. Their musical talents bonded them even more as they sang and played gospel music together.

Laura was a dynamo in the Tyus family; a supremely gifted piano player and singer, only her sister Mary Ruth had stronger vocal pipes than she. Arguably the most beautiful of all the Tyus girls, Laura had even won a few beauty pageants in her heyday. With Laura as a surrogate mother, Clarence attended eleventh grade at Fairview High School, where he made friends quickly and helped organize a doo-wop group called Alphonse and the LaVelles. Alphonse Hamilton was the lead singer and Clarence played lead guitar for the band, who hoped to be the next music sensation, like Frankie Lymon and the Teenagers. With dreams of grandeur, the group entered local talent shows in the area and fantasized about getting a recording contract. Led by Alphonse, the boys sang a few original numbers and some doo-wop classics.

The teeny bopper wannabe sensations were a hit with the locals in Flint, Michigan. They easily won first place in a talent show in nearby Ballenger Park, and a local paper publicized their appearance with a huge photo of the group. Decked out in identical suits and ties, Alphonse stood in the foreground with a microphone in his hand; and Clarence, clutching his guitar, stood in the background with four other singers who gave the camera thumbs up.

The boy from Brownsville, a rock solid tenor with his thirty seconds of fame under his belt, had finally found his passion. With stars in his eyes and a multitude of rhythm at his fingertips, he cemented his plans to be a full-time musician after he graduated from high school. His studies came pretty easily to him because he was endowed with a sharp mind. He especially excelled in math and science.

Clarence knew how to get along with all kinds of people: white, black, Asian, or Latino; he could share a laugh or break bread with anybody. The transplanted Yankee quickly became "the cool kid" at Fairview High School because he bragged incessantly about how he was from New York City. He didn't tell anybody he was born in Brownsville, Tennessee, mind you. At lunchtime, geeky and awkward kids sat mesmerized and hung on his every word with half-eaten baloney-and-cheese sandwiches as the fast-talking, inner-city kid told wild tales about his misadventures in Times Square and his daring rides on the Cyclone at Coney Island— and he had photographs to back up his stories. His high-pitched voice was clear as a bell, just like his mother's. He enunciated every word and rarely used slang or profanity.

My dad was amazingly comfortable in his own skin, even as bloody civil rights protests fanned across the South and the North and some racist whites were hell-bent on maintaining segregation forever. Clarence was aware of what was happening, but he was also aware of his own personal power; that much he had learned from his mother and her spellbinding hold on the Holy Ghost. That's why he couldn't bear to rubberneck his father's backsliding. In spite of the ostentatious nature of their sanctification, Clarence embraced the most fundamental tenets of the religion and, for the life of him, Clarence couldn't fathom why his own father, a fire-and-brimstone preacher no less, didn't get it. With about 700 miles between them, Clarence didn't obsess about the past; he kept his chestnut-colored eyes on the future.

Inebriated and irresponsible as he was in 1958, Fred was still mindful that he was on the brink of doing irreparable damage to his sons and his wife. He had relocated to New York City to construct a brilliant rainbow that would reach the next unborn generation; however, if he was going to be falling down drunk all the time, he realized he might as well have stayed in Haywood County.

Though plastered, he heard his wife's fervent prayers. Without expressing his admiration, he was impressed with her unwavering faith, not only in God, but in his miserable self. She was more than a wife; she was a friend, a best friend, who didn't kick him when he was down and refused to call him names as he wallowed in sin. Her resilience shamed him worse than his own dead mother's disapproving glance ever could. When he was sober, she peppered him with questions: "Do you know your boys are looking at you? You'd better not play with God!" and her favorite, "When God takes his hand off you, you'll be sorry then. You'd better repent and beg for forgiveness before it's too late."

The problem was that Fred craved the taste of tobacco and alcohol. It was bigger than him; it had become his bread when he was hungry and his water when he was thirsty. His small but strong physical frame called the shots and he didn't have the moral strength to override their addictive demands. His younger son, Van, didn't utter a negative word toward his father, but Fred looked in his son's eyes and knew that Van was deeply disgusted with him. No words needed to be said; the loosely hidden flash of abhorrence in his thirteen-year-old boy's eyes said it all. Fred went cold turkey.

As Fred quietly lay in his rumpled bed, a thunderous spiritual warfare broke out in his soul. It was a ferocious battle over whom Fred would serve, and the darker forces of his nature refused to let go of their stranglehold. Before leaving for her job cleaning houses, Opal left a pot of coffee on the stove and food wrapped in aluminum foil; she always prayed that he would be there when she returned from work. As Opal scrubbed strangers' bathtubs and toilets, Fred, stilled by both shock and amazement, watched as his body broke out in cold sweats and shook with a feign fever and physically urged him to get a drink or light up a cigarette. As he drifted in and out of consciousness during his crude detoxification process, he became paranoid, anxious, and suffered debilitating, throbbing headaches that aspirins could not quiet. He thought he heard voices in the closet, saw the devil's shadow in the kitchen, and believed angels were at his bedside, protecting him. When she returned home from work and found her disheveled husband in his faded pajamas and drenched with sweat underneath crumpled off-white sheets, Opal rubbed his forehead and repeated the word, "Jesus, help him, Jesus. Help him, Jesus."

She had never seen anything like that before and her first instinct was to scream with fright at the sight of her husband's eyes rolled back in his head with delusion, but she refused to give in to fear. As Fred tried to vomit but heaved nothing more than saliva, Opal spoon-fed her husband soup and crackers. He lost weight and his clothing hung on his body like a human hanger. Though Van practiced his guitar in the next room to drown out the pathetic sounds of agony, an incoherent Fred was unable to appreciate the music coming from the instrument he loved more than anything in the world.

After weeks of this vexation, Fred came to himself. He was able to pick up his Bible again, and he searched for stories about temptation. He re-read the book of Job. Job was stripped of his wealth and family and tempted to curse God to recover his loss but he famously refused to denounce God and lay in his own ashes for a long time. Fred was inspired with the idyllic moral of that story; in the end, God rewarded Job with more than what he had before. Fred hoped for the same ending for his own life.

The King James Version of the Holy Bible was the only book Fred had read since he had dropped out of the fourth grade. At thirty-seven years of age, the Good Book had become his foundation and personal roadmap for everything. Great poets, novelists, and biographers had penned seminal works that inspired millions around the world; Fred knew not even their names and didn't care to know. Led astray, there was a

Bible verse to support why he fell into the trap and for every high and low he experienced; there was a corresponding prophet or biblical figure to explain away his current station in life. Fred blamed his startling fall from grace on the devil, and that was that. Family history, personal responsibility and poor judgment did not factor into the equation at all. It was the devil and his army of demons that tempted Fred, and Jesus and his angels saved him from the bottomless pit. All who knew Fred, including his long-suffering wife and teenage sons, were more than happy and eager even to assign blame to the Prince of Darkness, rather than to Fred Douglas Wills.

By 1959, Fred was back on his feet, ready to return to Daystar Church, and he even got a job as a modestly paid maintenance man in an office building in Long Island City. The inner character flaws that led to this charismatic preacher's staggering demise were not addressed, scrutinized, or remedied; they simply went into hiding, again. Down, but not out, Fred was moving forward again. In his mind, life was hard, but, honestly, he had no idea what hard living really was. His Great-grandfather Sandy, during his death-defying stint in the Civil War, had paved a much better road for him. But Fred was ignorant of Sandy's sacrifice, and lived like a man without a personal history.

My Great-great-great grandfather Sandy Wills blazed a path for his great-grandchild on a summer night in 1863 when he and his brothers in bondage (Mack, Richard, James, Andy, and Dick Wills) made a daring escape for freedom. The summertime heat in Haywood County was notoriously oppressive, but not more so than the system that kept Sandy and his brothers from enjoying even the most basic freedoms in life. The sweltering conditions proved to be a perfect backdrop for their daring desertion; there was no need for winter clothing or shoes, which they probably didn't have anyway. God's green grass cushioned their feet and the moon's brilliant glow served as a guiding light during their sudden bolt for liberation. Somehow, they had gotten wind of Frederick Douglass' urgent plea. Neither Sandy nor his brothers could read it, but in March of 1863, Frederick Douglass passionately and urgently wrote in his self-named journal, *Men of Color, To Arms!* Using stinging metaphors with a preacher's prose, he wrote in part:

"The day dawns; the morning star is bright upon the horizon! The iron gate of our prison stands half open. One gallant rush from the North will fling it wide open, while four million of our brothers and sisters shall march out into liberty."

Government-imposed illiteracy apparently did not prevent Sandy and his brethren from hearing Douglass' message. They could feel that the hour was upon them and they had to answer Douglass' call not just for their own sakes, but for their yet unborn children. This was the generation of slaves who had finally evoked American patriot Patrick Henry's words: "Give me liberty or give me death."

Frederick Douglass, who was born in Talbot County, Maryland, around 1818, was a runaway slave himself. In thunderous speeches, he passionately condemned the institution that he had firsthand knowledge about. When Douglass was about twelve years old, his master's wife broke the law by teaching him the letters of the alphabet. His literacy was the beginning of his liberty. Soon he was able to read newspapers, and his eyes confirmed what his heart had always known: slavery was immoral and on its deathbed. After several failed attempts, Douglass successfully ran away from his plantation in September of 1838. After stops throughout the Northeast, he settled in Massachusetts, where he became a prominent abolitionist, agitator, author, and ultimately the most famous black man in America, perhaps the world. With prominent facial features and a dignified statuesque build, Douglass finally got the ear of President Lincoln. And when the Union army was brought to its knees in some rebel states, Lincoln blinked and agreed to allow both free and enslaved Africans to enlist in what the United States War Department initially established as the "Bureau" of Colored Troops in May of 1863. An astounding eighty-five percent of all eligible blacks, including runaway slaves, volunteered to fight in about 175 regiments, including cavalry, infantry, light and heavy artillery units which became known as the United States Colored Troops.

Presumably under the cover of night, on either August 22 or 23 in 1863, Mack, Richard, James, and Andy Wills left the plantation they called home for most of their lives, and ventured into what they knew would be everlasting life, one way or the other. If the four African runaways were caught, the Confederate soldiers were under strict orders to kill them on the spot. If they managed to make it safely to Fort Halleck in Columbus, Kentucky, they were prepared to fight to the death to end the despicable system that had tormented them and their parents and grandparents for generations. Even though the risk of death was high, it was still a win-win for the noble renegades; going home to Jesus was a much better deal than returning to the devil's workshop at the slave plantations.

The four young men left Haywood County with nothing but the rags on their backs and it's very doubtful they had shoes for their feet. It probably took about four days to walk the 105 miles from Haywood County to Fort Halleck in Columbus, Kentucky, which was one of the locations where colored soldiers were allowed to enlist. It was pretty much a straight line along the banks of the Mississippi. It's unclear how these slaves—who had never roamed freely—knew exactly where they were going, except to walk along the river's shore. Perhaps they were given direction by Union troops along the way or maybe one of them knew their way around the state from being hired out for jobs.

Columbus, Kentucky, had quickly become the Promised Land for runaway slaves, not only because it was conveniently located along the Mississippi River; it was also the intersection of several transportation routes. The slaves, who arrived at the Union outposts before the United States Colored Troops were officially organized, were considered contraband, and many were turned away and returned to their dreaded slave owners.

Federal troops burned plantations to the ground as thousands of slaves congregated at the fortifications, Army officials faced a real dilemma. They initially made them work, without pay of course, but then they were faced with the issue of shelter and food. The creation of The United States Colored Troops was born more out of necessity, than out of altruism, as thousands upon thousands of runaway slaves lived among the federal troops from 1861 to 1863.

The Wills men embarked on that dangerous trip and it was a terribly long walk; they had no idea which mile would be their last, and they feared that slave catchers were hot on their trail. In all probability, they quietly prayed as they walked along the way and quickly hid whenever they heard anything suspicious. They probably saw wild animals in their travels like possums and raccoons, which are in abundance in the woods of Tennessee and Kentucky, and they may have noticed that the rabid creatures lived freer than they did. As the courageous men made their way northward, the longest distance was to the Tennessee Kentucky border. When they finally crossed into Kentucky, they didn't have far to go. Finally, on August 27, 1863, the slaves became soldiers. They stood in line at Fort Halleck, home to the 4th Field Heavy Artillery, Company F, and observed the activity of the Union's busy federal camp. They were not the first slaves to make it there nor would they be the last. Their first order of business was to answer the questions from the enlistment officer. Lieutenant G.W. Fettermann filled out the rectangular form for each of the Wills men in what was called a Company Descriptive Book. The weary men answered the questions as best they could.

"My name is Mack Wills," he said.

When asked his age, Mack said eighteen. Of course, he didn't really know his exact age or birthday, but he probably knew that he had to be at least eighteen years old to fight in the Great War between the states. In fact, they all said they were eighteen except Andy, who declared he was nineteen. An assistant may have used a measuring tape to determine Mack's height, which was listed at five feet, six inches. Lt. Fettermann probably didn't bother to look deep into Mack's eyes, and flippantly wrote that he had black eyes, black hair, and a black complexion. In actuality, Mack was probably a deep brown, but what would a white officer see? Everything in his world was either black or white; that was part of the reason this terrible war had to go forth.

When asked where Mack was born, he said, "Nashville, Tennessee." But the most startling and downright repulsive part of the form is where it says "occupation." As he did with his other entries on the enlistment form, Lt. Fettermann wrote, in his most beautiful cursive penmanship, "slave."

Upon first seeing this, it literally took my breath away. Occupation: slave.

I couldn't peel my eyes away from the reprinted original scanned records from the National Archives. Occupation: slave. Really? Was slavery *really* a means of earning a living? Honestly?! Slavery is not an activity in which a person is engaged; that would be an occupation. Slavery is not a profession, a livelihood, or a vocation. Slavery is many things, but one thing it is not is an occupation. To add insult to injury, in the "remarks" section of the form, Lt. Fettermann added, "Owned by Edmund Wills Haywood Co. Tenn." As if to say, if the war is lost and the Confederacy wins, these slaves should be legally returned to Edmund Wills.

One careful and analytical look at this enlistment form and it's clear: slavery was not only disastrous for blacks, but for slaveholders as well. They had become amoral and demoralized toward blacks and they lost all sense of decency and compassion for people whose skin tones were different than their own. The fact that a distinguished officer in uniform could write, presumably without missing a beat, that a human being in America was a slave, a condition he most certainly would not have accepted for himself or his own children, is appalling. It would have been preferable to write something like "not applicable." Occupation: slave, yet another disturbing footnote in the annals of Civil War history.

"James Wills, sir," he stated to Mister Fettermann. It was the same drill. The enlistment officer noted that James stood five-feet-eight-and-a-half inches and it turns out he may have been just a few months shy of his eighteenth birthday. Documents show that James Wills, who later changed his name back to his father's surname of Parker, declared his birthday as November 30, 1845. He more than likely just made up that date in later years for legal reasons. James was the younger biological brother of Dick and, unlike the rest, he and his brother documented that his father was named Dick Parker and his mother was named Caroline Parker, both of whom were presumably born sometime in the 1820s. The couple probably married in a sham of a ceremony where the bride and groom were told to hop over a broom, and the officiating minister, overseer, or master declared, "Till death or distance do you part."

Slave marriages were not recognized in the state of Tennessee. Both James and Dick were born on Edmund Wills' plantation, which means their parents may or may not have remained on the plantation after their escape. James hair, eyes, and complexion were duly noted as black. The disheartening classification of "slave, owned by Edmund Wills, Haywood Co Tenn" was also jotted down.

"Haywood County, sir." That's where Richard Wills said he was born. Lt. Fettermann documented that Richard was eighteen years old and stood five-feet-six-and-a-half inches. He jotted the word "black" for Richard's complexion, eyes, and hair.

"I don't know, sir," was Andy's reply when asked where he was born. He was the only Wills man among the group who didn't know when or where he came into the world. It was a brief response that probably passed without notice, but his unsettling answer was devastating in its form, and lasting in its impact. Andy stood at five-feet-five-inches tall, and he had no idea how he got to Edmund Wills' plantation. For all he knew, he sprung up out of the ground just like a turnip seed and just happened to be a living, breathing thing. He was very close to my Great-great-great grandfather Sandy, and in a general affidavit filed after the war, he reported that he had even slept in the same shack as Sandy when they were slave children, testifying that he had met Sandy when he was nine years old. Andy had eyes, but no visual comprehension; he could not conceptualize his earliest years but this was the first time he could actually envisage a future. Andy's enlistment into the United States Colored Troops gave his life new meaning. Going forward from this point in his life, he could account for his whereabouts and his mission on earth. After the war, he would call himself Andrew, rather than the nickname Andy; it was a spirited move that helped him to define himself, at last.

August 27, 1863, was Independence Day for all four of these men. It was that great getting-up morning where they found the steel in their spines and the fire in their eyes. This was the day that they commenced a bridge between that great gulf separating slavery and freedom. Pro-slavery mutants had hoped the brains of black slaves had atrophied with the absence of education, but they gambled and lost. The minds of these gutsy and bewitching African men were as sharp as the bullwhip that scarred their broad backs. The time had come for these soldiers to lash back at those who would die to keep their lives obscured in that awful netherworld of bondage. James, Andy, Richard, and Mack likely didn't realize they were making history. They could not identity a single letter of the alphabet except for an X, nor could they add or subtract. But, they could point and shoot; it was time to give the devil his due.

In a stunning turn of events, Sandy and Dick, the oldest among the men, had not made the trip to Fort Halleck in Columbus, Kentucky, on August 27, 1863, with the other Wills men. The reason is anyone's guess. It's highly doubtful that they had cold feet; perhaps, they covered for the younger men and stayed behind to make sure Edmund Wills did not hire slave catchers with dogs to sniff them out in the middle of the night. There's also a strong possibility that Sandy and Dick wanted to take the whippings for their escape, rather than allowing a slave stool-pigeon to rat them out while under duress during a barbaric beating at the whipping post. Maybe Sandy lied to his so-called master, and assured him that Richard, Andy, James, and Mack would soon return or, if he was really slick, maybe he said they went to fight for the Confederate army to protect Edmund's property. There are dozens of possible scenarios, none of which have been recorded in the National Archives. But here's a safe bet: Sandy and Dick were probably savagely beaten within an inch of their lives for staying behind. It was no secret that they were close to the four runaways, especially Andy, whom he lived with. There was no way, Edmund Wills probably reasoned, that Sandy and Dick could not know where they went and why. Their sudden departures meant thousands in lost fortunes for Edmund Wills. They were "prized" slaves, if you will; they were young, strong, and able to produce more slaves for the plantation.

If Sandy and Dick were punished, there's a possibility Sandy was staked out, a common method of torture for rebellious slaves. Four stakes were driven into the ground and each arm and leg was tied to each stake. The overseer, or perhaps Edmund Wills himself, may have wielded a paddle and thrashed the soles of Sandy's feet until they were raw and bleeding. And in a final blow, the assailant whipped out a knife and slashed the bloodied blisters to prevent the slave from running away.

Maybe these barbarians stripped my great-great-great grandfather naked and tied him to a tree and whipped him mercilessly with anything and everything they could put their hands on, from limber switches to rawhide. There's also a chance they "bucked" Dick. That is, they fastened his feet together pushed his knees up to his chin, tied his hands together over his knees and put sticks both under his legs and over his arms. These vicious slaveholding men were diabolical in their deeds to torture and humiliate souls that yearned for the same freedom that slaveholders took for granted. They hatched repulsive schemes that vividly illustrated that the evils of slavery had rendered them inhumane and uncivilized. They may have had control of the shackles around my grandparents' necks, but in the process they became unrepentant sociopaths who lost hold of the better angels of their nature.

Whatever happened to Sandy and Dick at the plantation in the days following their brother's escape didn't change their minds one bit. Forty-five days later, on or about October 8, 1863, Sandy and Dick walked, or perhaps ran, in the footsteps of Andy, Mack, Richard, and James, and made a beeline for freedom. Dick walked the same 105 miles to Columbus, Kentucky, and enlisted with the same 4th Heavy Field Artillery, Company F on October 12, 1863.

"Dick Parker, sir," he said with a mark of defiance. Dick's legal last name was Wills, because he, like Sandy, was the property of Edmund Willis Wills, but Dick never forgot that he was named for his father, Dick Parker, and even in the pit of slavery, he had always embraced his biological father's identity.

More than thirty years later, in an affidavit for his pension, he stated, "When a slave before the war I belonged to Willis Wills who raised me, therefore was known as Dick Wills, but after the War I took the name of my father Dick Parker. I was named for him and have always been named Dick Parker, though called by the name of my old master Wills."

Lieutenant G.W. Fettermann wrote that his name was Dick Parker, unaware of the courageous act from a man whose emancipation began with the reclaiming of his namesake. It was the first warning shot from Dick Parker that the war over slavery had already been won.

The lieutenant also noted that Dick was twenty-two years old and stood five-feet-four-and-a-half inches. His complexion, eyes, and hair color were deemed "black." But in another pension affidavit in 1902, Dick described his skin color as "dark ginger cake," which was a popular dessert at the time that could easily be mistaken for chocolate cake, until you tasted the finely chopped fresh ginger, black pepper, and cinnamon. His characterization of his bronze skin was certainly more creative than the enlistment officer, who would have never associated a delicious confection with a person of African descent. It was all in the eyes of the beholder, and Dick Parker apparently viewed himself one of the sweeter things God made.

Dick went on to tell the lieutenant that he was born in Haywood County, Tennessee, and belonged to Edmund Wills. Like all of the other Wills men, he was signing up to serve a five-year term, assuming the bloody war would last that long. To my delight, "occupation" was left blank. Lieutenant Fettermann did not put "slave," as he did for the other Wills men. It's not clear why this happened. Could it be that Dick told him outright to leave it blank? Or perhaps the lieutenant finally realized in the weeks that followed that it was absurd to certify a slave's bondage as an occupation? Whatever the case, Dick Parker's occupation was left blank for the ages.

In another remarkable move, my Great-great-great grandfather Sandy was the only one that did not enlist at Fort Halleck in Columbus, Kentucky. One day after Dick signed up for basic training; Sandy enlisted at a federal installation in Union City, Tennessee, on October 13, 1863. Union City, just twenty miles from Columbus, was the other home for the 4th Field Heavy Artillery, and was about seventy miles from Haywood County. It's not clear why Sandy chose to enlist at this location, though he was still a part of the 4th Field Heavy Artillery, but he was with company G, while his brothers were with company F. Union City was located on the Mobile and Ohio Railroad, which war strategists knew was a major North-South thoroughfare. The Confederates needed to regain control of the critical city because they couldn't move supplies without control of it.

Sandy stood before the officer, without his brothers, and faced enlistment alone in front of Lieutenant J.S. Mauggy. "My name is Sandy Willis Wills." Lt. Mauggy, apparently thinking the young illiterate man with a Southern drawl misspoke, wrote: "Sandy Willis."

This simple clerical error led to great frustration in the years following the war. When Sandy's wife Emma applied for a widow's pension shortly after his death, she had to hire a lawyer to cut through miles of bureaucratic red tape to confirm that her husband's name was actually Sandy Wills. Numerous depositions were filed by soldiers who fought alongside Sandy and knew him during slavery to attest that his last name was not Willis but, in fact, Wills.

In a sworn affidavit dated January 20, 1896, Andy Wills hired a lawyer to dictate his testimony. Andy said, "He was known in the army as Sandy Willis. His full name was Sandy Willis Wills and in getting it on the books Wills was left off and they called him Sandy Willis." Had Sandy been able to read, he could've corrected it on the spot, but the enlistment officer was writing scribble for all my great-great-great grandfather knew. Sandy did not know even the fundamentals of reading and writing. Neither did

Andy. Even after all those years after the Civil War, Andy signed his 1896 affidavit with an "X."

As Sandy faced his enlistment officer, he stated his age as twenty-three and said he was born in Tipton County which was about thirty-seven miles South of Haywood County in Tennessee. Assumedly, without even raising his head to look at Sandy, Lt. Mauggy wrote "blk" for complexion, eyes, and hair color. When it came to occupation, the officer wrote "farmer."

Farmer?! There are two schools of thought here. Either Sandy told Lt. Mauggy that he was a slave and the officer wrote "farmer," which is unlikely; or Sandy himself described his occupation as a farmer. If the latter is true, then Sandy was far more liberated and more of a revolutionary than I could have possibly imagined. If Sandy uttered, "farmer," that means he did not allow the forces of slavery, mighty as they were, to define him. If Sandy declared himself essentially a free man living as a farmer, then that proves that he, too, had fought and won the Civil War long before he actually engaged in any skirmish or battle. This means Sandy was a free man even when he was shackled to an uncivilized plantation. Unlike his brothers, no one wrote on Sandy's enlistment form that he was "owned by Edmund Wills of Haywood County," and that's probably because Sandy instinctively knew that, despite evidence to the contrary, he could not be bought. His soul was not for sale, no matter how many unscrupulous slave owners claimed to have a receipt for his precious life. It's little wonder that Sandy stood tallest among the enlisted Wills men at five-feet-nine-and-a-half inches. Apparently, he believed in his freedom before he was legally free. The world looked upon him as a lowly slave, but that's not what Sandy saw in himself. He had endured the primitive social structure for all of his twenty-three years, but my great-great-great grandfather did not let it infect his soul. Whether the Union won or lost the war, Sandy was convinced that he would not return to Edmund Wills' plantation as a slave. He was a farmer in his imagination and, as unlearned as he was, he didn't need a textbook to teach him that his imagination was the most powerful force on earth. Sandy's mindset contained enough energy to break every shackle and pop every chain. As the Good Book he couldn't read said, "If the Son sets you free, ye shall be free, indeed." Sandy found freedom before the Civil War even ended and he escaped the jails that ignorance had built.

Sandy, Mack, Andy, James, Richard, and Dick were now privates in the 4th U.S. Colored Field Heavy Artillery Regiment. It was one of about 175 regiments comprised of black soldiers from every state in the Union. Confederate troops also forced some slaves to fight with them, which was such a pity. As the ultimate blow in the Great War, soldiers in gray uniforms manipulated other slaves to fight against their own freedom. There was truly no depth to which pro-slavery soldiers wouldn't stoop.

The Union's 4th U.S. Colored Field Heavy Artillery was formed at Fort Halleck in Columbus, Kentucky, in June of 1863 and it was mostly comprised of runaway slaves. For reasons unknown, it had gone through at least two name changes; it was initially called the 2nd Regiment Tennessee Heavy Artillery, African Descent, and then it was redesignated the 3rd U.S. Colored Field Heavy Artillery. There were two camps, the one in Columbus, Kentucky, where James, Mack, Richard, Dick, and Andy enlisted, and the other in Union City, where Sandy reported for duty. The company was commanded by Captain J. Shaw.

The regiments were exclusively led by white officers but, as the war waged on, a handful of black soldiers were promoted to non-commissioned officers. The first slap in the face that many black privates experienced was when they learned that they received a lower salary than their white counterparts. Colored troops were initially paid ten dollars per month and three dollars was automatically deducted for clothing, leaving them with seven dollars. White soldiers received thirteen dollars a month and there was no deduction for clothing at all. Blacks did not receive the same medical care or supplies as white soldiers, often waiting for days or even weeks for supplies or medical treatment. After a national outcry from soldiers and abolitionists alike, an embarrassed congress leveled the playing field by 1864 and granted black soldiers equal pay, and even made it retroactive. No further money was taken out of their checks for uniforms or anything else.

One might imagine the camaraderie that the newly liberated slaves experienced during their basic training. They shared a great deal in common for all had been stripped of their independence and grew up on plantations under the heel of ruthless overseers and masters. Their tears all followed the same trail, suckling brown boys unreservedly aborted from their mothers and fathers, and those that were fathers themselves probably never had the privilege of nurturing their own children before they were sold away.

But there were other disturbing realities to which the soldiers were completely oblivious. The brazen new recruits, who would soon be issued one hundred bullets, could not count them. Troops on the move, who came upon signs indicating cities and distances, couldn't read them. The privates who were issued money for their service to the Union Army could not identify the words or pictures on the monies they received. It could've been counterfeit; they would have scarcely known the difference, save for the size and texture of the currency. These warriors would have to feel their way through the war, just as they had to feel their way through slavery. Illiteracy had rendered the men disabled. Their razor-sharp motor skills served as a guidepost for the fighters; God help them if they needed to use their comprehension skills, they would be sitting ducks.

As a member of the United States Colored Troops, my Great-great-great grandfather Sandy and his comrades experienced many firsts as members of the military. It was the first time most of them had new shoes and certainly the first time any had been outfitted for a uniform. During their training, the newbies were handed muskets and revolvers and taught how to aim at a target and pull the trigger. A target was one thing, but a looming question surfaced: could the soldiers be trained to kill whites that they had been indoctrinated to love and serve, second only to God Almighty? Generations of colored folks had been taught to idolize their white neighbors to the point where many, in turn, despised themselves. The Union army didn't consider the psychological and pathological component of brainwashed slaves waging war against their masters; and the slaves probably didn't consider it a reversal of fortune, either.

It may have been the most traumatic about face that the colored troops had to quickly reconcile in their minds and hearts. The white men that the black soldiers had been taught to fear all of their lives, they were now sworn to kill. These black men, many of whom had been forcibly reduced to passive yassa' boss drudges, had to transform themselves into ferocious executioners. These soldiers, who as boys were taught to be afraid of even the white man's voice, had to suddenly awaken their sleeping giants and slay the goliaths of the land.

Sandy, James, Dick, Richard, Andy, and Mack Wills were traversing a spiritual middle passage. Instead of crossing that vast Atlantic gulf as their chained ancestors had from Africa to America, they were now navigating and repositioning their internal compass from fear to fortitude. Few brothers on earth have ever had a stronger bond absent of compatible DNA. It was time to fight and, if one or more should fall, they had to keep marching forward until their last breath. There was no turning back because there was but a steep cliff waiting behind them. Whether they had considered the enormity of their place in history was irrelevant as they suited up for battle. The curtain was going up and they were the barnstormers of this bold new act on the bloodied war-torn American stage. The world, especially England and France, were watching and taking sides.

Of all the eyes that had seen the glory of the coming of the Lord during the Civil War in 1863, these colored soldiers, who were married to their oppressors by surname and servitude, were ready for their baptism by fire.

"Forward, Hut!" That was the cry of the drill sergeant in 1863, as Sandy, Andy, Richard, James, Mack, and Dick learned how to march in lockstep with the 4th Heavy Artillery Unit as the companies trained for warfare. Tennessee was a hotbed of the Civil War and Confederate soldiers were especially enraged that the state was largely in the hands of Union forces. They specifically wanted the head of every slave who, in their view, had the audacity to wear a uniform and fight on the side of the enemy. But the new members of the United States Colored Troops were lionhearted in the face of war. They learned how to execute, fire, and clean their weapons and they mentally prepared themselves for battle, though they hardly knew what to expect and, in an ironic way, their ignorance of the epic battle assuaged their fear of it. If war was hell, then the valiant soldiers were fully prepared for the onslaught, because slavery was hell squared. If passion were the deciding factor of the conflict, then the former slaves had already won for a return to bondage was non-negotiable. In the weeks following their enlistment as soldiers, they were disengaged from the metal shackles that had constrained them both mentally and physically for all of their lives. Confederates were fighting for their principles, but my great-great-great grandfather and members of the United States Colored Troops were engaged in a crusade for black people yet unborn. It was no contest.

Tragedy struck the brothers before the first bullet was fired at the colored soldiers. Richard Wills got sick during the training exercises. The eighteen-year-old fell ill just four months after he enlisted at Fort Helleck in Columbus, Kentucky. Without warning, his body became wracked with pain and he had a cough that wouldn't quit. A high fever accompanied by bloodshot eyes sent him to the regimental hospital where he was immediately diagnosed with the measles, or rubeola, as it is sometimes called. As the virus ignited flat discolored rashes on his mahogany skin, Richard lost vital body fluids due to diarrhea. When his comrades and brothers-in-arms last saw him, they probably prayed that he would recover enough to see the war to its end, even if Richard couldn't fight with them. Richard, Andy, Mack, James, Dick, and Sandy had all risked their lives in that death march from Haywood County to Fort Halleck in Kentucky. It was such a shame to succumb to illness, just as they were prepared to stick it to the Confederates that they had hated so. As is often the case when death is in the air, the young men likely thought back to their childhood with Richard and remembered the few joys they shared together, even as slaves. They dreamed of fighting for freedom together and they had been prepared to die together. But Richard was dying alone on a military hospital cot. Civil War medicine left much to be desired; there was little that any nurse or doctor could do for him except watch him drift away.

Five days before Christmas, on December 20, 1863, Richard transitioned to eternal freedom and rest all by himself. In the company descriptive book, a clerk noted in the remarks section: "Died in Regimental Hospital of Columbus, Kentucky (Fort Helleck) on the 20th day of Dec 1863 of Rubeola and Diarrhea. Inventories and final statements forwarded to A G O December 22, 1863."

Perhaps the saddest footnote of all is the question of to whom were Richard's remains given. Certainly, slave master Edmund Willis Wills didn't want them. Unless the boy could work like a mule, Richard was of no use to him dead. Besides, the dead slave was AWOL from the plantation, which cost Edmund Willis Wills a lot of money and work.

Who *were* Richard's mother and father? Slavery, in its contemptible family arrangement, had erased Richard's heritage and robbed him of his birthright. He was a motherless child with no caretaker to wipe his fevered forehead or tend to his blistered body, and no one to bury what was left of him. His living and his death were essentially one in the same. As a slave, he had always been a dead man walking, no firm identity, no independence, and no legacy. The United States of America had sanctioned her citizens to shred his soul to pieces, save what they could use and appropriate for themselves. Richard Wills was gone and forgotten long before he had actually died.

His death was yet another reason why the War of Secession had to go forth. Andy, James, Dick, and Mack may have stood before Richard's diseased corpse and held a small funeral for him. Maybe they gave their beloved brother last rites and prayed for his soul to be reconciled with a freedom-loving God. There's a possibility that they saw Richard's death as an inspiration; harrowing as Richard's short eighteen years were, he died a free man in a soldier's uniform. There's a chance the entire 4th Regiment gathered to pay their last respects to Richard. Conceivably, they may have viewed his death not as a crushing blow, but a solid victory. Richard had come from many generations of slaves, but he was probably the first to die on his own accord. Imaginably, it was a celebration of how all the members of the 4th would leave the world. Death held no sting for these warriors; in fact, it held great promise. Like Lazarus, the diseased beggar in the Holy Scriptures whom Jesus brought back to life with the sound of his voice, the Wills men may have reckoned they, too, would leap from their graves, bound hand and foot, and hop right into heaven.

There was little time to mourn for Richard, for the arc of death was a shadow that loomed over all of their fragile lives. Death was probably not their overriding fear; the soldiers were likely more concerned that their combat not be in vain. Their oxygen-rich blood fertilizing American soil meant nothing, so long as their children and children's children were not property of anyone but God.

As the remaining Wills brothers defended Fort Halleck without Richard, they probably didn't look back. Richard didn't even get to fight the battle, but Andy, Mack, James, Dick, and Sandy were now firmly poised to win the war.

Enlistment forms of Sandy Wills and Dick Parker. To see the rest of the enlistment forms visit www.diefreethebook.com, http://www. diefreethebook.com.

3–446.

DEPOSITION A

Case of _Emma Wills_, No. _575,189_

On this _6_ day of _March 1900_, at _Ged_, county of _Haywood_, State of _Tenn_, before me, _J. A. Critchfield_ a special examiner of the Bureau of Pensions, personally appeared _Emma Wills_, who, being by me first duly sworn to answer truly all interrogatories propounded to her during this special examination of aforesaid claim for pension, deposes and says:

I am _49_ years of age; my post-office address is _Ged Tenn_ and I am by occupation a farmer. I am the identical Emma Wills who has made a claim for pension as the widow of Sandy Wills who served during the Civil War in the United States Army but I dont know in what company or regiment about he served in the same regiment with Andy Wills, Dick Parker, Jim Wills or Jim Parker as he is sometimes called Mack Wills & Gary Austin. I dont know any thing about the dates of his enlistment or discharge. He never served in but that one regiment that I ever knew or heard of. My said husband was named Sandy Wills and I never heard him called Sandy Willis except possibly by some one who would mispronounce his name. He always said he went in the army as Sandy Wills and I never heard any other name. His owner was named Willis Wills. He is dead.

I became acquainted with Sandy Wills about two or three years after the Surrender. He has always lived right here in this neighborhood both before and after the war. I was raised within

Page 5 Deposition a

One of the many sworn depositions Emma Wills gave when she filed for widow's pension.

**Fred as a blues hustler in
Haywood County**

**Opal before she joined the
Holiness church**

Clarence started playing guitar at age nine.

**My dad, third from left, was the standout in the
family right from the start.**

Opal and Fred in New York City

Fred had no idea how much his sons looked up to him.

Clarence and his best friend Frankie in NYC

My dad as lead guitarist for The Wearyland Singers.

Clarence loved being in the military.

Clarence as a paratrooper right before boarding plane

Ruth was the love of my dad's life.

Ruth, flanked by her conservative parents, Sallie and Hardy

Ruth and Clarence wedding day, 1965

**Clarence (seated), Billy Brown, Billy Ravenell and Van posing for The
Thrashing Wonders publicity photo**

Four

Misery in G Major

Being a teenager is tough enough in America, but for Clarence, it was next to impossible as he approached his senior year in high school in Flint, Michigan. He missed New York City and bragged incessantly about it to his new friends in Flint, but he didn't want to return home if his father wasn't sober. After a number of telephone conversations with his mother and Van, he felt assured that his father was no longer drinking and that the family was stable again. In 1958, Clarence was adamant about not witnessing any more acts of domestic violence, alcoholism, or any of the madness that seemed to seep into his parents' chaotic lives. Imagine a seventeen-year-old having to put his foot down on an issue like that.

When he got word that his father actually rented an entire house in Long Island City, Queens, and held a steady job, Clarence felt comfortable returning to the city he loved. Weeks before the start of the new school year at Long Island City High School, Clarence sheepishly returned to his parents' home on 27th Road in Queens—just blocks from the rooming house they had all once crammed into. He was comforted to see Fred lucid and clearheaded because, the last time he saw his beloved dad, the man was stoned out of his mind. Their father-son relationship was largely unspoken, but Clarence was extraordinarily sensitive to his father's shortcomings and he took Fred's failings personally. He secretly hoped for the best for his father and didn't badmouth him—ever. But much like his mother, Clarence believed in his father's redemption through the church. Holiness was their only way out of their living hell, and Clarence really did believe the Bible stories about the power of Jesus Christ and other disciples who performed miracles. He believed in the passionate gospel songs that sprung from the recesses of his mother's heart.

Aside from playing the guitar in church, Clarence, Van, and even Fred, were rather reserved in a church culture that embraced wild shouting and loud singing. Though they all had a knack for inciting church people to dance with their intoxicating guitar rhythms, none of them ever displayed any outward expressions of praise; it was as though they were too cool for that. Their mother, however, made up for their lack of expression. With a now-sober husband and both of her sons back home, Opal felt as though her prayers to Jesus had been solidly answered and she danced all over the church with an unspeakable joy. It was amazing that she had any joy at all because her husband had thoroughly humiliated her time and time again. She had been homeless, forced to drag her husband out of the gutter, and saw her eldest son flee to her relatives out of state for shelter. The only weapon she had at her disposal was prayer and it seemed to have come through for her again. Fred was sober; Clarence was back in New York, and Van was playing his guitar with his brother, again. All was well with Opal's world.

In his senior year at Long Island City High School, Clarence re-bonded with his best friend Frankie and got back in touch with his first love, Ruth, who was also a high school senior at Central Commercial High School on East 42nd Street and Third Avenue in Manhattan. It was a business school and Ruth was all about business. She excelled in typing, stenography, bookkeeping, and other clerical skills. Clarence loved that about her because, even though music was his first passion, he, too, dreamed of having his own business someday. Ruth dressed to impress at Central Commercial High, adorning herself in flowing pearls and arranging her hot comb-straightened hair in the popular beehive do.

As a black kid, Clarence was part of a tiny minority at the mostly white Long Island City High School, but no one really bothered him about his race. If they did, he knew how to talk his way out of trouble. In an attempt to fit in, like most boys his age, he caved in to peer pressure and often sneaked a cigarette after school with his friends and tasted the alcohol that seemed to captivate his father so. He knew it was wrong, but Clarence had a fearlessness and recklessness that few would have ever suspected of the mild-mannered church boy. During his final year of high school, he developed a unique skill of acting like a cool kid with his white friends at school; but when he was with his parents at church, he was the mild-mannered teen guitarist who had mastered the change up from D major to G major to make the church ladies and even the deacons dance in the spirit. He was very sociable on all fronts and appeared harmless to all who met him. Clarence walked this fine line between saints and sinners, alternately dipping his toe in the holy water and the devil's brew for the rest of his life.

Clarence's passion for music increased with his age and he often took his girlfriend Ruth to musical programs—gospel and otherwise. Clarence didn't hide his love of all kinds of music. Born so close to Memphis, he deeply appreciated country western music and the blues. But his parents made him feel guilty when he listened to the so-called "devil's music," so he hid his secular records and played them only when his parents were not home. Sam Cooke was the sole exception in their household. The newly minted soul singer had been a teen sensation in the gospel world for most of his young life. Born in Mississippi in 1931, Sam Cooke was born into a Christian family that had also fled segregation in the South and relocated to Chicago when he was a toddler during the Black Migration. His father, Rev. Charles Cook, was a popular Baptist minister who took tremendous pride in his children's talents, especially young Sam whose golden-piped voice was widely considered a gift from God. A sensation even as a young teenager, he was the lead singer for a local gospel group called the Highway Q.C.'s before he landed the gig of a lifetime.

The Soul Stirrers was one of the most renowned quartet gospel groups in the country and was led by a gritty full-throated Texas singer named Robert H. Harris, who was known by R.H. Opal, and millions of other church ladies loved Harris like a brother and adored him like a husband. In the late 1930s, he had pushed the a cappella group to new heights as they went from local chitlin circuits to national auditoriums with lucrative recording contracts. They were the biggest gospel act in American history, but in 1950, Harris shocked the gospel circuit when he abruptly quit the quartet to start his own group. The thirty-four-year-old singing legend was replaced by a lanky nineteen-year-old looker named Sam Cooke. Most thought it a joke that a kid would replace the great Harris until Sam Cooke opened his mouth, and then the debate was over. The young man's voice was blessed with a maturity and fervor that caused black women to shout and faint in the aisles. Harris had gambled and lost; the Soul Stirrers did not wither away without him, they only became bigger and better.

As Sam Cooke blossomed with the group, he made the group even sexier with the addition of a jazzy guitarist and drummer. But Sam was the man, and the Soul Stirrers quickly became known as "Sam Cooke and the Soul Stirrers." Clarence, Van, Opal, and Fred were all huge fans of Sam Cooke's records especially his rendition of "Touch the Hem of his Garment," where the crooner's voice glides over the lyrics describing the famous Bible story of the poor woman who just managed to touch the hem of Jesus' garment. Sam became the Elvis of the gospel world. Church girls made eyes at him and waited for him backstage to express their "appreciation."

But Sam had a dark side that the church folks didn't know about. He was a real swinger who loved the ladies a little too much, and he also loved the forbidden music—rhythm and blues. Fully aware of the fallout from singing the sinner's music, Sam recorded his first R&B song under an alias, but "Dale Cook" was immediately outed as a gospel turncoat. Had it happened after President Richard Nixon's resignation, it would have likely been dubbed Gospel-gate. Sam Cooke's departure from the Soul Stirrers in 1957 caused a major uproar in the black community but Sam was determined make some "real" money and sing to a wider audience than just black church people. More than a few black preachers based entire sermons on Sam Cooke's perceived betrayal of God and the church, and there were blatant forebodings of his demise.

Still, Clarence and Van and many other young people liked that Sam Cooke showed the world that he could do more than just sing gospel and indeed he belted out some of the most beautiful soul music ever heard like "You Send Me," which was a monster hit in 1957 and shot to number one on the music charts. Clarence tried to get his mother to listen to Sam Cooke, but she, like millions of other church folk, boycotted Sam because he went to "the devil's side." However, even Opal couldn't resist some of his popular songs like "Sweet Sixteen." If Clarence and Van caught her with her guard down, she couldn't help but enjoy the sweetness in Sam's voice that she had loved so well when Sam crooned glowingly about Jesus. But in between tapping her foot to his melodious voice, she constantly told her sons how she pitied Sam's open embrace of the fast life and, sure enough, Sam Cooke was shot to death in a seedy motel in Los Angeles after some kind of dispute over a prostitute. No one was happy that Sam died in 1964, but black church folk, especially Holiness people like Fred and Opal, chided their grown sons with a smirk and deadpanned, "We told you so."

Sam Cooke's untimely and tragic death didn't deter Clarence one bit. As he wrapped up his senior year in high school, he still had stars in his eyes. In fact, he was fully content with following the same path from gospel to rhythm and blues as Sam Cooke had done. Clarence had no fear of death and with every birthday he tempted fate more and more.

Unlike his younger brother, Van, Clarence enjoyed being a student. But Van, still bitter and distant over his parent's instability, had dropped out of school and didn't care too much about anything except his guitar. It was good that Clarence left New York for Michigan when his family became homeless, because he was able to create stability for himself and remain in one school; but Van had been tossed from one school to another and subsequently lost interest in academics even though he was smart as a whip. But Van was not nearly as aggressive, outspoken, or daring as his older brother Clarence, who understood that his ticket to success was punched by a diploma. If there was one thing that Clarence grasped early on, it was the rules of the game; he knew how to acquire credentials and unlike many blacks in Holiness, he didn't feel intimidated by anyone— white or black. This was a guy who wasn't afraid of anything, even when he should have been.

On graduation day, Clarence put on a suit and tie and, when he saw that his parents were getting dressed, he politely told them he wanted to go it alone. Opal was mildly insulted but didn't push the matter because she knew her son had already been through a lot, and the fact that he was graduating was a testament in itself. Clarence matter-of-factly explained to his parents, neither of whom had ever set foot in high school or attended a graduation of any kind, that he just wanted to be with his friends. His parents had done nothing to help him to this special commencement day; they did not provide stability during his school years and they had never really helped him with his homework. Clarence had been on his own for a long time, and he was only eighteen. Fred and Opal were good-natured people and wanted the best for Clarence and Van, but they had no clue how to govern themselves in the complicated world outside of their religion. This is why they fanatically embraced the tenets of Holiness; they were intimidated by just about everything else outside of religion. Just like their great grandparents who were held in bondage, they felt unworthy of the world's success. Jim Crow had taught them well that they were not entitled to wish for anything more than scraps; and indeed, scraps were all they had. Even Fred, with his lofty dreams, did not truly go about executing them with vim and vigor. He wanted to do things on "his" safe terms and make his own rules, and that was not how the game was played. But Clarence respected the rules and his understanding of the game took him far in life.

But Clarence's graduation was all a sham. Due to the instability of his childhood and the constant turnover at schools, he was short a math class and was not cleared to march with his fellow seniors as the band played pomp and circumstance. Deeply embarrassed, he told not a soul, not even Ruth, who graduated on time from Central Commercial High School and bragged incessantly about her graduation ceremony that was being held at Carnegie Hall, of all places. So when he walked out of the door, God only knows where the dejected boy went. Doubtful he went to the graduation, maybe he went to Coney Island or Times Square. But later that evening, he returned to Long Island City and strolled into Evans Bar on 28th Street. It was the typical Queens dive, with a dozen round tables and rickety chairs and a long wraparound bar. There was nothing special or glitzy about it, but the establishment held great fascination for Clarence through his younger years, probably because he was not allowed inside as a minor.

Armed with a draft card which certified that he was eighteen years old, and eligible to fight in the emerging Vietnam conflict and legally drink alcohol, Clarence celebrated his manhood by himself. It certainly wasn't his first drink; throughout his senior year, Clarence and his white, black, and Latino friends sometimes sneaked down Broadway's gritty streets in Queens and alternately took swigs and exchanged each other's spit from a bottle wrapped in a brown paper bag. The skinny narrow-faced kids chuckled with devious delight as they swallowed the bitter firewater, with hopes that no one witnessed their boyish clod; they could barely stomach the taste of the alcohol but they all wanted to imitate their fathers—especially Clarence. He had quietly wondered why his father was so enraptured by what some preachers jokingly called "joy juice" which had nearly destroyed his entire family on numerous occasions. Now it was Clarence's turn. Van, who was playing down the street in front of the house, saw his brother's shadow wrap around the corner of 28th Street. The scrawny fourteen-year-old dashed behind him and followed Clarence into the bar, cautiously remaining about ten feet away at the door's entrance.

Feeling like a man, but still looking like a boy, Clarence steadied his small frame on the bar stool and balanced his size-eight shoes on the circular footrest. In a cocksure gesture, he tossed a crumpled five-dollar bill on the bar and asked for a scotch with a beer chaser. The unimpressed bartender raised an eyebrow and didn't move an inch. Without missing a beat, Clarence reached into his back pocket, heaved a faint sigh of frustration and opened his wallet. He tossed his signed draft card onto the bar next to the money and eyeballed the tall, red-headed Irishman who stood before him with a wise-guy grin. The bartender flipped the draft card back to him and grabbed the bottle of scotch and poured it into a tumbler, topped off beer in a pint glass, and placed both drinks before the fledgling souse.

Eighteen-year-old Clarence, who stood about as tall as he would ever get at five-feet-seven-and-three-quarter inches, neatly tucked his draft card back into his wallet and secured it in his back pocket. As Van peered into the dark musky bar with amazement from the sun-drenched doorway, Clarence gripped the first glass with his right index finger and thumb and quickly choked down the booze and chased it with the second shot. With every gulp, it burned his virgin throat. His body violently shook and his head rattled left and right, and he squeezed his eyes tight. The amused bartender looked at the little squirt, having seen dozens of eighteen-year-olds recoil in the same manner before, and waited for the young man's next move. Clarence put another couple of bills on the bar and ordered a second round. Bemused, Van crept over to his inebriated brother and said, "If you don't like the way it tastes, whatchoo drinkin' it for?!"

Enraged, Clarence spun around on the stool and yelled at his lighter-skinned brother, "Get out of here!" The kid took off, but that was a moment my Uncle Van never forgot and would retell that story with vivid imagery for years and years to come.

Clarence was toasting his new independence. Finally, he was a man who could chart his own destiny and he had a firm plan in mind. He wanted to join a gospel group, make records, and travel the world as a famous musician. He didn't play his guitar the way his contemporaries did; he heard a different, fuller sound in his head, and incorporated those well-constructed rhythms with the blues, country, and church music he had heard all of his life. He knew from the reaction of church ladies who danced their shoes off when he played the guitar that he was onto something big.

He was a natural leader, too. In church, he learned how to separate voices into alto, tenor, and soprano sections, and he also knew how to play the piano to help singers stay in tune. Mixing in his affable manner made Clarence a pleasure to deal with on all fronts. Sure enough, a burgeoning gospel group in the western section of Queens snatched him right up. They were known around the city as The Wearyland Gospel Singers and the lead singer, David Stewart, hired Clarence on the spot as their lead guitarist.

They were seven young black men, all of whom were raised in different Pentecostal churches around New York City. Just about all of them were born in the South and were shuttled away from the brutal country towns with their parents during the tail end of the Black Migration. On the radio, they knew every word and beat to popular gospel songs performed by legendary groups like the Dixie Hummingbirds, The Swan Silvertones, The Blind Boys, and so many more. The Wearyland Singers were organized, full of talent and spunk, and hoped to get a record deal and go national, just like their gospel idols. They entered the gospel circuit as newcomers and were awed by what they saw when these gospel pioneers passed through New York City to perform.

These types of gospel groups had been around since the turn of the twentieth century and they traveled the chitlin circuit right alongside their sinful blues and jazz counterparts. Both split the black audience; the gospel groups courted the church-going Christians, and the blues and jazz artists courted everyone else. Many times the audiences overlapped because both musical genres were creating some of the most beautiful sounds Americans had ever heard.

Mainstream America basically ignored these Christian singing sensations, but millions and millions of blacks, saints and sinners alike, embraced them wholeheartedly. These groups sold millions of records on gospel labels like Decca, Specialty, MCA, and Peacock, which especially fitting because many of these flamboyant singers sometimes crossed that fine line between humble Christian messengers and pretentious self-obsessed entertainers.

Pioneering groups like the Soul Stirrers sang in churches, school auditoriums, and sometimes major venues like the Apollo Theater, to standing-room-only crowds coast to coast long before anyone had ever coined the phrases Rock and Roll, Rhythm and Blues, and Motown. Decades before the Temptations and the Four Tops, these were the real

McCoys who dressed in identical suits and stood shoulder to shoulder on stage and made crowds swoon to the spirit. Before Elvis and the Beatles hit TV host Ed Sullivan's show, The Dixie Hummingbirds lead singer Ira Tucker's vocal theatrics cast a spell on audiences. It has been argued that white and black wannabe singers watched these gospel greats from afar and transformed their spiritual acts into a secular one. It's no secret that R&B stars Jackie Wilson and James Brown grew up listening and watching dynamic gospel acts and imitated the Christian showmanship almost to the letter.

The Blind Boys of Alabama were probably one of the most copied gospel groups. Clarence Fountain, Jimmy Carter, Johnny Fields, George Scott, Ollice Thomas, JT Hutton, and Vel Bozman all met at the segregated Alabama Institute for the Negro Blind in Talladega, Alabama. In a sickening irony, staunch segregationists even separated people who couldn't even see the color of their fellow citizens. Nevertheless, the seven blind youngsters exhibited an astonishing talent for singing spirituals in 1939 and before long they took their show on the road. And what a show it was! Each member wore black sunglasses and, when Clarence Fountain wailed on stage about one day seeing his dead mother again with Jesus, folks in the audience cried and many fainted. The group sang with a fierce thunder in their soul, likely born out of their disability, and though white audiences ignored their blockbuster talents, black audiences went wild. The Blind Boys theatrics were endless and memorable, as they walked in hand-on-shoulder to deafening applause and danced feverishly in the spirit as the tempo of their songs like "Something to Shout About."

By sheer coincidence, The Blind Boys of Mississippi had formed a couple of years earlier at the Pine Woods School for the blind near Jackson, Mississippi. Galvanized by lead singer, Archie Brownlee, and his cohorts Joseph Ford, Lawrence Abrams, and Lloyd Woodard, the quartet was backed by a jazz band, which really helped them swing. There was nothing more intoxicating or infectious than seeing these men, who also wore black sunglasses, break into spiritual ecstasy, dance without shame, and never lose their balance or fall off stage.

These groups sang century-old Negro spirituals like "Swing Low, Sweet Chariot" and spiced them up with an up tempo beat and guitar. They commonly sang Thomas A. Dorsey's famous gospel tunes, like "Take My

Hand, Precious Lord." Dorsey was considered the "father of black gospel music" and was primarily responsible for infusing the blues into spirituals.

Dorsey grew up singing secular music and was famously known as Georgia Tom. He composed for blues legends like Ma Rainey in the 1920s. They created saucy songs with double entendre lyrics, such as their popular "Tight like That." But Dorsey's sinful days came to an end when his beloved first wife died while pregnant, and he viewed the tragedy as a calling to change his wicked ways. He never recorded another blues song again. The devil's loss was the church's gain, as Dorsey revolutionized the way African folks sang to God.

Fred, Opal, Clarence, and Van were deeply woven into this musical fabric. Whether they lived in Tennessee, Indiana, Chicago, or New York, they regularly purchased tickets to see a gospel program featuring groups like The Blind Boys or the Soul Stirrers. These musical programs, often hosted by a local Christian disc jockey, were their only form of entertainment, because most black Pentecostal church people were forbidden from going to the movies. But these programs were just as entertaining, if not more so. And Clarence wanted a piece of the action. He was a full-fledged member of the Wearyland Singers in 1960 when the group was booked to open for major acts like the ones my dad had idolized on the records. Interestingly, all of the men shared a common thread: they were all the great grandsons, and in some cases grandsons of slaves, and the African-born rhythms that once rang out from the cotton fields were now ringing out on a brightly lit stage, backed up by a band billed as a gospel extravaganza.

These gospel stars were the first celebrities Clarence ever met. Backstage, as all the groups waited in the wings for their cue, he was awestruck as he recognized famous singers like Claude Jeter of the Swan Silvertones, and Julius Cheeks of the Sensational Nightingales. Clarence especially enjoyed rubbing elbows with the guitarists he idolized such as Howard Carroll of the Dixie Hummingbirds. No matter how many millions of albums these superstars of gospel sold coast to coast, they were still reduced to singing in school auditoriums and storefront churches to make a living. Even though Jim Crow laws did not exist in the Northern cities, these mega-talents still couldn't get booked regularly at major venues like Carnegie Hall, and they were not welcome on major network shows like Ed Sullivan. The best they could hope for was the Apollo Theater in Harlem, and those gigs were few and far between because Jackie Wilson's sensual performances were a more exciting draw than the grown up church boys who sang songs from Zion. They made a joyful noise unto the Lord, but mainstream America turned a deaf ear to them.

Clarence and the Wearyland Singers learned quickly that all that glitters was not gold. Sometimes they were not paid after a performance and most times they were paid less than what they were promised. Splitting the money seven ways often left very little for each member. Fred, watching in utter disgust from the wings, bided his time and then he couldn't hold back any longer. "Boy, you wasting your time with that! Go get a real job and make something of yourself!" Fred often said this with a tinge of resentment, which sent my dad over the edge.

The older Clarence got, the more he despised his father's chastisement. He felt his father had no right to impose his beliefs upon anybody, considering his awful track record as the alleged head of household. Fred didn't bother to explain to his son that he had the very same musical dream not so long ago, and he was brokenhearted when no one recognized or seemed to give a damn about his musical prowess. The best thing his talent had ever got Fred was a free bus ticket to New York. He didn't want to see Clarence experience the same disappointment. But, of course, Fred did not speak with such candor or understanding. He barked his arrogant orders at Clarence. The boy quietly suffered from haunting memories of periods of abandonment at the hands of his father and, though the pain was largely unspoken, it was ever present.

Van was becoming more and more reclusive; Clarence harbored a silent rage, and Opal, the grand wizard of them all, pretended nothing too bad had ever really happened and blamed it not on Fred, but on the devil. Worst of all, Fred never apologized to his impressionable sons who adored him more than anything and, with every birthday, they grew more and more resentful. Fred didn't just break their hearts, he shattered their souls by being a hypocrite in church, beating and berating their adoring mother, losing his dignity as a drunkard and—sin of all fatherly sins—being unable to provide for the family, rendering them homeless at times. Fred kept a stiff upper lip and almost seemed to dare anyone to even mention his transgressions, and no one in the family did.

Initially, Clarence took pleasure in defying his father's wishes that he get a "real" job. He spent his days doing odd jobs for small change and practicing songs for the group on his guitar. At night he took an evening course to make up the class that caused him to miss graduation, and later he joined the other members of the Wearyland singers for rehearsal. One day when Fred overheard Clarence complaining to his mother about how some of the singers were late for rehearsal and how he needed more money, Fred chimed in with his "I told you so's," and Clarence jumped up in his father's face and told him to mind his business.

But one look in his mother's distraught eyes and he immediately settled down. If there was one person in the world he did not want to cause any further pain, it was his mother. She had suffered so much and had been so terribly humiliated that Clarence couldn't bear to disappoint her any further. So he bolted for the door and made the most daring move of his life in 1962. He went to the Recruiting Station on Main Street in Flushing and enlisted in the United States Army.

When Clarence stood before the enlistment officer, neither he nor the enlistment officer had any idea that my father was a Civil War legacy and that his Great-great grandfather Sandy Wills probably walked barefoot to an enlistment station in Tennessee to fight for his unborn children and grandchildren's freedom. Clueless of this amazing piece of genealogy as he stood before a recruiter, he gave his name as Clarence Douglas Wills. And unlike his great-great grandfather, he was able to sign his full name in script. Times had so dramatically changed since 1863 when Sandy enlisted. In the ninety-nine years since his daring move, the army had become fully integrated with a number of blacks in high positions in the armed forces, and their futures were brighter than ever before. The same year that Clarence entered the Army as a private in New York, there was one African-American captain—also from New York City—who would go on to make history in the decades to come. Colin Powell was poised to shatter barriers in the Army as the first black four-star general, the first black joint chief of staff, and later, the first African-American secretary of state.

In January 27, 1962, it became official. Clarence brought home two certificates. One was his high school diploma from William C. Bryant Evening High School, which awarded him a certified diploma. This was a first for the Wills family and it pretty much went unnoticed. The second was a Certificate of Acceptance addressed to Fred and Opal from the station commander which read:

> I am very pleased to inform you that your son, Clarence Douglas, has successfully passed the mental, moral, and physical examinations required of applicants and is now qualified for service in the United States Regular Army. I heartily congratulate you on the choice your son has made in applying for the enlistment in one of the world's finest military organizations, and feel sure that he will be a credit to the United States Army and to our country.

During this time in 1962, President Kennedy was facing trouble in Vietnam, but the situation had not yet escalated. Thousands of American military personnel were flowing into South Vietnam in a strategic attempt to protect the rural population from insurgents. Few Americans even knew where Vietnam was on the map, and there was little indication when Clarence entered the force that this small movement would escalate into a bloody conflict that claimed thousands of soldiers' lives and forever changed the political and cultural landscape in America. Oblivious to what lay ahead, he had one pressing question for his station commander: could he bring along his guitar when he shipped out to Fort Dix in New Jersey? The answer was yes.

With that, Private Clarence D. Wills returned home to Long Island City to pack his belongings into a long, green duffel bag as Fred, Opal, and Van watched in silence. Clarence was always up to something new and different, but his latest move was a whopper for his parents and his brother Van. No one knew when or if Clarence was coming back. As he packed his personal effects, he talked about traveling overseas and told his mother and brother that he planned to take advantage of every opportunity presented to him.

When the lead member of the Wearyland Singers called Clarence to express his remorse over his leaving the group, Clarence encouraged them to give his brother a shot. Ever since Van dropped out of school, all he did was practice his guitar and he was really getting good at it, so he joined the group. As Clarence loaded his bag on his back, he kissed his mother goodbye, and she urged him to keep his Bible with him at all times and make sure he wrote home. Opal was not happy that her boy was leaving, but she understood that, as a man, he had to venture out on his own and chart his own course. She not only loved her son, but she respected him. Fred, on the other hand, was bitter and said not a word. In truth, he was probably bitter because he was ashamed that he had not been a better father and was not due the respect he felt he deserved. Swollen with arrogance and filled with fear for his son's future, Fred waited for his son to say goodbye to him, and Clarence waited for his dad to make the first move. Both waited in vain because Clarence eyeballed Van and said goodbye and turned and walked out the door as his mother tearfully said, "God Bless you, Son, I'll be praying for you. I love you and take care of yourself, hear?"

"Alright, Mother. I'm gone." Clarence said.

The deafening silence ruined yet another special moment for the family of four. Fred failed to see that his behavior was irredeemable in the eyes of his sons but both Clarence and Van were broken in secret fragile places beyond repair. If they had only talked about their pain, maybe it would not have festered so badly but, in a misguided attempt to maintain the family's status quo, everyone held their peace. They all had an unspoken agreement that forbade unseemly behavior. Fred and Opal had already been through that, and the violence between them was so devastating in the end that it was understood that they didn't want their teenage sons to engage in such repellant behavior. So with broken hearts and dejected spirits, they all tried to go along and get along. Poor things, they had no clue that holding their peace would soon manifest itself as rage, depression, and recklessness. They were perfectly content while playing music together in church with Fred, Clarence, and Van on their respective guitars, and Opal on the piano; but when the music stopped, they had no way of expressing their true feelings and they didn't want to go there, anywhere. It was misery in G major.

Opal didn't dwell much on the past, she was the only authentic "saved and sanctified" one among them, but the boys continued to feel that they were due an explanation and an apology from their father. They wanted their dad to say, at the very least, "sorry" for not being a better father and tell them that it wasn't personal. Fred, oblivious to their need for closure, went on his way, essentially telling his sons to suck it up and learn how to be men in this wicked world. After all, Fred had a remorseful story as well; no one said "sorry" to him when his mother died and left him and his young sisters and brothers to basically fend for themselves and tiptoe around a drunken father. No one told Fred "sorry" when the winds of fate knocked him down, so he didn't see why he needed to apologize to anyone. Stuff happens, he figured. And hypocritical and unrepentant as he was, he re-anointed himself as holier than thou and walked and talked like a preacher.

When Clarence boarded the military bus that was bound for Fort Dix in New Jersey, he pitied his father and swore to himself that, when he got married and had his own children, he would never be like his dad.

Clarence's entry into an integrated army in 1962 was the result of a hard-fought battle. The United States armed forces had been strictly segregated until the end of World War Two. President Harry Truman finally ended the national disgrace that started when my great-great-great grandfather enlisted in the United States Colored Troops during the Civil War. The U.S.C.T. was separate and unequal from the rest of the Union troops as they fought mightily to stop the Confederacy in its tracks. As the war raged on in late 1864, the Confederates had reluctantly recruited slaves into their military but, unlike the Union Army, they did not create a separate branch for them. Although they were fighting against their own interests, slaves were not segregated within the Confederate army. Though their military mission was misguided to say the least, blacks fought right alongside whites and slept and ate with them, too. But the devil was in the details, as the Confederates were reluctant to give them weapons in their sick attempts to persuade blacks in gray that slavery was good for America. No one can blame the black soldiers aligned with the Confederates, because, as in slavery, they had no choice—they had to fight with the enemies of their freedom, or die. It was as simple as that.

Although the United States Colored Troops were shamefully separated from the rest of the Union Army, I'm very grateful that my Great-great-great grandfather Sandy and his brothers were on the right side of the war—especially as the war shifted to the Union's favor by 1865. The Civil War, which started in 1861 and decimated the South's countryside and claimed the lives of thousands of young men, black and white, slave and free, in blue and gray, was nearing its end. When it initially broke out, no one imagined how doggedly determined white Southerners were to keep Africans in chains and at their exclusive disposal. Even President Lincoln underestimated the intense grip that half of America had on black bondage. Had General Ulysses Grant not effectively choked the life out of the South, where civilians and Confederate soldiers were practically starving to death, the Confederacy might have continued their fight until every soldier in America was killed.

Shortly after the New Year in 1864, white federal troops started to ship out of Fort Halleck in Columbus, Kentucky. They ranged from baby-faced, gung-ho lads who lied about their age to enlist, to hardened men in their mid-thirties. The soldiers were loaded down with artillery and other equipment and they were prepared to kill Confederate soldiers in gray. But as with most forts, the eager newly independent black soldiers, equally prepared to fight, but were ruefully left behind.

Andy, James, Dick, and Mack Wills, and the hundreds of their brown compatriots with Company F of the 4th Heavy Artillery regiment were ordered to stay put, along with some white army soldiers as a garrison, to protect the fortified position, particularly from guerilla attacks. Colonel William H. Lawrence was the commander and Peter Dobozy was his lieutenant colonel. It's not clear if my Great-great-great grandfather Sandy's Company G joined them from Union City under the leadership of Lieutenant Dearborn. There were eight companies of the 4th Heavy Artillery ranging from A to H with nearly 600 men, most of them runaway slaves.

The Confederates were relentless in their mission to take back Tennessee from federal troops, so garrison duty wasn't exactly a walk in the park. At any moment, guerillas were liable to attack the fort and leave death in their wake, which is precisely what happened on March 6, 1864. Military records show that black soldiers from the 4th Field Heavy Artillery Company E fended off about thirty guerillas, who were feverishly trying to get between the breastworks and the brigade. These small groups of red-faced combatants seethed with rage that proud Africans were adorned in military uniforms and kept watch over federal military installations. Their gunshots sometimes rang out in the middle of the night, and the black soldiers from the 4th had to be prepared to drive them off, or die trying.

Although many of the soldiers were probably restless at the fort, they were certainly made to understand the consequences of losing control of the coveted military post. The general consensus among most white officers was that black privates were wholly incapable of engaging in combat, and most expressed and argued this point as though it were a scientific fact. These white officers, though members of the Union Army, did not in any way view themselves as freedom fighters or anything of the sort. In fact, some resigned their commissions because they were appalled at the thought of serving in the United States military to merely emancipate slaves. The very thought of such a mission repelled many white officers, who saw their duty as preserving the original Union; they literally couldn't care less about blacks, whom so many white soldiers deemed as inferior human beings.

But the 4th Field Heavy Artillery in Columbus, Kentucky, was a strategic location, as it was initially part of the Confederacy's western defensive line. In fact, thousands of slaves were used to build fortifications in western Kentucky for the rebels' cause. The very thought of slaves now defending it for federal troops was more than many Confederates could stand. The Wills soldiers stationed at Fort Halleck were part of a sort of subunit for the federal installation. In addition to their regular picket and patrol duty, they were sometimes whisked into minor skirmishes, but they never engaged in a major battle like the renowned 54th Regiment from Massachusetts, which was the inspiration for the movie, *Glory*, starring Denzel Washington and Morgan Freeman. But the 54th, which led the famous assault on Fort Wagner in South Carolina in 1863, was the exception, not the norm for members of the United States Colored Troops. That is certainly not to say that my Great-great-great grandfather Sandy's service to the Union army was any less commendable; their lives were at stake and, at any point, they could have been slaughtered wholesale, like the unfortunate soldiers at nearby Fort Pillow in Tennessee.

On April 12, 1864, African-American soldiers throughout the country got wind of a massacre involving black troops at the hands of white Confederate soldiers that shocked not only the United States Colored Troops, but the nation.

Fort Pillow in Henning, Tennessee, was about 100 miles from Fort Halleck in Kentucky and about forty miles from Memphis. The fortification was situated on a high bluff near the Mississippi River and surrounded by a ditch. It was built in 1862 by Confederate troops and named for Brigadier General Gideon Johnson Pillow, who had no clue that his name would be forever linked with what some military historians call one of the most shameful moments in American military history.

Guarding the fort were about 300 black soldiers from the 2nd U.S. Colored Light Artillery and the 6th U.S. Colored Heavy Artillery as well as about 300 white soldiers from the 13th Tennessee Calvary. For the first time in their lives, these black soldiers had a real responsibility and were treated like men, but there was no time to revel in their newfound liberty because Major General Nathan Bedford Forrest was on the march with about seven thousand Confederate soldiers. The garrison at Fort Pillow was outnumbered right from the start of the ambush, as sharpshooters took defensive positions shortly before midnight.

There are conflicting reports of what happened in the morning hours of Tuesday, April 13, 1864. Some say the soldiers guarding Fort Pillow laid down their arms and surrendered as an avalanche of men in gray approached, some on horseback wielding the Confederate flag. But General Forrest's' reports at the time indicated that federal troops kept their weapons pointed at the Confederates and did not surrender. Whether the entire garrison surrendered or not, the horrific outcome of the fort's invasion speaks volumes. Almost the entire unit was slaughtered. There were reports that irate Confederates savagely bayoneted black soldiers who, by some accounts, had fallen to their knees and begged for mercy as prisoners of war. Although twenty Confederate soldiers were killed in the battle, about 500 soldiers—both black and white—were mercilessly executed. Some were decapitated, with reports of brains littered among the dead. Even civilians, many of whom were married to soldiers at the Fort, were shot in cold blood and drowned as they fled to the nearby Mississippi River.

But the letters at the time really told a more haunting tale. Major General Forrest wrote in chilling detail:

"The river was dyed with the blood of the slaughtered for 200 yards...It is hoped that these facts will demonstrate to the Northern people that negro soldiers cannot cope with Southerners. We still hold the fort."

Forrest's callousness to the atrocity illustrated how paranoid the Confederacy was about the legitimacy and potential victory of the United Sates Colored Troops. To the Confederates and their cold-hearted supporters, the importance of maintaining the enslavement of my Grandfather Sandy and the millions more in bondage cannot be overstated. They had been thoroughly indoctrinated with the belief that people of color were lower than dogs, and they were hell bent on proving it, even at the expense of their own precious lives.

Other witnesses of the so-called Fort Pillow Massacre revealed in their personal letters just how horrific this event was. Confederate soldier S. H. Caldwell expressed the horror in a private note to his wife.

We are just [back] from Fort Pillow which fort we attacked on Tuesday the 13, 1864, and carried by storm. It was garrisoned by 400 white men and 400 negroes, and out of the 800 only 168 are now living. So you can now guess how terrible was the slaughter. It was decidedly the most horrible sight that I have ever witnessed. We took about one hundred and 25 white men and about 45 negroes and the rest of the 800 are numbered with the dead—they are heaped upon each other 3 days...

As word of the carnage at Fort Pillow spread, there were strong reactions across the North. Biographers noted that President Lincoln was "besieged with calls for retribution" as news reports sensationalized the devastation at Fort Pillow. Some felt President Lincoln should have made a public statement about the massacre because he knew the terrible risks associated with the establishment of the United States Colored Troops and was, in effect, responsible for their safety. Weeks later, President Lincoln briefly addressed the Battle at Fort Pillow, expressing his remorse and accepting responsibility for the event.

The fact that President Lincoln acknowledged the deaths of black soldiers was probably enough to give my Great-great-great grandfather Sandy and other black troops reason to fight on. At last, the spilling of black blood mattered to someone. For generations, blacks had been whipped, beaten, tortured, executed, and lynched—and in the eyes of most whites it was par for the course. But with the highest authority in the union expressing regret over black blood, a new day had indeed dawned in a divided America.

In the wake of the massacre, undeterred members of the U.S. Colored Troops wailed "Remember Fort Pillow" as a rallying cry. Garrison duty was not so mundane, if it ever was, for black soldiers. Although it seemed true glory was lost or won on the battlefield, the U.S.C.T. proved that it was also won or lost guarding the fort.

After the massacre, the Confederate soldiers abandoned Fort Pillow and took Union horses and supplies along with them. Tennessee was solidly in the hands of the Union, and to stay meant they would soon face the same bloodbath that they had just executed on the Yanks in even greater numbers. They left their blood-soaked Confederate flags on the decimated fort and fled for the hills the very same night. However, unshakable colored troops, including those with the 4th Field Heavy Artillery, held their ground. Surely, my great-great-great grandfather, who was just miles away from this bloodbath at Fort Pillow, knew that General Forrest's men were full of hubris nearby, preparing to destroy more fortifications and slay more colored soldiers.

My heart swells with pride when I consider how in the face of this imminent danger, not one of the Wills soldiers went AWOL. As the air of western Tennessee reeked with the smell of horse carcasses mixed with the cadavers of former slaves, these fearless soldiers summoned the courage to remain steadfast in their quest to be free citizens. Their resolve was non-negotiable; should they fall in their noble mission, they were sure that their deaths would not be in vain and now, their blood would not simply be washed away with the rain. As members of the military, they were assured that their duty and their sacrifice would be remembered. And they were right. I never had the privilege of laying eyes on Sandy, but his blood pumps through my heart. Every day I thank him for his service not only to his country, but to his family. He stood his ground so we can stand tall.

If there ever was a great war, this was it; terrible in all of its proportions and hateful in all of its deeds. My Great-great-great grandfather Sandy, along with Mack, Andy, Dick, and James, held steadfast and now victory and freedom, permanent freedom, was in their sights. They were the truest of any freedom fighters that the United States had ever known. Slavery had robbed them of their parents, their education, their stability, and their God-given right to roam free on the planet Earth. It took hundreds of years, but these African men were about to become the first wave of a new breed of Americans, whites included, who would die free.

Five

Happy, Free, and in Love

In 1962, Clarence, a twenty-year-old bachelor, dreamed about his darling girlfriend Ruth as he moved into the army barracks at an army installation named for a Civil War veteran. Filled with ambition, Private Clarence D. Wills was part of the 5th Training Regiment at Fort Dix in New Jersey. The bustling training center in Burlington County was named for Major General John Adams Dix—a little factoid Clarence learned just moments after he stepped foot on the military grounds. He felt right at home with his new comrades, just as he had during a cadet program he joined during his senior year at Long Island City High School. For a child who had been yanked from one state to another for much of his childhood, it turned out Clarence longed for and even appreciated the strict regulations and order of the military.

In his locker, he kept his personal clothing, a five-by-seven, black-and-white picture of Ruth, which she signed, "To Clarence" at the top right hand corner, and "Love Ruth" in the bottom right corner. She looked dazzling and sophisticated in a delicate blouse draped in pearls and her hair was swept up with a bang that covered her high forehead. She was truly a vision of loveliness. Clarence glued her picture on the back of a larger piece of cardboard so it wouldn't bend, and colored the border orange. He was infatuated with Ruth and hoped to marry her when he returned to New York. Also inside his locker was a small, red, leather-bound Bible that was just a little larger than the size of his hand, and his black-and-tan electric guitar. He was one of only a handful of privates who brought along an instrument, and that alone made him a standout.

DIE FREE

At the end of a long day of training in mid-1962, Clarence, who made friends fast, entertained troops with his guitar rendition of The Isley Brother's hot new hit in 1962, *"Twist and Shout."* Black, Latino, and white soldiers chimed in on the chorus of *"Shake it, shake it, baby,"* while Clarence led his comrades with his smooth tenor voice. *"C'mon, baby,"* and they repeated, *"C'mon, baby—work it on out!"* Their voices bounced off the walls of barracks and the black guitar player, as he was initially known, became one of the most popular new recruits. He was a free, happy spirit who genuinely liked people.

As cranky soldiers rose before the break of dawn every morning, Clarence was the one to head to the showers with a joke or some other wisecrack about a whacky dream he had. Even though he was born in the South, he had not a trace of a Southern dialect or drawl. The only way anyone would detect that he was a Southerner, was if they looked at his birth certificate, because he rarely admitted it. Like many transplanted blacks, he hated the South and everything it represented, especially with news reports that blacks were still being harassed and murdered by racist mobs. He prided himself on being a New Yorker, even though he wasn't a native son.

Although he liked to clown around, Clarence was on a serious mission. He sought guidance from his commanding officers about what path he should take to make the most of his military experience on Uncle Sam's dime. The first thing he did was enroll in the Supply Clerk Course, which he completed within six months of his training. By June, he got his first certificate of many from the Department of the Army. Clarence's Certificate of Training read: This is to certify that Private Clarence D Will ID number Ra 12 656 114 has successfully completed Supply Clerks Course, MOS: 760.

In an ironic twist, the enlistment officer spelled my dad's surname wrong, much in the same way they had misspelled his Great-great grandfather Sandy's last name nearly a century before during the Civil War. While Sandy's dilemma was "Willis," they incorrectly spelled Clarence's last name as "Will." In all of his paperwork and certificates, he had to neatly write an "s" in black ink at the end of his last name. (People *still* mangle my last name, which consists of one simple vowel and four consonants; and it's spelled exactly the way it sounds. I never understood the mystery about our family's last name, but at least there's a precedent for all the ridiculous fumbling.)

Clarence's first army award was signed by a lieutenant colonel and dated June 8, 1962. This meant he was certified and qualified to deal with military equipment and logistics. With that, he moved at the speed of light and always kept his Bible, Ruth's picture, and guitar in tow.

After successfully completing combat training at Fort Dix, Clarence was shipped to Fort Bragg in North Carolina, where he took a number of courses at the Army Education Center and then he jumped into another world. He was shipped further south to Fort Benning in Georgia, and enrolled in the United States Army Infantry School whose motto was simply "Follow Me."

During the summer of 1962, Clarence checked into the sprawling military campus and met his drill sergeant, went through initial processing, was issued his uniform, and assigned to a company. As he had done at the two previous forts, he carefully unpacked his guitar and his Bible, along with his other belongings, and placed them in his locker. Training with the 82nd Airborne Division's Special Forces was not for the faint of heart. Wake up call was at 4:30 a.m. sharp, sometimes, 3:45 a.m. Breakfast was served at five in the morning. The future paratroopers were guaranteed a busy day filled with exercise, procedural training, and a host of other classes. But they all looked forward to one singular moment: when they could jump out of the plane and release their parachutes. It was the ultimate adrenaline rush for my dad and his fellow soldiers.

The first week was "ground week" when soldiers practiced maneuvers outside the plane. The second week is known as "tower week"—when they trained to exit the plane from mock towers, and the third week is the real deal: jump week. Clarence made sure he brought along his camera and took plenty of pictures to document the exhilarating experience. In stunning black-and-white photographs, I see my dad—the only black face in the group—in his jump uniform with an "airborne" patch on his shoulder. He is smiling for the camera right before boarding the plane. He's holding his helmet with both hands, and his parachute, reserve chute, and harness are strapped to his sturdy body as he stands surrounded by more than one dozen men, all dressed like him.

The road to becoming a jumpmaster is an intimidating one. It's an honor that was off limits for black soldiers until 1944 when the first all-black paratrooper unit was formed, known as the Triple Nickels. Prior to these courageous soldiers—it was believed that blacks didn't have the guts to jump out of planes. And it certainly takes guts because there's always a chance of a complete or partial malfunction, which could mean instant death or serious injury.

With the eagerness of a child, Clarence gleefully cheated death every time he jumped out of a flying airplane and floated into the blue sky. High above, with the sound of the plane's engine whizzing past his ears, he was free as a bird. The closest to the moon as he would ever come, Clarence looked at the world below him and relished in the glory of being above it all. The sounds of whistling winds as he made his rapid descent on the wings of gravity with the earth below slowly came into focus. This was the ultimate maneuver that he believed really separated the men from the boys: could you stare death in the face until your parachute opened? If not, have a seat, look up and watch me, boy! That was my dad's macho attitude.

Jumping out of planes was a unique military experience that not every soldier had the nerve to do—and those that had the nerve were held in high esteem. It's no surprise that my father pinned on his wings and sewed a paratrooper patch onto every leisure jacket he had for the rest of his life. He knew his airborne experience was special, giving him serious street credibility everywhere he went. It was the ultimate he-man experience and my bad-ass father, who jumped to glory over and over in the army, walked with a self-assured confidence until that fateful day in September when gravity and fate finally caught up with him on the Williamsburg Bridge.

As Clarence mastered the techniques of jumping—always keeping your eyes open, chin on the chest and elbows tight to the sides—he was given his paratrooper wings. During his down time, I found that he scribbled on a notepad "Tell the girls I've gone to rest, Pin my wings upon my chest, I'm Airborne!"

That stimulating experience says a lot about my father. He was a risk-taker who deliberately teetered on the brink of danger, particularly the danger of death. I'm not exactly sure why he consistently positioned himself in these compromising, though honorable, positions, but it was an eerie foreboding of what was to come.

As a full-fledged paratrooper, he was shipped overseas to Saint Andre, Evereux, France, in 1963. While he was there, he learned of the assassination of John F. Kennedy and it greatly disturbed him because the young Irish politician was the first president my dad had ever voted for, as soon as he was old enough to vote. As Clarence sat in the barracks in the foreign country, with his guitar on his bunk, the soldiers listened to heartbreaking and shocking accounts of their dashing commander-in-chief who was murdered in cold blood in broad daylight, next to his beautiful wife. These were the days before CNN and cable news; information was very slow in getting to the American soldiers in Evereux, France. The one thing they all knew was that America would never be the same when and if they returned home.

While overseas, Opal regularly wrote her son touching letters, which were scrawled with a barely legible penmanship befitting a young girl who paid more attention to boys than her teachers in her youth. In her letters, she always shared Bible verses that he should read and she always wanted to know when he was coming home. Clarence always wrote back, as well, addressing the letters, "Dear Mother." He never acknowledged or asked about his father, which was a quiet indication of the seething rage he had for Fred. He loved his mother with every ounce of his being. He loved Opal because she never found fault with him and always searched for the best in him, even if he was wrong. Her grace always prevented him from unleashing his vexation at his father.

Were it not for his mother, Clarence would've probably stopped speaking to his father long before. He cared about his dad and, as a kid, idolized him; but as a man, he saw another side of his father that sickened him. For one, he didn't like the way his father toyed with religion. Though he did not outwardly express his sanctification the way his mother did, Clarence embraced the apostolic doctrine almost as much as Opal did. He believed that God was the center of everything and it was very dangerous to act one way in public and another behind closed doors. And that was Fred to the letter. In church, he wore a suit and tie, and hollered sermons from a pulpit, but behind closed doors he had a real problem with drinking and adultery and had repeatedly humiliated his wife and sons. Half a world away in 1963, Clarence could not understand why a real preacher, who professed to know the Holy Scriptures, would dare deceive an all-knowing God who knew and saw all.

Clarence didn't profess to be saved or holy, but he was a believer. In the army he drank alcohol and smoked with his fellow soldiers and learned the intimate French words that attracted and wooed the young French gals, but he did not have the audacity to proclaim himself a minister. He was just a guitarist who loved music. Some of that music happened to be gospel, but Clarence loved doo-wop, jazz, country, blues, rock and roll, and he even appreciated classical music, especially sonata's involving string instruments. He tried to teach himself to read music, but he had learned by ear, and he was most comfortable sounding out rhythms on his own.

Naturally, when a small group of soldiers in his company struck up a band during his stay in France, Clarence became a charter member. As the lead guitarist of the group, he taught soldiers—one in particular named Scottie—who thought they knew how to sing, how to really hold a note. He created a set of music, ranging from bluesy numbers to popular songs like the 1963 hits, "Up on the Roof" and "On Broadway" by the Drifters. These were easy songs for untrained voices because many of the chorus lines were more spoken than actually sung. Clarence was the only one with more than ten years experience singing in churches, choirs, and a professional gospel group, so the band mates all naturally followed his lead. They performed in clubs mostly during the weekends in Paris when they were off-duty and the French girls loved them. They even slept in the club over the weekend—and Clarence took a black-and-white photograph of the bed he slept in. He liked to joke that French girls always pretended to know Elvis Presley, and acted like Elvis was their best friend. He snickered as he imitated them in broken French: "Oh, oui, oui, we've known Elvis for years…"

No matter what Clarence did during these galvanizing years of his young life, he always managed to strike up a band. When he was a pre-teen, there are photographs of his darling narrow, chocolate face, bracing a guitar that was bigger than his entire upper body, with his singing aunts and cousins behind him. His adorable and affable spirit always gravitated to the sounds of the guitar and the songs from the heart.

Clarence's duty in France was about much more than a band, of course. He was on the short list to ship out to Vietnam, which had not yet escalated into a full-blown conflict. President Lyndon Johnson was faced with an international dilemma the moment assumed office after Kennedy's death. At issue: how to stop the communist North Vietnamese from taking over South Vietnam. Every year that went by in the mid-sixties, the situation became worse and worse. More and more American troops were sent in to fight communism. In 1961, the year before Clarence entered the army, only 2,000 American troops had been deployed to the region. By 1964, there were 16,500 U.S. soldiers in Vietnam. He was more than ready to ship out from France to the emerging quagmire in Southeast Asia. The young brash paratrooper wrote in letters to his mother and to Ruth, both in New York, explaining that he couldn't wait to be sent to Vietnam to fight.

My poor Grandmother Opal may not have been well educated, but she knew that was the last place on earth she wanted her son to go. Clarence didn't have the vantage point that Opal did. The American television media had become increasingly critical of the war and it's poorly defined mission, but Clarence was only being fed the military's point of view from his end where, to some soldiers, it was viewed as honorable as the battle in World War II. He didn't go through all of this training for nothing, he thought. He wanted to get involved with some real combat and return as a war hero.

Opal prayed. As she continued her daily rituals at church, she testified and pleaded with God openly, that her son NOT be sent to war-torn Vietnam. She knew that her son loved to flirt with danger, but this was not a game, and she had heard about the young black church men who had returned from Vietnam in flag-draped coffins. Fred didn't say much during this time. Reserved, he always let his wife do much of the talking and the praying. But in his heart, he loved his son and, naturally, did not want to see Clarence hurt or killed.

God must have heard Opal's fervent prayers again because in the end, Clarence never did go to Vietnam. But he did have a terrifying brush with death without ever stepping foot in Asia. His letter to his mother dated December 1, 1964, explains it in full:

> Dear Mother: I received your present. But I have much better news. I've received the Holy Gost.[sic] Let me tell you how it happened. There is a strange type thing people smoke. It's called Pot. While I was playing Sunday night, a man came up to me and gave me a "block" of it. I decided

to wait until latter to smoke it. Mother, I'm crying. On payday night, I put all of it into one cigarette and smoked it. And, Mother, I died. I was running thru the hallway here begging people to help me, but they couldn't hear me. And just so I would know that it was for real, God let me come to life while begging one guy to help me, then he took life away from me again. So I thought about my Bible in my wall locker. So I ran to my wall locker. And as soon as I got to my wall locker, he took my life away. I'm crying again. I ask him for one more chance to try and he gave it to me. I opened my wall locker and grabbed my Bible. I pleaded with him, Mother, and he had mercy. He showed me that he could take away my senses without taking my life. He let my body stand on the side of my bunk and talk to fellow soldier about how crazy I was, and my soul was standing there watching my body perform. My soul said to my body that, "He can't hear a word you are saying." So I stoped.[sic] My friend told me to get in bed so, in order not to be sent to the crazy house, I laid down. As long as I laid on my stomach down with my heart pressing against my Bible, I was in sort of a trial zone. Mother, the devil was fighting hard.

Mother, last night God took my life at least six times. And each time he gave it back, I was more grateful. I laid on the bed and cryed [sic] like a baby. Man cannot play with God. He had to force me to accept him. And I thank him for it. Mother, let me tell you what else he did. He took me up into the sky and let me look down at my own body. He started to take me through some big area but, we thought it would be best to come and see you before I went there. Mother, my soul was floating around in space. I met your soul up there, too.

I'm not going to say any more right now. So bye for now. I leave here Jan 10, 1965.

Love, Clarence.

Clearly, my pop smoked some really *really* bad weed. Having never been a smoker myself, I have read my father's tearful letter to his mother dozens of times and, each time, I am struck in different ways. As a journalist and wordsmith, I can't help but feel a twinge of pain when a twenty-two-year-old man misspells simple elementary school words like "stopped," "ghost" and "cried." It breaks my heart to know that his lack of stability during his childhood had this much of an impact on his academic performance. He made up for this deficiency in later years by becoming the first college graduate in the Wills family.

I am moved by his perfect recollection of his hallucinations and delusions. The fact that he grabbed his little red Bible, placed it to his heart, and laid on his stomach deeply touches my soul. He was trying to physically put the Word of God in his heart, as if he were a little boy trying to please his devout Christian mother. Clarence viewed this experience as a vicious battle over his soul when he wrote: "Mother, the devil was fighting hard." It clearly illustrates that, though he were a sinner, he fully embraced the same religious principles as his parents. A fast-talking, guitar-playing, flirting-with-death wise-ass he may have pretended to be; but deep down, he begged God to live to see another day. He wasn't a full-throated hot shot; he was just "acting cool." That whole fearless routine was nothing more than a stunt; Clarence wanted to live and enjoy life to its fullest and finally he had been scared straight. Actually, I don't think his entire experience was hallucinatory. I really believe that something or someone really did take him through some "big area" and he wanted to see his beloved mother before going there. Again, it's worth pointing out that there's no mention of his father anywhere during this frightful experience.

The most fateful part of the whole letter was where he wrote, "Man cannot play with God. He had to force me to accept him. And I thank him for it."

If this entire experience was based in any kind of reality, other than smoking a bad joint laced with a hallucinogenic substance, then Clarence would prove to have a short memory. For all of his begging and pleading with God to give him "one more chance," in a few short years, my dad would thumb his nose at not only God, but at his beloved mother, his faithful wife, and his five dependent children. This peculiar apparition only scared him straight temporarily.

But, for a time, Clarence did indeed try to fly right in the wake of that horrifying experience. He stopped drinking and smoking while stationed in France and he changed his tune on the guitar. In late 1964, the Motown sound exploded with some really catchy tunes and the soldiers wanted Clarence to play them, but he refused. As his mother taught him, songs about lust and sex were the devil's music. So, he went back to playing gospel music when he was off duty, and his comrades hated it with a passion. They wanted him to play "The Way You Do The Things You Do" by Temptations, and the white soldiers begged him to play "Do Wah Diddy Diddy" as sung by Manfred Mann. Clarence flatly refused and instead played songs like "I Shall Not Be Moved" by the gospel quartet, The Harmonizing Four, who became famous in the post-war era by singing traditional spirituals with a modern fervor. A few of the black soldiers who had also grown up in little Pentecostal churches in the South, appreciated Clarence's sudden turnaround, but the white soldiers thought it was stupid and boring.

In a strange way, they felt Clarence had betrayed them and judged him as weird and no longer fun to be around. Feeling uncomfortable, he no longer yearned for military combat and decided against extending his military stay. He wanted to go home and get back to church. Shortly before he left, one of the soldiers broke the neck of his guitar and left it dangling off of his bunk. Clarence was devastated when he found it, but he said nothing and did not report it. He would later say that it felt like someone broke his arm.

In January of 1965, Clarence returned to his parents' house in Long Island City a seasoned and mature military man. Fred, Opal and Van sat spellbound as Clarence explained how his guitar got broken in half and how he almost died. His captivating stories of jumping out of planes and singing in France made them very proud, especially Van, who would soon be drafted into the very same army during the conflict in Vietnam. Ever timid, he did not dare follow in his brother's paratrooper footsteps.

The first and only gift Clarence purchased when he returned home was a brand new Wurlitzer piano for his mother. He had listened to Opal play on broken down, secondhand, and out-of-tune pianos all of his life, and he had always dreamed of buying her a new one to call her own. The piano cost five hundred dollars of his hard-earned money from the Army, and Opal begged him not to do it, but his mind was made up. This was his special way of letting his mother know just how special she was to him and how much he loved her. For his father, he bought nothing.

However, Clarence was even happy to see his father. Fred had really straightened himself out and was saving money to build a church in Astoria. My Grandfather Fred, who had the gift of gab, had formed a bond with an old man who had a huge building on 11-15 30th Avenue in Astoria, directly down the street from Astoria Housing Projects. The man told Fred that he could rent out the colossal block-long building for a couple of hundred bucks, and that he was welcome to make a church out of the bottom, a little store off to the side, and he and his family could live upstairs. Fred's original vision—which he crystallized in his mind during his first trip to New York City—had finally come true.

Clarence was actually excited for his father, because he figured that maybe if Fred built his own church, he would walk a straight line forever. Besides, Clarence reckoned, everybody makes mistakes in life and, while he was in the army, he had certainly made his. In an instant, all was forgiven. He vowed to help his father build what would be called "Light House Church" and just about every dollar he earned went into that effort. This was, without question, the happiest time in all of their lives. Clarence used all of his smarts from the military to turn the century-old building into the field of dreams.

Clarence was hired at United Parcel Service and was so respected that they quickly made him a manager with a full benefit package. He worked routes all over Manhattan. While Clarence was in the military, he had heard repeatedly that computers were going to change the world one day and that, if anyone wanted to get ahead of the curve, they'd better learn the basics of the emerging technology now. So he enrolled in the Data Processing Institute in Manhattan to get in on the ground floor of cutting-edge technology.

In fall of 1965, Clarence popped the question to the girl he had adored since he was fourteen. Every young man in New York who saw my mother in action wanted to claim her because she was classy, intelligent, and super sexy. Ruth was also ambitious and loved beautiful things. She was a girl who designed and sewed her own dresses, and she hated a filthy house. She was perfect for Clarence, and Clarence was perfect for her. She worked as a secretary in midtown Manhattan and during his lunch break they held hands together and ate lunch in Central Park or sat on the steps of the grand museums along Fifth Avenue's Museum Mile.

Clarence talked about how he planned to join either the police or the fire department, and still moonlight as a musician with a new gospel group he had joined called "The Thrashing Wonders." Most importantly, he talked about making big money in the near future. He had dreams of buying real estate—thanks to his military service he could get low interest loans, establish money generating businesses, and put his yet unborn children through college. He told Ruth how he grew up poor, shuffled from pillar to post, and he vowed to never be that way again. Ruth firmly believed in his vision and the couple married on December 18, 1965.

Both had been raised in shabby storefront churches and neither envisioned themselves getting married in a small sanctuary. So my mom chose a picturesque traditional church called Antioch Baptist Church in Jamaica, Queens, for the pre-Christmas wedding, which she says she was inspired to do by a popular magazine at the time called *December Bride.*

Both Ruth and Clarence's father's were ministers, so she had a family friend named Rev. Charles Leader marry them. In a slender wedding dress that my mother had fashioned herself, she walked down the aisle, holding her father Hardy's arm, with a white veil over her face. Her youngest sister, LaPearl, was her maid of honor and Clarence's best man was his only brother, Van. Their union was a joining of two Holiness families, both of whom had originated in the South and relocated to New York.

On my mother's side of the aisle were her sisters: Dorothy, Alma, and Elaine. Her brothers, Horace, Clinton, and David, were on hand as well as Aaron, whose baby son sat in his lap, nursing a bottle. Within a few short years, my mother gazed out of her kitchen window and watched police bolt into her brother Aaron's apartment building next door to hers—only to find out that her sister-in-law had shot her brother to death in cold blood when the scorned wife suspected Aaron was cheating on her. On my parent's wedding day in that charming church, everyone was young, happy and full of promise but tragic outcomes, similar to my Uncle Aaron's, awaited most of them, including my own father. It was such a shock to the older generation of Southern-born folks who had relied faithfully upon their religion to prevent exactly these kinds of tragedies from happening. One by one—they watched their children succumb to drugs, alcohol, or murder.

After the wedding and brief reception, which was held in the church's basement, Clarence and Ruth moved in with Opal and Fred. Proving to be as fertile as her mother (Sallie), Ruth got pregnant right away with me, and I was born precisely nine-and-a-half months after their wedding, just weeks after Labor Day in September. My dad had openly hoped for a boy and had the audacity to express disappointment that I was a girl. He was used to having a brother, and a father, and lots of male soldier buddies around him. I was a new phenomenon to the daring and dashing paratrooper. But he quickly got over it, and I was warmly welcomed into their household where I felt like I had two mothers and two fathers; my parents were both twenty-four, my Grandma Opal was just thirty-eight and my Grandpa Fred was forty-three. Not one of them had gray hair yet and all of them were still in the prime of their lives. I was tossed from one set of arms to another like a precious pink poodle.

My dad and grandfather continued to work on the new building in Astoria. Grandpa Fred made daily trips to junkyards and literally built the church out of scraps, and odds and ends that he found while rummaging through mounds of debris. Night after night, he sawed wood to make an altar and a pulpit. He laid carpet, painted the church, and helped wire new lights in the emerging sanctuary. From 1965–67, the father and son worked hard to make the place suitable for church downstairs and living quarters upstairs. My grandfather wanted our family to move into the building, but my mother resisted the idea. The place was still too junky and drafty, and there were rats, mice, and huge cockroaches everywhere. Clarence agreed with my mother and, when my grandparents finally moved out of their house in Long Island City, my dad moved his wife and daughter to a comfortable public housing project in Rockaway, Queens called Hammels. My brother, Clarence Jr., whom I nicknamed Big Boy because he was a huge baby, was born in September of 1968 and our move was to be transitional housing for our expanded family. Clarence planned to purchase a house on Long Island—particularly in Roosevelt or certain parts of Freeport where more African-Americans lived. But we grew to adore the sprawling housing complex where we bonded with the Courtlandt and Haynes families next door on the seventh floor. Vance, Simone, Vanessa and Kenny Jr. were close in age and were my favorite playmates. In the meantime, Clarence took the city exam for the fire department and waited for word. The fire department was more than ninety-five percent white in 1969 and the city had no objection to keeping it that way at the time. My father loved a challenge and, heaven knows, that was a big one.

While waiting for the results, Clarence continued doing what he loved most in the world: playing his guitar and singing gospel. The fledgling Queens group called The Thrashing Wonders was led by a soft-spoken young man named Billy Brown, whose singing voice was like thunder when he sang, but a whisper when he talked. He was the most sincere and polite man you'd ever want to meet and he and Clarence had become the best of friends. Both had been invited to join the distinguished Masons Lodge number 173. Other members of the group were Billy Ravenell, another vocal powerhouse; his brother Preston Ravenell; and a phenomenal bass singer named Joe Warren. Because so many people respected Billy Brown, who was also a devout church deacon, the group was able to book lots of gigs opening for major recording gospel artists like Shirley Caesar and The Dixie Hummingbirds. Clarence was able to put his stamp on the group with his sophisticated jazzy style of playing on his brand new and very expensive electric guitar, custom made by Gibson with a fancy carrying case. After a childhood filled with hand-me-downs and secondhand junk, everything Clarence purchased as an adult had to be brand new and top shelf.

My mom and dad were the picture perfect couple as the turbulent 1960s drew to a close. Blessed with a girl and a boy, and bright hopes for the future, it seemed that the wind was at their backs. But the seeds of their demise had been planted so long ago that they had forgotten they were even there. Clarence had never fully resolved his troubled childhood and, though he tried to pretend it was in the past and he was over it, the poison was still in his heart. My mother, who tried to ignore her own temper when it flared up occasionally, had never resolved her own shortcomings either. So the happily married couple followed in their parents footsteps and used sanctified religion as a means to a peaceful end. Instead it was more like putting a Band-Aid on cancer. Slowly but surely, the poison inside the two lovebirds would spread until it became a full blown sickness. In the meantime, both pretended not to see it coming. My brother Big Boy and I, and my future unborn siblings, were soon caught in the middle.

I'd like to think that Clarence would have taken his life more seriously had he known about his Great-great Grandfather Sandy Wills' tenure in the army during the final years of the Civil War. In summer of 1864, Sandy and other members of the 4th U.S. Colored Heavy Artillery continued their garrison duties as Major General Sherman's forces annihilated the South, reducing hundreds of thousands of acres of land to rubble and ash. It was a strategic move to literally force the stubborn Confederacy to surrender.

As Sandy and the former slaves defended the fort, the soldiers no doubt rejoiced with word that Confederate General Robert E. Lee's army was coming unglued from all directions in late 1864. Less than one week after General Lee surrendered his legendary Army of Northern Virginia, John Wilkes Booth shot President Lincoln in Washington, D.C., on April 14, 1865. Lincoln died the next day.

Although Lincoln entered the war in 1861 as a pure politician, stating emphatically that his mission was purely about saving the Union rather than freeing the slaves, with time and intense pressure from abolitionists like Frederick Douglass, the president accepted that the abolition of slavery was part and parcel with preserving the Union. But the death of "Uncle Abe," whom many slaves came to view as their father, was arguably the worst blow of the war.

As blacks lionized Lincoln's memory and legacy, they also quietly celebrated their newfound legitimacy as free human beings who could now roam the country and do as they pleased without answering to a slave master. In the spring of 1865, the Civil War was over and my Great-great-great grandfather Sandy Wills was finally a free man. Having lived on the brink of death for about two years from 1863–65, Sandy was probably cautiously optimistic when he learned that the Confederate armies had surrendered. He had lived his entire life as a slave—an experience that robbed him of his parents, his family legacy, and his education, but not his dignity. Sandy may have been illiterate but he could hold his head high as a man who helped topple an evil systemic institution that was once impenetrable. Sandy, my warrior of an ancestor, was a critical part of United States history.

But there were fewer celebrations in Tennessee and Kentucky. Garrison duty for Sandy, Andy, Dick, James, and Mack continued until June of 1865—when the entire 4th U.S. Colored Heavy Artillery shipped out of Fort Halleck and relocated to Pine Bluff, Arkansas. The soldiers marched with their heads held high as white officers repeatedly documented the outstanding conduct of the colored soldiers and praised them as having "acted nobly" and "exceeded expectations." The most dramatic about-face was likely from Colonel Steven Hicks, who had vehemently opposed the enlistment of black troops. He wrote, "...permit me to remark that I have been one of those men who never had much confidence in colored troops fighting, but those doubts are now all removed, for they fought as bravely as any troops in the fort."

Sandy Wills and his now "brothers in freedom" left Edmund Wills' plantation in Haywood County as slaves, but in 1865, at least one of them was promoted to corporal. Dick Wills Parker, who defiantly reclaimed his blood father's name and dropped his slave master's surname of Wills when he stated his legal name during enlistment, was appointed a non-commissioned officer on October 5, 1865. Parker's upgrade was most certainly a personal victory for all of the Wills men who marveled at the stripe on the shoulder of Dick's uniform. What an incredible stamp on American history that these former slaves left for the ages. Most of them walked to the enlistment station—to fight in one of the most devastating civil wars to ever occur in the history of humankind. They summoned up the courage and dignity to walk in the shadow of death and they emerged on the side of victory. Dick Parker's stripe was well earned and deserved, and it was a stripe for all the proud black men of the 4th U.S. Heavy Artillery who championed the American flag even though Old Glory did not protect her children of color. But none of that mattered in 1865, because the taste of freedom was so sweet in their souls that the sting of racism temporarily lost its power.

Sandy Wills became the first in our family to become a free citizen of the United States. When the first of the Reconstruction Amendments was ratified by twenty of the then thirty-six states in December of 1865, Africans who had been forced into bondage for centuries could finally exhale. The thirteenth amendment had, at long last, abolished slavery in the United States of America, even though a handful of states such as New Jersey, Texas, Delaware, and Iowa had initially rejected it. Mississippi, an especially cruel cradle of hatred in the South, did not ratify the thirteenth amendment until March 16, 1995.

Christmas took on a special meaning in 1865 as my great-great-great grandfather remained on duty in Pine Bluff, Arkansas, but celebrated the birth of Jesus Christ as a man who was suddenly in charge of his own destiny. He, and all of the members of the United States Colored Troops, had accomplished a remarkable feat in the annals of human history—they had overcome a seemingly insurmountable institution of slavery, which had been sanctioned from the highest levels of government and begrudgingly accepted by blacks, as well. Every trick in the book was used to keep Africans in bondage, and most of those tricks worked. Supporters of slavery manipulated God's Holy Bible; they snatched brown babies from the breasts of their weeping mothers, and they reduced proud strong men to timid boys. However, some of the Africans escaped, others purchased their freedom, and many untold millions died in their silent protest against the wicked system that robbed them of just about everything God gave them. But Sandy Wills was one of the lucky few who had the opportunity, as a child of this heinous establishment, to help issue slavery's death warrant. Unable to sign his name, he brandished a weapon that was stronger than any gun; he executed it with his sheer force of will. The historic thirteenth amendment was the first amendment adopted in the nation in about sixty years. The United States of America was just shy of her ninetieth birthday, and the so-called peculiar institution, which tormented millions of Africans, was legal no more.

As the victorious soldiers continued their duty in Arkansas in 1866, the Wills men almost lost Corporal Dick Parker to disease. The newly branded non-commissioned officer contracted small pox, a highly contagious virus characterized by large sores on the body. Civil War medicine left much to be desired, as a high fever accompanied by unsightly lesions peppered his face and entire body. But Dick Parker had a lot to live for now. With slavery behind him, he could envision a future of whatever he so desired. Stuck in the regimental hospital in Pine Bluff, Dick's body slowly recovered from the fluid-filled blisters that could have killed him and, after he regained his strength, the corporal returned to duty on January 28, 1866.

One month later, on February 25, 1866, the 4th United States Colored Field Heavy Artillery Regiment, which was established in spite of protests from whites who thought slaves were too ignorant to fight, was mustered out of service. Some of the deactivated soldiers, many of whom refused to return to their old plantations, returned to Columbus, Kentucky, near Fort Halleck where a Freedman's Bureau had been established.

The Wills soldiers, now honorably discharged, were eligible to receive a war pension if they were injured during the war. Because they were all illiterate, members of the Freedmen's Bureau helped them fill out the paperwork. All of the men who sustained injuries received a pension, except Sandy, because the enlistment officer misspelled his name as Willis, and the War Department rejected it because there was no record of a Sandy Wills having served in the U.S.C.T. It was probably a crushing blow for the young veteran, who desperately needed, deserved, and had faithfully earned the money. Like most of the soldiers, he probably suffered from hearing loss due to the constant firing guns and canons and numerous other injuries. But Sandy found himself with no recourse; it was his word against the United States War Department, and that was one battle he couldn't win. How does an illiterate former slave, who cannot even identify the letters in his name, prove that his last name, Wills was misspelled Willis? Dejected, Sandy never received a single dime of his pension money. It was a damn shame.

Even more celebrations of freedom were short-lived as millions of African-Americans found themselves homeless and jobless, with broken families, and lives in shambles. And not to mention, millions of blacks were starving, nearly to death. Many wept openly because they were desperate to reunite with children, parents, and other relatives who had been sold and separated from them during slavery. Others wanted to get legally married and assimilate themselves into society as free people.

In spring of 1865, the United States Congress had established the Bureau of Refugees, Freedmen and Abandoned Lands, commonly known as the Freedmen's Bureau, which addressed those needs and much more. There were locations all across the country and for a short while it was effective in bringing order to a chaotic situation. The bureau opened four thousand schools for black people, along with a number of colleges, which at least one quarter of a million African-Americans took advantage of across the country. To the best of my knowledge, Sandy did not take advantage of these schools, but at least two of the Wills men did. In official military correspondence in later years, I discovered that Dick Parker and Mack Wills were indeed able to sign their full names, unlike Andy and James who continued to sign their names with an X.

Sadly, with two steps forward that the newly freed men and women took, there were plenty of former Confederate soldiers and former slave masters who violently pushed them back. The first casualty was the controversial promise of forty acres and a mule. The Freedman's Bureau actually had nothing to do with this; it was a special order created by General William

T. Sherman before the Civil War had actually ended. As Sherman's mighty army dislodged white slave owners from their vast properties in the South, the general mandated in January 1865 that Africans take over the abandoned lands stretching from South Carolina to Florida—forty acres per family—to resettle. In some cases, the Army threw in a mule for plowing. Within months, about ten thousand freed slaves took over the plantations they had once been held hostage on. President Lincoln's successor, Andrew Johnson, revoked the order and returned the land to the former white owners shortly thereafter. Some blacks worked out an agreement to remain on the property as sharecroppers; others left in anger. The sudden about-face was a sign of what lay ahead for blacks, who finally became American citizens with protection under the law when the fourteenth amendment was ratified in 1868. By this time, Sandy, Dick, Andy, James, and Mack had all returned to Haywood County, Tennessee. All of the men were eligible bachelors under the age of thirty and they apparently resettled in the same little shacks, not as slaves, but as sharecroppers.

Like millions of other penniless blacks whose primary skills were farming, my great-great-great grandfather was assigned a particular plot of land and, at the end of the season, he was supposed to get a share of the crop, usually around one half. But, history shows, that the illiterate sharecroppers were regularly cheated out of their fair share, and could not calculate their debts, including food and shelter, which the plantation owner deducted. So essentially, they were still in a lose-lose situation. The only difference was they could leave at any time they pleased. But Sandy didn't leave Haywood County. Neither did Dick, James, Andy, or Mack. Instead, they started dating the young girls they met at functions at the Colored Methodist Episcopal Church in their Haywood County's enclave of Brownsville. All of the Wills veterans still embraced the same Christianity they had been taught as slaves, and they were all probably very religious and continued to adapt and bend the conservative rituals and songs to fit their African rhythms and style. Songs about freedom and gratitude still rang out in the church, which was a stunning blending of voices that ranged from the highest of sopranos to the deepest of basses. They didn't read hymn books, because most of them still couldn't read. The songs that they did know were burned into their hearts from the many years they had sung the melodies while bent over in cotton fields.

In 1868, Sandy met Emma West Moore and the two were smitten. Many years later, Emma was required to describe how she met Sandy (in sworn statements when she hired a lawyer to obtain a widow's war pension). Through these precious documents, we get a full and beautiful picture of their historic courtship. They were charting new territory as a free African-American couple. In generations past, slaves were paired together, sometimes against their will, to reproduce children for the benefit of the slave owners. It was a particularly disgraceful slap at holy matrimony. But Sandy and Emma were the first of millions of newly freed Africans who dated and decided on their own terms whether they actually liked each other.

According to the sworn depositions, which serve as a fascinating account of their lives, Emma was born a slave to Dolphin and Millie West. They were owned by a slave owner in North Carolina whose last name was West. At some point during her childhood, Emma was sold to another slaveholder whose last name was Moore. It's not clear if she was separated from her parents or not, but she became known as Emma West Moore. Some knew her as Emma West; others called her as Emma Moore. From the sound of her testimony, she was a gentle, dignified, and assertive young lady when she met Sandy during a period she calls "after the surrender" in Haywood County. Her's was an interesting choice of words. She didn't say "after the war;" she verbally referred to it as "the surrender." This may mean, at least in her view, that the war had been over long before the Confederates finally gave up. My Great-great-great grandmother Emma met Sandy about two years after the Civil War ended, around 1867. Born around 1851, she was probably the picture of beauty at the age of sweet sixteen. One census record describes her as being mulatto—which means she was probably of a light brown or yellow complexion. Although they lived about two-and-a-half miles from each other, they had never met. She admitted she had known "his people," meaning his relatives or close friends. Sandy and Emma, head over heels in love, married on February 11, 1869, in what must have been an elaborate wedding for two former slaves. It certainly appears that she had maintained a strong bond with the Moore family even though they once owned her, because she had her wedding ceremony, as she put it, in a deposition "right in the white folk's house." She was especially close to Joel Moore, her former slave owner's son, and he and the rest of his family were present at Emma's marriage ceremony to Sandy. Neither had ever been married.

This congenial relationship and bond between former slaves and former slave holders is not one that is discussed, but it should be. It is a natural reflex, especially for African- Americans, to assume that all black slaves hated their white masters, but clearly, in my family, this was not the case. Legal documents I obtained from the National Archives in Washington tell a much different story, and it's not one laced with hatred or vitriol.

Personally, I am saddened and disgusted that my great-great-great grandparents had to suffer through slavery, but Emma apparently came through the oppressive system without a trace of resentment or anger in her heart. I think I am angrier about slavery 150 years later, than she was when she actually went through it. Emma apparently fully embraced the tenants of Christianity and forgave, perhaps to a fault, the very people who had rendered her illiterate and a social outcast. How she managed to do this, I will never know, but this much I do understand: My great-great-great grandmother was graceful, affable, and extraordinarily kind, even in her teens. There's a strong chance that she lived most of her young life as a house slave and was not subjected to the bitter winds and brutal sun that the field slaves were. Her bond with her former slave master's family was so strong that, after Sandy's death, they helped this illiterate poor black widow hire a lawyer so she could get the pension that Sandy never saw.

Emma, due to her youth and naiveté, probably never fully appreciated that she was being held against her will. She likely saw the Moore family as her own family and maintained a cheerful countenance through it all. She hadn't yet had any children snatched from her and she apparently knew where her parents, Dolphin and Millie, were, as well as her siblings. So, in her eyes, she had no problem getting married in the Moore's big house, which she continued to work in as a day laborer for many years after the surrender.

The popular view of post-Civil War relationships of resentment and even violence was obviously not part of Emma's brave new world of freedom. In 1869, just a couple of years after the United States of America finally recognized her as a human being and a citizen, Emma West Moore Wills was happy, free, and in love.

The marriage of Sandy and Emma was evidently the talk of the little town of Brownsville in Haywood County. A colored Methodist minister named Sam Williams traveled from Memphis to join the couple in holy matrimony. During the reception, guests, black and white, were even "served" dinner. In later depositions to prove she was the widow of Sandy Wills, Emma named wedding servers such as Nelson Moore, who was probably a fellow slave that she grew up with on the plantation. Among the wedding guests were Sandy's comrades who were as close to him as any brother could be: James, Andy, Dick, and Mack, all of whom testified in later depositions on Emma's behalf that they were present at the couple's marriage ceremony. I'm guessing that at least one of them stood as his best man—though it's not explicitly stated. Other guests at the wedding were Elmira Moore, Charley Bailey, and, as Emma succinctly put, "many others that live around here."

But as whites and blacks happily gathered in the Moore's big house in Haywood County, Tennessee, to jointly celebrate, probably for the first time ever, there was a quiet movement to put an end to such interracial merriment. The Ku Klux Klan had been born in the same state where Emma and Sandy were married. They were mostly hateful veterans of the Confederacy who were determined to undo every forward step that blacks made in the wake of slavery. They used violence, intimidation, and harassment to restore white supremacy in the United States.

Whenever the federal government tried to include blacks in local and national governments, the Klan used all of their power and influence to stop it. Thousands of former slaves had educated themselves and established businesses and homes and, torch by torch, the Klan did everything they could to burn them down. This is probably why Sandy and other black members of the United States Colored Troops laid low and did not brag about their heroic duty during the Civil War. Tennessee was the last place that a colored soldier would show off his uniform or brag about his duty, because Sandy knew he would have been hung from the highest tree in Haywood County. Even Emma admitted, after her husband's death, that she didn't know anything about his enlistment or discharge. The only thing she knew was that he had served in the army with James, Mack, Andy, and Dick. Imagine living as someone's wife for twenty years, and knowing next to nothing about her husband's military career.

After their splendid wedding day, my great-great-great grandparents settled into a sharecropper shack, which they did not own, and forged ahead. Emma obviously continued to work at the Moore House, presumably as a beloved domestic, and Sandy went back into the fields. A proud soldier who ably defended his fort and mastered the techniques of warfare was reduced, yet again, to picking cotton. What memories he must have had as he returned to the monotonous work of his youth. The proud uniformed soldier had come full circle and was back to wearing raggedy overalls in the cotton field. The sounds of gunshots were now but a memory that became more distant with time. He did his small crucial part to end slavery but, at a glance, nothing had really changed.

Emma was still in the master's house, doing what she had always done. Sandy was still in the field, doing what he had always done. The only difference was they could walk away from Haywood County at any time, but where exactly would they go? They could have relocated to another city and become sharecroppers somewhere else, but they would have been isolated from their friends and family who loved them.

If Sandy could learn the art of war, he proved that he was capable of learning anything—but as the white supremacy movement gained strength in his hometown, racists decided they didn't want blacks to go to school or church with them. These are the same folks who had black women, like my Great-great-great grandmother Emma, to nurse and breastfeed their children from the cradle on. These are the same Southerners who depended on my Great-great-great grandfather Sandy to help turn the tide of a war that was nearly lost to the rebels. Slavery notwithstanding, blacks and whites were inseparable from the moment both races hit the shores of North America. White families regularly included blacks in their family portraits and in all intimate parts of their lives. They wept at each other's funerals and rejoiced at the births of each other's children. They had built America together, and blacks obviously did the brunt of the backbreaking work, while whites enjoyed the fruits of their labor.

Now suddenly as the bloody 1860s drew to a close, whites had issued a virtual national memo that black citizens were to be shunned as if they had leprosy. Never mind that the two races had, however awkwardly, bonded together in name and blood. With the dawn of a new decade in 1870, a few zealous racists managed to convince an entire nation that my great-great-great grandparents—and those who looked like them—were a scourge of society. And that new underground Civil War would last for a very, very long time.

Firefighters at Engine 1 grew to love my dad.

Clarence at his finest as he walks his namesake into Light House Church

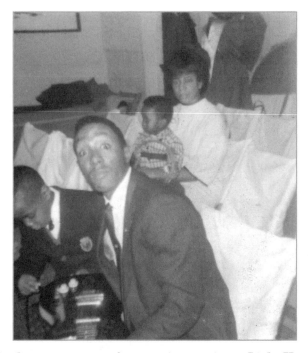

My dad, the deacon, prepares for morning service at Light House Church.

Elder Wills in his self-styled pulpit inside Light House Church

Sunday School children begged my grandfather to open candy store
before worship service begins.

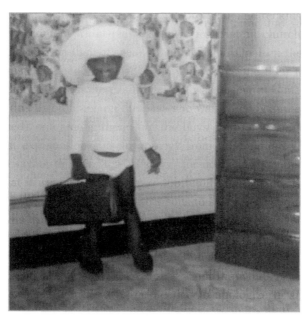

My dad loved to take silly pictures of me.
We had lots of fun together.

Big Boy and I are seated on our dad's motorcycle.

Dad was the first college graduate in the Wills Family.

Clarence as a distinguished mason

Big Boy and me at my 8th Birthday party in Rockaway Beach

Dad as a staff sergeant in National Guard

Dad from the window of our beachfront apartment in Ocean Village

Two vehicles my Dad cherished: his fire truck, and his bike, named Jessica.

The beginning of dad's downfall

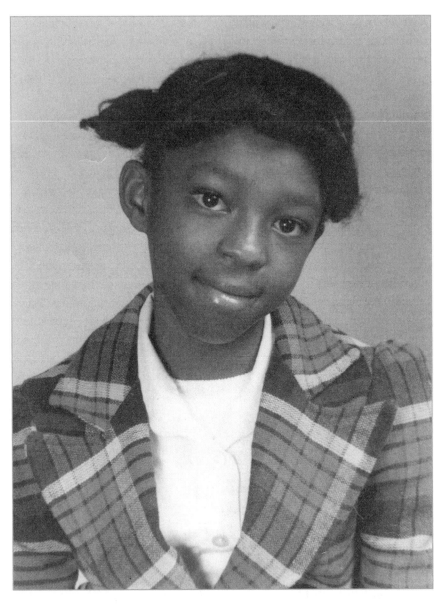

During my late elementary school years, I was deeply worried about my dad. He had checked out from us.

I call this "the last photo." My dad became unrecognizable.

Dad's brothers from the fire department carry his casket into church.

Dad's thuggish friends from the motorcycle club followed the funeral procession all the way to the cemetery. We were horrified.

A family photo shortly after my dad's death. I refused to smile.

Grandpa Fred proudly walked me down the aisle in place of my dad in 1994.

Fred and Opal renewed their vows during their 50th wedding anniversary in 1991.

Big Boy and I in 2010 hosted an event for people with disabilities at the Apollo theater in Harlem. He stole the show!
COURTESY: Alonzo Boldin

Thirty years after my dad's death, we have expanded as a family, but Clarence is still missed.
COURTESY: Alonzo Boldin

As long as I live, I will honor, protect, and defend my father's legacy.
COURTESY: Tony Gale

Six

Straight out of Central Casting

After a couple of years of hard labor by Clarence and Grandpa Fred, Light House Church opened its rickety doors in spring of 1967. It was christened with the blessing of Fred and Opal's new pastor, Elder Joseph Morgan, who was the founder of another church called Holy Temple in Corona. He promised to provide support for the church until it was able to survive on its own. The sanctuary, which my grandfather was still putting finishing touches on, held its first Sunday school with three young children, the oldest of whom was seven years old. My grandmother, Sister Wills, as she told the young trio to call her, taught Bible stories for an hour, starting at ten o'clock in the morning. The little ones were so impressed with her enthusiasm that they promised to bring all of their friends from Astoria Projects and their parents, which they did.

By the following Sunday, there were about one dozen beautiful, eager brown faces staring at my grandmother as she handed out Sunday school lesson plans and crayons to the youngsters, who enjoyed learning about the roots of Christianity in the Holy Bible. They didn't care how the church looked at all. The walls were painted a dull yellow and there were exposed light bulbs with strings attached and hanging down. Odd-looking framed pictures that my grandfather found at the junkyard were conspicuously hung to cover the unsightly portions of walls that could not be smoothed over. There were wooden folding chairs with cloth covers that my grandmother made fitted over the backs, and hard un-cushioned pews that didn't match. My grandfather used steel pipes as coat racks, and chairs he found from an abandoned shoe shine shop were placed in the back as

148

extra seating. He hung a small American flag on the back wall of the pulpit, which was uncommon in Holiness churches. Exposed wiring was wrapped with black electrical tape, and the microphone over the rostrum was strung from the ceiling and hung down in front of the speaker's face. More than a few preachers, in a fit of excitement, yanked out the microphone. The only new things were the items that Clarence purchased with his salary, staying true to his rejection of secondhand stuff. From a Christian bookstore on West 43rd Street, across from Port Authority, he purchased a gold-plated offering plate that visitors and members lined up to place their crumbled dollar bills and spare change.

Worship service followed at 11:30 sharp and, slowly but surely, one family after another, mostly from Astoria Housing Projects down the street, streamed into the curious little handmade church that bore huge signage that said, "Light House Church of our Lord Jesus Christ of the Apostolic Faith, Inc., Elder Fred D. Wills, founder and pastor. An eleven by fourteen picture of Jesus Christ, under glass, hung next to the sign.

Clarence was the first member anointed a deacon by his father, which means that midway through the service he was responsible for raising an offering and, as an added bonus, he played his cherished guitar alongside his father and was accompanied by his mother on the piano. My father also assisted my grandfather during his sermons as a reader, which meant my grandfather told the congregation which chapter and verse to turn to—and then he shouted to my father "READ!" Clarence stood and read the Bible verses until my grandfather said, "Now, stop right there." It was actually a long-standing tradition that started with illiterate preachers in the nineteenth century who actually could not read the Bible. The scriptures were read aloud for the preacher by the one person in the church who was literate.

In a Southern preacher's prose that was peppered with chants like "Thank the Lord" and "Glory to God," and admonitions that cross-referenced an ancient biblical figure to one's present day misery, my grandfather held his audience captive for a solid forty-five minutes—with church members alternately leaping to their feet, with shouting of "Amen, Elder Wills!" "Preach it, Elder Wills!" and "That's the truth, anyhow!"

I rattled my little tambourine as my grandfather's voice peaked to various highs and lows and sometimes members wept and even fainted with guilt after feeling implicated by my grandfather's fiery words. Neither

Broadway nor Hollywood could ever have staged a better drama than what I witnessed every Sunday morning for my entire childhood. They were all straight out of central casting.

My mother served as the church secretary, recording in a professional ledger book how much money was raised in the offerings, what lessons took place during Sunday school and any other church business that needed to be recorded. One by one, some members who had grown to love Elder and Sister Wills, began to defect from Holy Temple and other churches throughout the city and join Light House. Sister Sowell, an older dark-brown-skinned lady who spoke very quickly and reeked of unadulterated joy, was one of the earliest members. She was a poor domestic worker, but she was truly rich in spirit. As my grandmother ebulliently sang songs and banged out rhythms on the piano in sync with her husband and oldest son on their respective guitars, Sister Sowell added percussion by beating on pots and pans with a big spoon or a stick. Born in what my grandmother called "the Carolinas," Sister Sowell was one of many Southerners who felt right at home in the little church.

There was also Sister Carrie Boyd, a rail-thin single mother who had a string of beautiful girls. Sister Boyd was an outspoken and forthright woman from Georgia who had no problem telling you how she felt even if she hurt your feelings. No matter to her, she didn't care much about your feelings anyway if she felt she was telling the truth. But she had a lovable quality about her that made her memorable despite her tough exterior. Her granddaughter LaShawn and I were like sisters and we did everything together. Sister Sistrunk also joined my grandparents' fledgling church. Second only to my grandmother, she was the strongest singer in the church and quickly became the go-to person for music. As word of the young church spread, young and old mothers who were born in the South and their children, most of whom were born in the North, began to stream into the storefront house of worship. There was Sister Bland from North Carolina, with her talented daughters, Violecia, Sheila, Glenda, and Helen at her side. Sister Lomax brought her entire brood from Astoria Housing Projects: from the oldest kids, Barry, Linda, and Carol, to the youngest, Judy, Randy, and Denise. Another dynamo, Sister Angie Grant who heralded from Georgia, brought her daughters and her many grandchildren.

My grandfather's small but cozy church, which uncomfortably seated about sixty people, swelled within a year to almost seventy-five people, the overwhelming majority of whom were women and children. There were also some real characters in the mix, notably Elder Lafayette Sims. He was a tall, barrel-chested, light-skinned minister with a resounding voice who had a personality that rivaled TV sensation Flip Wilson, the black comedian who broke barriers in 1970 by headlining his own variety show. With a boisterous and jolly laugh, Elder Sims knew how to hold an audience's attention and evoke a laugh or a tear, as he memorized entire poems and Bible verses and recited them with great fervor like boxer Muhammad Ali. He was married to a woman named Juanita and they had three children, Joanne, Valerie (who was my best friend in the church), and Lafayette Jr. My Grandfather Fred and Elder Sims had a lot in common with their troubled past, but they tried their best to stay in church to overcome their weaknesses.

Amazed at the rapid growth, Clarence, by default, became a mentor to many of the young boys and men who were mesmerized by the way he played guitar, and they insisted he teach them the basics. My father, a generous spirit, always obliged and passed around his guitar to one boy after another after church was over and taught them the same chords he learned as a boy.

I was barely in kindergarten, but I breathed in this entire melodrama with a prurient fascination. The best part of the entire service, by far, was the music. My grandmother, whose rich voice overpowered everyone else's, was a stone-cold singer, with a trained and disciplined deep-alto voice that soared and made everyone stand to their feet. Opal could have easily been a professional gospel singer like Mahalia Jackson, but my grandma always told me—as I wove her long salt-and-pepper hair into a French braid on Saturday afternoons—that she could never leave her husband and boys to "go singin'" on the road. It was the world's loss, believe you me. Sister Wills really belted out songs when my father hit just the right lick on the guitar, which prompted her to stop singing and dance in the spirit. I always sat right next to her on the piano stool because I just adored her so much. It has always been remarkable to my family that I didn't play the piano, for all of the years that I spent literally pressed against her side as her fingers zipped along the ivory keys.

No one, including myself, really understood the origins of my grandparents' and father's musical style, which was a cross between the Grand Ole' Opry in Nashville—complete with my Grandfather Fred's

Tennessee yodel—and the House of Blues in Chicago. The churchgoers, unaware of the musical roots, clapped their hands and stomped their feet to the swinging gospel beat. During the many times when my grandfather became ecstatic over the music he said to the church crowd, "Boy, we havin' a time! I say, we havin' a time!"

Everyone shouted in return, "Amen, Elder Wills!"

The dozens of people in the church didn't know about my dad's courageous military history or that Clarence had become so disillusioned with his now pastor father that, as a teenager, he once moved away. Few, if any, understood that this was music that was steeped in sounds from slavery; no one discussed ancestral roots in this little church and few really understood what made the other tick. They simply smiled and sang along— and seven days later, they did it all over again.

Aside from my grandmother, whom everyone saluted as a real woman of God—my father was the standout in the church, even more so than my grandfather, Pastor Wills. Always dressed as neatly as a pin on Sunday morning, with his equally polished wife, Ruth, nearby; Clarence moved in church like a military man on a mission. He was deliberate and precise in all matters big and small. He started to tune his guitar to my grandmother's piano at 11:25 a.m. sharp. My grandmother routinely hit the "C" key on her Wurlitzer piano that her son purchased for her, and Clarence adjusted the levers at the top of his guitar strings until the two instruments were perfectly in sync.

Pastor Wills was always just a few minutes late because the children begged him to open the candy store during the half-hour recess between Sunday school and worship service. I always stood off to the side of the tiny store and watched like a manager as my grandfather sold hordes of the latest penny candy like Now or Laters, Bazooka bubble gum, jawbreakers, and lemon drops. The bright-eyed children, dressed in their Sunday best, handed Elder Wills quarters, nickels, and dimes as they happily departed with enough candy to rot their teeth for a lifetime, myself included. As with the church, my grandfather built the candy store with his own hands and purchased the candies wholesale from retailers in Long Island City.

Almost a half century later, a few of the thousands of kids who streamed through his quaint little candy store send me messages, saying things like: "I still remember your grandfather's candy store. He was the best." And my grandpa really was the best, and very friendly with the children who passed by going to and from the elementary school, P.S. 171, which was just a couple of blocks away.

Thirty years later, I was especially tickled when my colleague and fellow reporter, Dean Meminger, passed along a message to me from his relatives who once lived in Astoria Projects. They told Dean to tell me that how well they remembered my grandfather, and his candy store, and how he "looked scary like an undertaker." I laughed so hard when Dean told me that because I suppose, to some kids, my grandfather did look a bit frightful. Not only did he walk with a noticeable limp, but he had the highest cheekbones and brow bones imaginable, which protruded from his very pleasant face. When he looked at you, his whole face really looked at you. Of course, people now pay good money for exotic bone structure like that; but to children, my grandfather's face drew double takes.

At eleven-thirty on the nose, my father strummed his guitar, I lifted my little tambourine, and we waited for my grandmother to sing the first song. Others in the congregation joined in and clapped their hands, and some boys played the bongos to keep time. After a short prayer, they had testimony service where some people rose from their seats and told the most heartbreaking stories you'd ever want to hear. They'd ask everyone to pray for their son or daughter who was struggling with drugs or alcohol, or to pray for a husband who had disappeared, or a job they had suddenly lost. My grandmother always peppered these sorrowful testimonies with an "Amen." For most of the churchgoers, such confessions were the only form of therapy they ever had in their harrowing lives.

About halfway through the service, at twelve-thirty, Clarence put down his guitar and raised the church offering. I enjoyed watching my dad take control of the service and position the small table in front of church. He never had to ask for the audience's attention because he had a commanding presence. Like clockwork, he opened his red leather-bound Bible, the same Bible that he pressed against his heart in the army when he almost died from smoking laced weed, and read the entire twentieth chapter of Psalms, the King James Version. The poetic and popular book of the Holy Bible is full of sacred poems that reflect Israel's faith.

In this particular chapter, there is a lyrical and commanding appeal for believers to give freely of their money. Rather than my father begging people to open up their wallets, he let the Bible do the talking. With my grandmother playing a melody on the piano, he routinely read and perfectly enunciated all nine verses, which began:

> "The Lord hear thee in the day of trouble; the name of the God of Jacob defend thee. Send thee help from the sanctuary and strengthen thee out of Zion. Remember all thy offerings and accept thy burnt sacrifice. Grant thee according to thine own heart and fulfill all thy counsel."

But it was something about the way Clarence read the seventh verse that captured everyone's imagination: "Some trust in chariots and some in horses, but we will remember the name of the Lord our God."

Unlike many ministers, including his own father, Clarence was not a screamer or a yeller when he spoke before the congregation. He spoke calmly with authority, passion, and zeal. And when he said, "Some trust in chariots, and some in horses, but we will remember the name of the Lord our God," he punched the words "chariots" and "horses," and briefly paused to allow the church members to think about what he just read. What he was saying, and what he in fact believed at that time, was that most people, church folks included, put their trust in other things rather than God.

Some black folks in New York were notorious for spending their hard-earned money on "the numbers," an underground gambling consortium based out of Harlem. They also wasted their money on alcohol and drugs, and other illegal activities, which reaped them nothing but pain and heartache. But my father, in his own sublime way, chided them to sow their money in the House of God, where they were sure to reap great dividends. With his call, the adult members lined up row by row and put their money into the golden offering plate, which my father always shined before placing it on the table.

The offering ranged from thirty to fifty dollars and, on a holiday like Easter, where there were visitors, it might top one hundred dollars, but rarely more than that. My grandfather never got enough money from the offerings to make ends meet, and he always had to supplement church income by doing odd jobs around the city during the week and, of course, keeping the candy store open as long as possible. A few members paid ten percent of their salaries, referred to as tithing. My dad was especially meticulous about this until the day he died. If his check from the fire department was $302.62, he wrote a check made out to Light House Church for $30.26. There were certain principles in Christianity that he firmly believed in, and that was one of them.

The good news from the fire department came in late 1969. My dad was twenty-eight years old. He passed the written fire exam with flying colors and was admitted to the Fire Probationary Training School on May 16, 1970, which was situated on a twenty-seven-acre waterfront facility. Clarence and the other members of his class were known as "probies." They went through rigorous training on Randall's Island, a small mass of land adjacent to Manhattan. My dad had recently purchased the most talked about and best-selling car perhaps in American automobile history: a sparkling, royal-blue 1969 Volkswagen Beetle. The unmistakable German-made car was practical and affordable. Clarence handled the four-speed manual transmission with ease as he traversed the Van Wyck Expressway and the Grand Central Parkway in Queens. He was a fast but very safe driver, and I was always planted in the right rear backseat, taking in the views of the city—gasp—without a seatbelt.

Clarence was one of two black men among thirty-three assigned to the Probationary Fireman Training School. Although they did not roll out the welcome mat for him, the senior members of the department showed my dad a grudging respect when they learned of his military duty, especially his paratrooper experience and the time he served stationed in France. Clarence's experience gave him bragging rights among the cadre of Irish and Italian fire captains.

Learning the ropes was almost child's play compared to his paratrooper exercises, as he easily mastered the training rigors and fire procedures and tactics. When a vacant building on the training grounds was set ablaze, there was not a speck of fear in my father's eyes as he forged into the inferno the same way he had jumped out of a moving airplane. He boasted to his wife that he passed every test with flying colors and that he was looking forward to the big graduation when our entire family could attend. He brought home a picture of his graduating class which he, as usual, immediately framed. My dad is one of four men sitting with his legs crossed on the ground, wearing the standard soft-blue, fire department-issued shirt. Like all the men, he wore big fire boots, his fire hat with his last name written in black magic marker across the top, and he has a pleasant smile on his face. It was the dawning of a new era in the fire department, with two black fire officials seated nearby in white hats. The city was entering a fresh decade, 1970, and New York City was being pushed to include more African- Americans into its previously all-white fire department ranks.

Clarence's graduation from the fire academy was memorable, for me in particular. My grandparents were there, along with my mother and my little brother, Clarence Jr. I had no idea what was coming. My daddy was easy to spot, as being one of only two black firefighters and, being a preschooler, I followed his every move. But when the group of new firefighters simulated a fire exercise where they walked into a burning building, I absolutely lost my mind. I'm not sure anyone had fully clued me in that my beloved father was graduating from fire training school and that he was entering a burning building to put the fire out because that was his new job. It was all an exercise, but all my young, teary eyes saw was my dear daddy entering a hell hole, and I had a full and complete breakdown.

The audience on the lawn, which was filled with Irish and Italian families and scores of children, was startled by my preschool tantrum. I was terrified because I thought my daddy was going to die. I knew that walking into a burning building wasn't a good thing. It was an eerie foreshadowing of how concerned I was, even at a young age, for my father's safety. It was not a typical concern of a child who had not yet finished kindergarten, but I was somehow instinctively aware that my daddy liked to quite literally play with fire. I would have this fear for my entire life, until I saw him for the final time in an elegant casket. With wide, adoring eyes, I always gazed up at his fetching face and felt that something terrible was going to happen to my father one day, and I dreaded that fateful moment every step of the way.

By 1970, my father was initially in denial, but my mother realized there was something wrong with my brother, Big Boy. It was the immunizations, my mother pleaded—her son couldn't take it. My mother had to pin my strong little brother down as the nurse pulled his small brown arm forward and injected a huge needle into his flesh—as Big Boy screamed bloody murder. The poor child was traumatized so badly that my mother had to keep candy in her purse to give the tearful child as a reward after it was over.

After a series of shots at a local health center down the block from our housing projects called Pryme, (my mother says) my brother broke out in a violent fever and was never the same. Suddenly, my happy bouncy brother became sullen and withdrawn. He didn't talk to me anymore and we no longer played our silly little games. He just looked at me as I sang the theme song to our favorite television show on PBS called **Sesame Street** and he didn't sing along. When my dad plopped him in front of our floor model state-of-the-art color television, I remember being startled by my brother's near-catatonic state.

"What happened to Big Boy, Mommy?" I asked over and over.

Distressed, my mother didn't have an answer for me or my father. As I entered kindergarten at P.S. 183 in Rockaway Beach, Queens, my mother stayed in Pryme Community Health Center, waiting hours on end for specialists to explain what was wrong with her toddler son. "Autism," one doctor finally explained after a battery of tests. None of us knew what the autism was, but we all quickly learned about the neuro-developmental disorder that is characterized by social impairment and other repetitive behaviors. In short, my brother acted unlike anyone else in our neighborhood and some insensitive people started to call him "Cheryl's retarded brother." It was very hurtful to hear such things, but my mother and I continued to embrace Big Boy in spite of his unique behavior. I didn't care what was different about him, he was my baby brother and I loved him to pieces. I was confused and didn't quite know how to handle him at times—especially being an awkward kid myself—but I was my brother's keeper in every sense of the word. I felt an obligation to protect Big Boy from the hostile attacks. My brother became obsessed with two things and two things only: cartoons and drawing. He watched animated shows with rapt attention and tried to emulate them in voice and appearance. He would raise his finger and pretend to write things in mid-air and drift off into his own world. My dad didn't know what to do or how to react. He never said anything about it to anybody except my mother. He wasn't ashamed of Big Boy; I think he just accepted my brother's disability for what it was. His outward reaction conveyed: "Stuff happens." However, he was disappointed to know that his namesake would never be the daredevil that he was. I remember a few years later when my dad tried to teach both of us to ride a bike. I picked it up right away, but Big Boy just couldn't get it. It was just the three of us on a bright summer day in a park in the Hammels housing projects. I remember my father's blank expression as he helplessly watched Big Boy sprawled out on the ground and screaming, "I can't, Daddy! Leave me alone!!!"

As a result, my brother rode a plastic mobile toy called a Big Wheel for years and years—even when he was too big for the low-ride tricycle with one huge wheel in the front and two smaller wheels in the back. My dad pretty much just shut down his emotions and did nothing to help my brother. He barely even spoke to him because he no longer knew what to say to the little boy who was curiously content in his own world—and no one was invited in.

My dad also entered another world when he walked into Engine 1 Ladder 24 on 142 West 31st Street, right across the street from Madison Square Garden. There were no bells and whistles or balloons when Clarence, the first black to ever report for duty at the oldest firehouse in New York City known as Midtown Madness, stood before the captain, checked in, and was issued badge number 6658. Black firefighters had routinely been assigned to areas in the Bronx and Brooklyn, but never Engine 1. The firehouse, dwarfed by highrise office buildings on either side, boasted a huge red garage-like door with two fire trucks inside.

As Clarence was directed to the area to hang his fire coat, boots, and hat, he received hateful glares from the white firemen who stood with arms firmly folded, and frowns on their faces. As he was introduced to his new "brothers" one by one, they gave him the cold shoulder and refused to even look him in the eye or shake his hand. My dad had lived in many places across the country, from the seat of the Ku Klux Klan in Tennessee to the remote areas of France and, he later recalled, the most hateful treatment he ever received was in New York City, of all places. When he was assigned his bed upstairs, he overheard an argument among the firemen who loudly protested that they "didn't want to sleep next to the nigger" and to "put him somewhere else."

As long as no one put their hands on him, my dad told my mom night after night, everything would be okay. Initially, Clarence was afraid to eat the food his fellow firefighters cooked because he feared they might poison him. So my mom always prepared his food, which he took in plastic dishes. There were one or two firefighters who did not engage in this mob mentality, though. They made a little small talk with Clarence once in a while to let him know that not everyone hated him. But those that did were fierce in trying to run him out. He joined the Vulcan Society, the official organization of African-American firefighters—and was urged to file a formal grievance, but he refused. He felt he could overcome the harassment without making it any worse. But it got worse before it got better.

Some frosty mornings, when the fire alarm went off in the house, my dad and the other firefighters sprang into action, quickly dressed, and slid down the pole. He'd put his feet into his fire boots and find them full of ice water. Angered, he quickly poured them out and hopped on the truck and said not a word. When he told my firebrand mother these stories, she was horrified and wanted something to be done. My father simply called them "stupid young clowns" and assured her that soon they would tire of their pranks and get used to him, because he wasn't going anywhere.

Clarence found a great way to distract himself from these fools by going to college. He enrolled in New York City Community College, which is now called Borough of Manhattan Community College, in what was another historic first for the family. While other firefighters watched television and listened to music, Clarence sat at a table with his college textbooks and yellow highlighters. He was glad no one in the house talked to him, because he was able to study in peace. The commuter college was located in Lower Manhattan on Chambers Street, just a stone's throw from City Hall. I still have his textbooks, including a number of books on Frederick Douglass, particularly the abolitionists' autobiography called "My Bondage and My Freedom," which means my dad took an interest in African-American history while he was in college. Little did he know that his great-great grandfather, Sandy Wills, was such an important part of that thread in American history.

Every Sunday, we still went to my grandparents' church, which was starting to hit its stride. My grandfather had an assistant pastor named Norman Harris, who was a policeman in New York City. He also had a wife, Dorothy, and several children. My father held a deep respect for Elder Harris and, when my father really lost his way in the end, Minister Harris was the only man who tried to get my father to turn from his wicked ways.

Meanwhile, Grandfather Fred imposed the strict Christian rules that he saw in place in Indiana in his church. Women were not allowed to embellish themselves and once again my mother flaunted those rules. But as head of his own church, he went one step further. Citing scriptures, he discouraged his members from seeking medical treatment—right down to eyeglasses—because they should depend on Jesus to heal their bodies. It was a deadly and dangerous precedent that he put in place, which eventually contributed to his own death. From the pulpit, my grandfather admonished the poor worshipers, "Do you believe Jesus is a healer? If you believe it, then you know he can heal your eyes, your body, anything—it can be done in Jesus' name."

My grandfather was fanatically adamant about this and, if he saw a member of his church wearing eyeglasses, he openly pitied them and questioned their faith. His logic seemed reasonable to many as he preached about Jesus raising Lazarus from the dead. "If he raised Lazarus from the dead, then healing your eyes, or your ailments is easy—ain't it?"

My Grandmother Opal believed this hook, line, and sinker, but not everyone in the congregation went along with it; some just listened and went to the doctor anyway. Others were offended, thought he was nuts, left, and never came back. A scant few, my parents were not included in this number, believed what he said wholeheartedly.

Near the conclusion of every Sunday worship service, my grandfather used Goya olive oil, which was on sale at every supermarket in the neighborhood, prayed over it, and anointed members' heads with oil in a "prayer line." One by one they stood in line and whispered in my grandfather's ear how they wanted God to heal their various ailments from arthritis to back pain and, in some cases, cancer and heart disease. My grandfather motioned for them to put both of their hands up and he put his hands on their heads and prayed feverishly out loud as some of them trembled, cried, and a few fell prostrate onto the floor.

My grandmother and father always serenaded this part of the service with a song that sometimes went on for ten or fifteen minutes, depending on how many people were in line. Elder Wills really and truly believed he was doing God's work and did not see anything wrong with what he was doing. If you died from not going to the doctor, then it was God's will. If you went blind due to glaucoma, then it was God's will. If cancer ravaged your body and rendered you disabled, then it was God's will. It was all about "faith" in my grandfather's eyes, and he was by no means the only one who believed this. He had seen preachers walk on fire coals and not have their feet burned and he had witnessed miraculous healings at Christian Revival meetings around the country so he felt like he was in good company.

Elder Wills also baptized thousands of people of all ages in a pool that he built himself off to the other side of the church. It was critically important that Christians were baptized in the "name of Jesus Christ" as opposed to the "Father, Son, and Holy Ghost." If you were baptized any other way, you had to do it again the right way. As a child, I saw so many of his baptisms that I collect paintings of the sacred ritual to this day. Of all of the things I witnessed, that was the most moving thing I had ever seen in my life, even more intriguing than seeing people lose their consciousness and speak in other tongues—where it sounded as though they were speaking Hebrew or an African ethnic language. With their arms folded across their chest, and dressed in white, each baptism candidate was asked by Pastor Wills if they repented of their sins. Then he proclaimed, "I now baptize you in the name of Jesus Christ for the remission of your sins and you shall receive the gift of the Holy Ghost." And with a thunderous splash in ice-cold water, he dunked their entire body down in the water and lifted them back up. Upon experiencing this, many broke out in praise, others wept openly, and still others danced right in the water.

To me, as a child, it looked like the scariest thing ever—as though you might drown or something. My grandmother always sang the same song: "Take me to the water—to be baptized." The entire ritual was steeped in tradition. Upon further reflection, many of these folks thought their lives would instantly change for the better—most times it did not. The same misery they left at home was waiting for them upon their return. But for a brief shining moment in their lives, their sins were washed as white as snow.

The Thrashing Wonders were still a local sensation in New York in the early 1970s and Clarence still managed to be a part of the group for which his brother Van was now the lead guitarist and music leader, although Clarence missed a lot of rehearsals due to his college classes and his job at the firehouse. Van lived in a room upstairs from the church, but he did not venture downstairs on Sunday morning to join Clarence and his parents. He kept his father at a distance and feared his father might disappoint him if he got too closely aligned with him. The only time Van went into the church was to rehearse with the Thrashing Wonders where he set up a reel-to-reel deck and recorded many of the rehearsals to critique at a later date.

One day, while waiting for the other members to show up, Clarence and Van hit the record button and played and sang together exactly as they had done as children, except now both played their guitars in a far more sophisticated manner and each had their own styles. Van plucked the strings of a Chet Atkins Tennessean made by the popular guitar-making company, Gretsch. It was a vintage guitar that Van played and polished with pride until he drew his last breath. Clarence played his own vintage guitar that was made by the Gibson guitar company. In this rare instance, the two brothers sang and played as if they didn't have a care in the world. Van sang the high parts and Clarence sang the lower parts of gospel songs like their favorite, "Standing by the Bedside of a Neighbor," written by gospel pioneer Thomas Dorsey, but made famous by The Dixie Hummingbirds. They also sang songs such as:

> *Only Jesus can heal the sick…*
> *Only Jesus can raise the dead…*
> *There is nothing, too hard for him*
> *because he'll do everything he said*
> *He can save your soul*
> *He can set you free*
> *He can give you*
> *everything you need…*

These were compositions they learned from listening to the radio, but the premise was in line with their father's thinking. The brothers were both grown men in their late twenties now but, in their hearts, they were still the little boys who believed in their parents' religion. I had the forty-year-old reels converted to CDs when I was writing this book so I could hear how they sang and played. Their music is soulful and touching.

I heard Billy Brown, the lead singer of the Thrashing Wonders, interact with my dad and uncle and the other singers—and their camaraderie was inspiring. They loved to sing gospel music, and money was secondary, unlike now where money comes first for most gospel artists.

When my mom got pregnant and had my sister Crystal in 1972, we had to move across to a larger apartment in Hammels Housing Projects, building 81-04, where we had three bedrooms. Crystal was an adorable little girl with soft curly hair and big brown eyes. My mom was "on birth control," but that didn't stop another pregnancy, less than one year later, that took my parents completely by surprise. In 1974, Celestal AND Cleavon entered our family in an unexpected twin birth. I was eight years old and I felt like

God had given me two living dolls. Celestal strongly resembled my mother and Cleavon strongly resembled my father.

During this time, my father did something that put him on the fast track for success—and death. He bought a motorcycle. By now, his fellow firefighters had finally stopped harassing him and treated him like one of the guys. After word got around that Clarence was a mason, a paratrooper, and a non-commissioned officer in the United States Army National Guard, they finally realized that he was no pushover and had earned his two stripes the old fashioned way. In a flash, they went from hating him to loving him.

The new Honda bike was convenient on a number of levels. First, Clarence was always on the go and now he could get to his destinations in less than half the time. Second, he could park his motorcycle inside the firehouse and not worry about parking the royal-blue Volkswagen on the street and risk getting a parking ticket. And third, it satisfied and fed his adrenaline rush for speed and risk-taking. It all started out so innocently, as most tragic endings do. The best part was when he placed me and Big Boy on the back of his motorcycle and rode us around in circles. It was better than a ride at Rockaways' Playland as we wrapped our small arms around our daddy's waist and screamed for the entire forty-five-second ride. On perhaps two occasions, we visited the firehouse where he and his fellow firefighters taught us how to slide down the fire pole—which was the coolest thing ever. One firefighter helped us wrap our legs around the top, and two firefighters waited at the bottom for our big drop.

Clarence made history—again—as the first college graduate in the family. We went to that graduation, too, and my daddy, for the first time in his life, wore a graduation cap and gown. I remember saying "Congratulations, Daddy" over and over again. He had earned his associate's degree in applied science (A.A.S.) from New York City Community College and quickly transferred his credits over to The John Jay College of Criminal Justice on the west side of Manhattan where he majored in fire science with hopes of earning a bachelor's degree.

We were busting out of our three-bedroom apartment in the projects and my mother couldn't take it anymore. Ruth saw construction a half mile down the road of a new private development that was called Ocean Village. As the white buildings were erected with terraces and all the amenities one could imagine, my mom reserved a five-bedroom apartment in a townhouse that was still being built.

When we moved in, it was like gated paradise with white sand castles in the sky. Located right off of Rockaway Beach Boulevard, it was nestled along the subway trestle that guided the fabled "A" train to its last stop on Mott Avenue in Rockaway. Everything was new in our five bedrooms, one-and-a-half-bathroom flat that was on the second floor. Almost all of our windows overlooked Rockaway's boardwalk and the Atlantic Ocean, which, as children, we took full advantage of. We were still within walking distance of Rockaway Playland—albeit a long walk of about two miles. There was a community wading pool, a huge basketball court with four different baskets, a shopping center, and even a giant tree house with a seesaw. The floor of the tree house was pink and we created hyped up games of tag called "no touching the pink"—which meant you had to run from the person trying to tag you but you couldn't step foot on the pink ground. An oceanfront neighborhood that was once like the Hamptons to the rich and famous in Manhattan a hundred years ago—was now our beachfront hood, and we all loved living there.

We quickly made friends with hundreds of other kids our age like Eddie Torres; Gregg, Steve, and Vicki Bassett; Angela, Darianne and Tonya Hawkins; Wendi Lucas; Lonnie and Robbie Riles; and adorable twin girls known as Tina and Flo. We had a friend nicknamed Gweek Gweek, whose real name was Cascius Turpin. I never knew why we all called him Gweek Gweek but nobody called him by his real name, not even his family. My new best friend was Patricia Davis, who was my age and the same zodiac sign, Libra, and we were as thick as thieves. We spent the night at each other's apartments, did our homework together, and talked for hours on end on the telephone. My mom and her mother, Bernice, became very close as well. Trisha and I mercilessly teased a cute Puerto Rican kid who lived one floor below her named Louie Troche and we danced circles around him, singing the 1955 rock classic "Louie, Louie." He told me thirty years later on Facebook that we "tormented" him with that song. We got a good laugh at that.

As creative and restless inner-city children, we took wholesome all-American games and unwittingly added speed and violence to them. It was the happiest time in all of our young lives and kids today would probably be arrested for playing the games that we did for kicks. Some were simple street games like "kick the can," which was a slick New York City version of the suburban game of "hide and seek." With a pack of say twenty rambunctious children, everyone had to hide outside, while one person turned around, closed their eyes, and counted to ten. In front of the stoop of the building, a beer or soda can was hastily placed in front and, as the person looked for hidden players, they had to run back to the can and tap the can on the ground three times and say, "I see Wendy." Then Wendy had to come out from hiding and sit on the stoop also known as the base. Eventually, as more kids are pointed out, they sat on the stoop and waited anxiously for a child to come running at the speed of light and "kick the can"—before they could be found out, and everyone on the base ran free to hide again.

As a Long Islander, I tried to get my son to teach his coddled friends our fun game of "kick the can." He told me, "That's whack, Mom."

I needled him as a punk, Long Island snot and told him that he didn't know what fun really was.

A far more dangerous childhood game was called "Hot Peas and Butter" and it is truly legendary among city kids. If you ever played it, you never forgot that you did it. It involved a long leather belt with a sharp edge. As kids sat on the stoop or base, one person was selected to hide the belt in the community's parking lot. It was usually stashed away in a car bumper or under a loose hubcap or something. After hiding it, the child returned to base and said, "Hot peas and butter come and get your supper!" With that call, dozens of children ventured out to find the belt. The person who hid it constantly screamed who's "hot" or near the belt and who's "cold" or far away from it. This could go on for fifteen even twenty minutes and then the climax! The person who found the belt gets to violently whip and thrash every child until they ran hurriedly back to base. In the summertime, if you were wearing shorts, you really felt the sting.

Such a game now seems preposterous, but for summers on end we played this game with great joy and anticipation. And we were obviously not alone. When I Googled, "hot peas and butter," I found it everywhere like the Urban Dictionary, which describes it as a "fun-ass game in which one person hides the belt and asks a group of people to find it and you get to beat the s*** out of your family and friends."

I laughed hysterically when I saw that online. There's an African-American woman online named Kelli who sells "Hot Peas and Butter appealing gifts." On her website she wrote, "I chose the name Hot Peas and Butter because it was one of my favorite childhood games growing up in Brooklyn."

There's a children's musical group called Hot Peas and Butter, which has a Wikipedia entry. It may seem like a sick game but, trust me, you haven't lived on the edge until you played Hot Peas and Butter.

We played with fire when we routinely set garbage cans ablaze on the beach—and watched the fire burn itself out. We had relay races on the rickety boardwalk, which was so close that it seemed to be part of our home. We hit the beach for picnics and just to goof off every day— even on a school day. The boys played touch football in the sand and the girls often walked along the jetties and watched the waves crash along the huge rocks. Girls and boys alike played another popular street game called Scully where we dipped candle wax into a milk bottle top and used it as a game piece. Using chalk on concrete, a kid drew a five-by-five foot square box that resembled tic tac toe. The object of the game was to go from the starting line outside the box—to each of the thirteen numbered boxes. As one player tries to go from box to box, the opponents could knock you out of the box by flipping the bottle cap smoothly along the ground with their thumb and force you to start over again. It was much better than checkers or chess, as we lay on the sandy ground with our bellies rubbing the concrete and one eye closed as we aimed our bottle caps straight for another to win the game.

All of our silly little games, especially our paddleball tournaments where my friends Walter Robinson and Yvette Martin were the respective king and queen of the court (really a side wall of one of the buildings in the complex), came to a grinding halt when we heard the thunder of my dad's motorcycle roar up to our townhouse building. If I was jumping double Dutch, I hopped right out of the two ropes and ran to the parking lot. All of the kids in Ocean Village stood back in amazement as my cool-looking dad, clad in a Fonzie-style leather jacket and bright-red helmet, revved the engine to let everybody know he was home.

I was extra proud because I knew how lucky I was to have a father at home, as more than half of my childhood friends did not. Daddy always wore boots when he rode his motorcycle, even in the summertime, and had black leather gloves to match his coat. He walked upright with great authority, and all of the kids gathered around his bike to see it and sit on it. The only thing that made him angry was if they sat on it when he was upstairs in the apartment, which quickly led my father to put a cover on it every night and lock it with a bicycle lock.

Out of nowhere, something happened between my Grandpa Fred and my dad. There were ugly rumors about my grandfather doing things in the dark that were suddenly coming to light with other women. Clarence was incensed and deeply embarrassed not only for himself but for his mother. How could his father do this, now that he had everything he wanted? He had a church, a candy store, his son and wife by his side, as well as grandchildren. My father watched his dad preach from the pulpit about fearing God and admonishing and chastising those who fell into sin, only to learn that his father hadn't changed much at all.

Van wasn't surprised, which is why he never allowed himself to get too involved in the church, only popping by on special occasions. He knew his brother was setting himself up to get his feelings hurt. And, oh, how my dad was crushed in the wake of these unconfirmed rumors. On his final Sunday at Light House Church, Clarence searched his father's eyes for confirmation and found it. Fred couldn't look his son square in the eye. Demoralized, Clarence walked out of the church and told my mother he was never going back to Light House. And he meant it. If there was one thing my dad couldn't stomach, it was an unrepentant hypocrite, especially when that person claimed to be a preacher. *How could anyone in their right mind try to con God?* my father wondered. With that, Clarence decided he would not be a hypocrite. If he was going to be a sinner, he'd stay out of the church—and that's exactly what he did.

One of his friends joined a motorcycle club called "The Newcomers" and asked Clarence to join, too. My dad's membership with these low-life men and women would eventually redefine him in the worst way. This astute military man, who was never late for an appointment or a class, suddenly started to lose track of time.

Our loving and fun daddy, who walked through our doors in the middle of the night and put his cold hands on our warm bellies, soon moved away from us. The dutiful son and deacon, who read the poetic Bible verses in Psalms 20 with zest and passion, put the Holy Book in a bookcase and forgot about it. The guitarist, who played the most beautiful melodies that most of his fellow church-goers had ever heard, stored his treasured vintage instrument back in its case and tucked it in the back of his closet.

When I was ten years old in the summer of 1977, New York City exploded in a frenzy of madness. From the city's financial collapse to the rumble at Yankees Stadium as the boys in pinstripes chased the championship ring, everybody, especially my dad, was coming unglued. Billy Martin—the headline-grabbing manager of the New York Yankees— had a public hate-fest with the ball club's first black superstar, Reggie Jackson. Jackson was better than good and, as children, we clamored for a chocolate bar that was named exclusively for him. Their contentious relationship was splashed all over the pages of the New York dailies as Jackson, AKA Mister October, became the media's whipping boy—in spite of his undeniable talent on the field which led the team to the World Series that year. Every day I clipped newspaper articles of the baseball drama and wrote my own commentary about how I wanted to eject Billy Martin for nearly coming to blows with his star player in a Boston dugout.

Then there was the infamous fiscal crisis. Social services were being cut left and right. Even my dad was laid off from the fire department for two days before he was reinstated. New York's political establishment hated President Gerald Ford for not rescuing the city out its doldrums and union workers were threatening to walk off the job. Embattled Mayor Abe Beame was up for re-election and had fierce competition in the form of a flamboyant congressman, Ed Koch, and a future democratic icon, Mario Cuomo.

If that wasn't enough drama in 1977, we were all afraid of a madman with a gun who was on the loose. I was scared out of my wits of Son of Sam, David Berkowitz. He had murdered a young lady with a 44 caliber pistol in Forest Hills, Queens, which was not too far from our apartment complex in Rockaway Beach. Then he followed it up with two murders in the Bronx, which was also nearby. When *Daily News* columnist Jimmy Breslin released the letter from this nut job, none of us happy-go-lucky kids in Queens were able to play outside for a while. The letter said, "I am the Son of Sam. I love to hunt. Prowling the streets looking for fair game— tasty meat. The women of Queens are the prettiest." We lived in Queens, I was about to turn eleven years old, and we were sure this monster was going to eat us all alive. We didn't play Hot Peas and Butter that summer because our parents thought he was going to hit the Rockaways next.

Then the lights went out! On July 13th, a Wednesday I will never forget, lightening struck a bunch of power lines, and the city was in the dark for what seemed like the entire summer, but it was actually just two days. Amazingly, our lights didn't go out because Rockaway Beach was the only city neighborhood that got its power from Long Island Lighting company system. But my mother still sealed all of the windows closed with sticks and put furniture in front of our door—because looters in Manhattan, The Bronx, Brooklyn, and Queens turned the city upside down. It was as hot as hell in our apartment and our fans only circulated hot hair. We just suffered through the blistering heat until my mother allowed us to open our windows and get the fresh breeze from the Atlantic Ocean again.

After a few more attacks that summer, a crazed David Berkowitz was finally busted by police in mid-August. Our parents let us go back outside and play for what was left of the weirdest summer of our lives.

And where was my dear father during this time? He was literally riding high and acting like the motorcycle stuntman and entertainer Evel Knievel. Clarence must have hired a professional photographer to capture a picture of him driving his motorcycle up a slender steel beam as the amateur daredevil jumped about twenty feet. Jumping out of planes wasn't good enough for this grounded paratrooper, now he had to fly through the sky on his treasured sport bike. At a glance, no one could have guessed that this audacious biker had five little brown children at home anxiously awaiting his thunderous return. In the summer of '77, my daddy lived like a free-wheeling bachelor in the hell zone that was New York City. After he had died, and I saw the photos of his motorcycle jumps—all I could do was shake my head and think, ***What a guy!***

Clarence wouldn't have been so flippant about his life had he understood the bridge that got him there. He was lashing out at his father in a way that would have made Emma and Sandy recoil with horror. In spite of their difficult lives, they never turned their back on their family. They were poor people who never had an opportunity to work for the government, but they worked the little plot of land they had and made the best of it. They were honorable people that survived the most dishonorable system America had ever embraced: slavery—and yet they maintained their dignity and their decency in spite of it all. My dad may have jumped out of planes, but he didn't learn how to jump out of disappointment. His answer was to run and act reckless to prove his childish point. Even our illiterate great-great-great grandparents knew better than that.

As the post-slavery South struggled to redefine itself in the new decade of 1870, Sandy and Emma were settling into the rigors of a newly established family with the birth of their first child, William. Like every milestone in their humble sharecropping lives, William's birth was also one for the books. He was among the first free children born in many generations of enslaved Africans in the United States. He entered the world as a bona fide American citizen, unlike his parents who were just slaves and had no rights, citizenship, or protections under the law. The thirteenth, fourteenth, and fifteenth amendments acknowledged their existence and made them citizens whose male members could vote. I can only imagine the joy they had for baby William, whose new free world was full of promise. William would never be sold away from Sandy and Emma under any circumstances. Although the family did not take advantage of the government-run colored schools in Memphis, which was about fifty miles away, William would not be beaten or whipped if he wanted to learn how to read and write on his own. His life belonged to his parents, not to a greedy slave master or overseer who treated him as a mule. Emma and Sandy, for the first time ever in African-American families, had the privilege and the honor of loving their child and teaching him how to survive in a free, albeit still dangerous, country.

Best of all, Sandy and Emma could record the day he entered the world for all posterity. William Wills was born on February 3, 1870, in Haywood County. My Great-great-great grandmother Emma, who was barely twenty years of age, had acquired a sense of order and a respect for recordkeeping that was remarkable for her young age. She knew she had the historic opportunity to document her firstborn's birth, which is exactly what she did, even though she couldn't write it down herself. In later years, when deposed by her lawyer to give testimony about her past, she admitted that every one of her children, except one, was born in her former slave master's house, the home owned by the man she gently referred to as Mister Moore. The white folks who once owned her, now treated her as a daughter in their very own home.

The former slave-holding Moores apparently gave Emma a family Bible where she had Mister Moore's younger son, Joel, write the name and birthday and location of her son's birth. With every successful delivery, all nine of them, she had Joel Moore inscribe the name of each child as well as the day they entered the world. What a stunning feat for a young lady—a former house slave—who grew up in one of the most suffocating and cruel systems of human bondage in the history of the world. My Great-great-great grandmother Emma emerged from slavery with such grace, poise and, best of all, a sense of legacy. Recorded in her very intimate testimonies, made when she applied for a widow's pension after her husband Sandy's death about twenty years later, college-educated lawyers quizzed this woman and repeatedly asked her for the spelling and birthdates of her children. She humbly replied, "I don't know, but I know my Bible is right."

She toted what presumably was a large King James Bible, which contained her historic legacy of freedom and, one by one, the lawyers jotted down the names and birthdates of her offspring. Alex Wills, my great-great grandfather, was born on September 20, 1871. Sandy Wills, named for his courageous father, celebrated his birthday on August 8, 1873. Adolfus Wills (who Emma nicknamed Dolphin after her own father) was born on October 2, 1875. Emma's first girl, Mattie Belle Wills, was born on September 7, 1877. John Henry Wills was born on August 3, 1879. Walter Wills was born on January 25, 1883. Emma's second girl, nicknamed Puss, was born on August 25, 1886, and the youngest, James, was born on March 28, 1889.

Emma guarded her family's Holy Bible with the greatest of care and the lawyer wrote down everything she said on March 6, 1900. Referring to Joel Moore, she said, "…he also set the dates of their birth down in my Bible as each one was born. I had nine children by Sandy Wills, eight of whom were living when he died and one was born the next month after he died."

The personal punch in the gut for me was the lawyer's signature of her name in a beautiful cursive handwriting, and in between her first and last name, is an X, bordered by tiny scribble that read, "her mark." My brilliant, exquisite great-great-great grandmother left her mark on American society in more ways than just an X. One of the many painful truths about slavery was that the lives of slaves were forgettable. I do not know and may never know my forbears who lived prior to the life of my Great-great-great grandfather Sandy, which is very unfortunate for me and my family. They were probably beautiful people who were stuck in an impossible situation but did the best they could with what they had. Because Emma took a stand, 150 years later, I can document her courageous actions in this book.

History shows that she was unique. When I review the records of some of the other soldiers, their children's birthdays are either left blank or just the year is noted. I'm sure they considered it an accomplishment to even record the approximate year. I do not assume that they were negligent; life must have been dizzying for the newly independent former slave women. My dear Emma was extraordinary because she clung to the records contained in her precious Bible, which she could not even read. She believed in herself and her reason for living. She fiercely believed in the Bible stories she knew so well. She could not spell Jesus, but she trusted the man she called her savior to guide her footsteps.

Her fortitude and dignity makes her the "Mother Mary" of our genealogical line. Like her veteran husband Sandy, she didn't need an education to know right from wrong. As she did during slavery, she "felt" her way through the world, and her razor-sharp intuition led the way. Her signature remained a humble X, but she saw to it that every single one of her children learned how to sign theirs. The 1900 census shows that Mattie Bell, William, John, and the youngest girl, Priscilla, who was thirteen at the time the federal workers stopped by their home, were all documented as being able to read and write. What an extraordinary accomplishment for a young mother, born a slave. She did not just settle for being a shadow that entered the nation quietly and left with barely a whimper. Emma West Moore Wills wanted the world to know that she was born, got married, and had children. And thanks to her smarts, her Holy Bible, and the United States Census, we know it now and forever. Emma didn't fight in the Civil War, like Sandy, but in her soul was a warrior who insisted that her children reap the benefits of her husband's sacrifice. A true self-effacing mother, she demanded for her children what she didn't demand for herself: an education. She set the bar very high for the entire Wills family for generations to come.

Clarence never knew of his Great-great grandmother Emma's legacy, but she may have mystically guided his steps as he set the bar she created even higher some two generations later. She'd be pleased to know that not only do I read and write—but I read the news to millions of people every day. She must be smiling ear to ear in heaven not just for me, but for all of her grandchildren who will never forget her sacrifice.

There were, however, some things that surely tormented Emma and her husband Sandy. Aside from the few country doctors, most of whom were not certified M.D.s, a simple illness could easily turn deadly. At least three of Emma's children were casualties of disease. The year 1893 was probably the worst year of Emma's life. That spirited teenage bride, who somehow inspired her former slave master to host her nuptials in his own home, buried three of her nine children—two in the same year. There is no record of what caused their deaths, I'm all but certain it was due to disease. The first sharp blow was little James, who passed away at just three years of age in February of 1893. Less than one month later, Sandy Jr.—who was nineteen years old at the time, died on March 22. It's very possible that the same disease claimed both of them. Emma must have been devastated, for losing two of your own children within weeks is almost more than any mother could possibly bear. But the worst probably came in 1898, when her first born daughter, Mattie Bell, a wife and mother herself, died on November 28, 1898, just months after getting married. In a deposition Emma says, "She died right here in my house." Mattie wed a man named Bill Bond, and he was literate as well. They had one child named Nales who was still a young child at the time of her death. Mattie Bell was just twenty-one years old when she passed away, and Emma was living with her along with Mattie Bell's three siblings, William, John, and Priscilla. Emma was young by modern standards, just forty-seven years old. Her bright life, full of historic firsts, saw one blow after another. Her husband Sandy's death was probably the worst of them all.

My great-great-great grandfather (who walked in the shadow of death to an enlistment station during the Civil War and fought courageously for his unborn children's freedom) died on February 8, 1889. There's no record or explanation of how this brave warrior died, but Emma was pregnant with little James when her husband drew his last breath at the age of forty-nine or fifty (no one knew his exact birthday).

What a desperate sight it must have been to see Emma, with her swollen belly, lean over her veteran husband's casket for that final goodbye. The handsome man who Emma described as "taller than most," hopefully left the world a proud man. He had eight children, one on the way, and just about every one of them knew their birthdays, and could read and write—a major milestone for the first free children born after slavery's end. Sandy's children could make money and count it, too. He fought in a great war to make it so. A sharecropper farmer his entire life, he kept his feet on the soil and his heart close to God.

Sandy also died a poor man. Official records show he owned no property and had no assets worth noting except one horse. The ultimate slap in the face came from the United States government, who did not, as required by law, offer to place him in a military cemetery in Tennessee. I tried searching for his gravesite and God only knows where his final resting place is, perhaps in an unkempt grave in a colored Methodist church.

Shortly after Sandy's death, Emma applied for a widow's pension. The United States War Department put her through hell and treated her like a lying criminal every step of the way—which federal officials did more to members of the United States Colored Troops than to white pensioners. The voluminous documents reveal a paper trail of discrimination. There are general affidavits, sworn depositions, doctor's reports, proof of marriage— and documents with the word "rejected" stamped in huge letters at the top of the page. It's little wonder that Civil War scholars have proved that injured black soldiers were less likely to apply for their rightful pension in the early years. The numerous depositions she filed, and the dozens of testimonies from soldiers who served with Sandy, gave me a near complete picture of my family tree on which much of this book is based. But I'm sure Emma didn't imagine her great-great-great granddaughter's future biography as she was dragged from one law office to another to prove that her husband did in fact serve and was honorably discharged.

The roots of her struggle stemmed back to the chronic misspelling of the family surname: Wills. The first lines of Sandy's discharge paper, officially filed on February 25, 1866 read:

> Know ye, that Sandy Willis, a private of Captain Judson
> B. Francis Company G 4th regiment of the U.S. C. Art.
> Heavy, volunteers, who was enrolled on the thirteenth day
> of October one thousand eight hundred and sixty three to
> serve three years or during the war, is hereby discharged
> from service of the United States.

When Emma initially filed for money that she was perfectly entitled to for herself and her minor children, she experienced a runaround that had to be especially humiliating and confusing for a woman who could not read or write. Although Sandy had an "Oath of Identity" on file in Washington, D.C., where he personally appeared before a justice of the peace five years before he died, and attested to the fact that he was in fact the identical man to the "Sandy Willis" in his discharge papers, and signed it with his X, The United States War Department Record and Pension Division ignored that documentation and coldly wrote: "The name Sandy Wills has not been found on rolls of Co. G 4 U.S.C.H.A." (Co. G 4 U.S.C.H.A is an abbreviation for Sandy's military unit, Company G. 4th United States Colored Heavy Artillery.)

With that rejection, Emma dealt with a complete circus-like atmosphere that forced her to pay what little money she had to a lawyer named Mr. C.M. Sweet. Lawyers during that time made a small fortune off of black soldiers and their widows because, not only did they have to file the paperwork, they also had to write for them, which was probably an extra charge. The poor former slaves had no idea what was written on the papers. All they could have was blind faith that the process was moving along as they signed their X at the bottom of the page.

My Great-great-great grandmother Emma was seeking financial support for herself and her minor children Mattie Bell, John, Walter, and Priscilla, all of whom were under the age of sixteen. Each child was worth a whopping two additional dollars; Uncle Sam put Emma through all of this drama for eight quarters per offspring. The attorney alone charged her ten dollars for his services, which was an awful lot of cash in the 1890s.

It took an astounding three years for Emma to cut through the red tape to get sixteen measly dollars—stretching from 1890 to 1893. The Department of Interior, Bureau of Pensions Special Examination Division, sent out dozens of questionnaires to soldiers who also worked in the 4th U.S. Heavy Artillery in an attempt to confirm Sandy's military experience.

The very first question was: "Do you remember the soldier Sandy Wills AKA Willis as a member of your company?" Most veterans like Allen Beard, Ephraim Green, and Peter Buckley simply had their lawyer or relative write the word "Yes."

Some like Abraham Dearborn wrote, "I remember Sandy Wills well." Others, like his former fellow slaves and brothers in bondage who fled Edmund Willis Wills' plantations with Sandy, hired a lawyer to give exhaustive descriptions of Sandy on Emma's behalf. James Wills and Jack Dyson gave a lengthy testimony for a general affidavit together, which read in part: "We were fellow soldiers with Sandy Wills in the late Civil War and were mustered out together...Claimant has no property and no income except from her daily labor. We have known claimant since her marriage to Sandy."

Mack Wills also filed an affidavit to vouch for Emma's claim to which he was one of the few who could actually sign his full name as opposed to an X.

Andy's long affidavit confirms that he and Sandy were slaves together: "I belonged to the same man he did before the war, lived and slept with him." I was intrigued by the fact that Andy did not refer to himself as a slave. These proud soldiers had obviously moved on with their lives. Veteran Corporal Dick Parker, who joined Sandy during their fateful trip from the plantation, also characterized his bondage in a most unique way: "I have known him since we were small boys and we belonged to the same man, Willis Wills, before the war." Like Mack Wills, Dick Parker also signed his full name.

There are more than a dozen other people who legally swore that Emma and Sandy never divorced, and that she never remarried after Sandy's death in 1889. They also attested to the fact that she was a moral woman without scandal or blemish and that her children were all fathered by Sandy.

Of all of the affidavits and testimonies, none is more compelling than Emma's multiple depositions fully describing how she met her husband and just about everything else that happened in between their marriage and his death. She, too, had a special way of recalling slavery with his comrades: "He and Andy Wills, Mack Wills, Jim Wills, and Dick Parker were all fellow servants."

That's a polite way to put that they were slaves—held against their will, without hope for an independent future, until the Civil War broke out. Slavery had become a normal way of life for all them; they were born into it and knew nothing else. I am proud of the dignity these African-Americans had in the wake of their nightmare of slavery. Amazing.

After the war's end, Emma was not the only one fighting for pension money. I obtained pension records from the National Archives for Dick, Andy, and Mack Wills, as well as their widows and, just like my Great-great-great grandmother Emma, they were intimidated and harassed by the War Department's constant request for more information. Their first hurdle was that Civil War veterans could not collect a pension until age sixty-two, but the harsh reality was that most black men did not live that long in the nineteenth century. Sandy died when he was about fifty and that was pretty much average. So Dick Parker, Andy and Mack Wills all hired attorneys to make the case for why they were due a pension before the age of sixty-two.

Dick Parker, who had been promoted to a non-commissioned officer, was initially rejected outright when he applied in September of 1902. The government sent his lawyer a letter saying there was no record of a Corporal Dick Parker with the 4th U.S. Heavy Artillery. Citing a "clerical error," they reopened his case in October of 1902. Dick Parker went to doctors who testified that he had heart disease and was blind in one eye. He had to make up a birthday for legal reasons and he chose October 11, 1841. After months and months of back and forth with the government, they finally gave the veteran fifty dollars a month. The department of Interior, Bureau of Pensions, asked the distinguished veteran humiliating questions like: "Were you a slave? If so, state the names of all former owners, particularly your owner at the date of your enlistment."

Corporal Dick Parker, still less than a human being in the eyes of the Uncle Sam, replied, "Edmund Wills owned me when I left house and I was a slave."

In spite of the slights from the country he had fought to protect, he wrote on January 24, 1903, "I pay taxes and I vote." Reading between the lines, he seemed to demand to be respected as a man with that statement. Dick Parker was a hell-raiser in his own way right from the start.

But when his widow, who also happened to be named Emma, tried to apply for a widow's pension after Dick died on May 7, 1924, at the age of about eighty-three, they put her through the same hell as my Great-great-great grandmother Emma Wills went through. The War Department found out that, while in slavery, Dick married a woman named Roxanna, and they refused to give her and her nine children the money they were entitled to until they could prove that Roxanne Parker was not alive. After demanding a marriage license for slaves, which the federal government knew full well they could not provide, a witness named Ernest Reed finally had to explain the obvious in a sworn affidavit, "…there was no public record kept of marriages of colored people where he married Roxanna and the record can't be found…"

It was the same drill for Andy who was legally named Andrew Wills. He was married to a woman named Susan Yancy for more than fifty years. They married on Christmas Day in 1867 and had about eleven children.

And just like my Great-great-great grandmother Emma, she kept the birth dates of all of her children in her family Bible.

Andy was actually shot by cannon fire during combat during the Civil War in 1864, but the Department of Interior's Bureau of Pensions treated him like an embezzler trying to steal from the country he so honorably served. Andrew designated his birthday as April 10, 1840, and when the federal government demanded proof of his birth—shame on them—he had to issue a sworn affidavit on October 28, 1907, that read: "Clerk of the Circuit Board of Haywood County, Tennessee, Andrew Wills, who made oath in due form of law, that he cannot furnish any public record of his birth or verified copy of date, because no such record is kept where he now lives or was kept when he was born…The reason he has no family record is because he himself is unable to read or write, and his parents likewise were unable to read or write."

It's so absurd that Andy Wills actually had to give sworn testimony to explain away a system that denied him human rights, as though everyone forgot how the evil deeds of slavery robbed Africans of their humanity. The treatment of these veterans is a stain on the flag.

After having his pension request outright rejected in 1886, Andy hired a lawyer and provided numerous surgeon's certificates detailing his hip injury where doctors wrote "walks with marked limp and body thrown to the left side." The loud blasts of the cannon also left him deaf in the right ear, and the government still sent out scores of letters to the illiterate soldier about his "alleged" injury. More than twenty years after nearly being shot to death during the war and paying lawyers exorbitant fees, the federal government sent Andrew Wills a check for six dollars a month commencing in 1892. That wasn't even enough to pay the lawyers' fees. He died on January 4, 1919, at around the age of seventy-nine.

Mack was the only veteran among the Wills brothers who eventually left Haywood County and relocated to Halls, Tennessee, and he was the only one who actually owned real estate, which was valued at about five hundred dollars. He had fifty dollars in his bank account at his death. When he died in 1921, his daughter Mollie Wills rightfully filed an application for burial of a deceased soldier. Mollie was roundly rejected and the federal government wrote, "pensioner left sufficient assets to meet expenses of his last sickness and burial." In 1920, his pension had increased to fifty dollars a month because he was over age seventy-five. Medical reports indicated that he suffered from varicose veins, rheumatism, deafness, and senility. His lawyer charged sky-high fees of ten dollars per filing, which was highway robbery for the poor old veterans. Like the others, he was initially rejected for his "alleged" medical conditions, and pension executives wrote that his illnesses were "not notable." His wife, Lizzie Johnson Wills, preceded him in death on September 14, 1895. They had twelve children.

There were no pension records for James Wills. Like my Great-great-great grandfather Sandy, James probably didn't want to be bothered with the bureaucratic red tape and, judging from what the other veterans went through, who could blame him?

However, of all of the depositions, and I have thousands of pages, none are more compelling than my Great-great-great grandmother Emma. Her words give me a bright and clear picture of the gentle and intelligent woman that she was. Over the years, Emma was called upon time and time again to give depositions to the War Department, even after her children died, to prove that she was who she said she was, as if the dozens of sworn affidavits, depositions, and legal documents were not proof enough.

She apparently remained close to Joel Moore, her former slave master's son, for her entire life. One year before she passed away, forty-six-year-old Joel Moore gave yet another sworn deposition vouching for Emma's character on March 6, 1900. He wrote that he knew Emma for all of his life and added that "she belonged before the war to my father and she has always lived right around this neighborhood." Joel Moore further added, "I think she has lived a straight honorable life. I have heard no talk at all against her character."

Joel Moore confirmed that he was the one who recorded the births of her children in his deposition when he wrote, "I do know that the ages of said children as recorded by me in said Bible are correct for the several entries were made by me soon after the respective birth when the date was fresh in my mind." Joel Moore and (it seems) everyone that ever came in contact with Emma Moore loved her to pieces—whether they once owned her or not. She was an extraordinary woman who lived in America during an extraordinary time.

Emma died a couple of years after her twenty-one-year-old daughter, Mattie Bell, on May 31, 1901. Unfortunately, there's no description of her funeral, but I can safely assume it was one of the bigger ones, because most of her surviving children—except Puss and Walter, who were minors—

were married with children. My great-grandfather, Allen Wills, who was also born in Haywood County, was about four years old when Emma passed.

My dear great-great-great grandmother possessed a sharp mind and never took her freedom for granted. Although she probably spent her entire life working for the Moore family, first as a slave, later as a paid laborer, Emma West Moore Wills laid the foundation for her future generations. I can almost hear her saying: "Make sure you stay in the books and learn all you can while you can."

Curiously, Emma probably never had any time to herself. Most of her children were born within two years of each other—some closer than that. Every time one started to learn to walk, another one was cooking in the womb. She was a multi-tasker before that term even became popular. She tended to her children and the farm, and performed endless chores from cooking and sewing to cleaning and organizing. All of this—mind you—before indoor plumbing, bathrooms, electricity, and heat. Emma managed to be a working mom, still making the short walk over to the Moore's big house to do more chores in addition to the ones she did at her own modest shack (which she rented). The only thing of value that she ever owned was one horse.

But Emma was wealthy in many other ways. She kept the pressure on her children to read and write and probably persuaded Joel Moore or one of his children teach her brown children. She had vision—good for her! Despite her illiteracy, she successfully fought for her husband's pension that she and her fatherless children were perfectly entitled to. Good for her! I would do just about anything and pay any amount of money to get my hands on my Great-great-great grandma Emma's Bible. Just to see with my own eyes how she knew that their lives were not in vain and her cherished Bible entries show that she didn't want her children to be forgotten. I can't even begin to imagine what she may have looked like, because there are no photographs that I know of. But I do imagine that she had strong arms and hands. During her short lifetime, it appears she spent the bulk of her time tending to everyone's needs except her own. She was probably the type of loving mother who ate dinner only after the children finished eating. The happiest and most carefree day of her life was probably her wedding day, when she may have donned a white dress or gown and fallen into the arms of a loving husband and proud veteran who had helped win the war. That was probably the last time she focused exclusively on herself. Every move she made after that, for the next thirty years or so, was strictly for her children, and her grandchildren, and generations yet born. I'm so grateful to know her name and her legacy. Emma and Sandy, the original freedom fighters of our family, are the reason I am free today.

Seven

A Scorned Daughter Redeemed

My dear father, exceptional in all he had touched, in a way that would have made Sandy and Emma unabashedly proud, stumbled into the arms of another woman who I will call "Maria." My mother was adamant that I not dignify Maria's affair with Clarence by using her real name in this book. My father had been dead thirty years—and I thought my mother was over it. But as I sat on her living room couch in her Long Island home, she clearly was not. "Do not use that b****'s real name, you hear me?" my mother said softly but firmly. I was a grown woman, but I felt like a little kid as my mom gave me the look of death.

"Okay, Mommy, I'll change her name to Maria.

"Don't forget, either," she snapped.

I smiled at my mother in return, but I was stunned that she was still a scorned woman after three decades.

"He should be taking care of me and, instead, you are. He should be taking care of his mother, Sister Wills, but instead you are. Makes me sick," my mother added.

I had no idea that my mother was still smoldering beneath the surface. Even I was over my dad's affair and had forgiven him long ago. But upon further inspection, I could see why my dear mother still seethed with rage. I was in no position to judge her; that much I knew.

Clarence met Maria just three days after my ninth birthday on October 1, 1975. I know this because my dad had become so disillusioned with his life and his responsibilities that he kept a photo album diary of his affair with this Latina lady, who was at least ten years his junior.

I guess he went through a mid-life crisis a bit early, because he was only thirty-three years old. The photo album is difficult to look at because it so vividly illustrates that my father had become woefully negligent toward me, my four siblings, and our mother—to an unimaginable and incomprehensible level for a man of his smarts and his ambition. I can understand why my mom remains angry.

The illustrated cover of his illicit photograph album says it all: a blonde-haired woman and a dark-haired colored man are locked in a loving embrace in a field of what appears to be flowers. When you flip it open, on the inside top left corner in my beloved father's handwriting (this is the man I loved more than anybody in the world), were the words: Property of Clarence and Maria, Love Forever, October 1, 1975, thru eternity.

The first time I saw this album, many years after my father's death, I was mortified. To think that I loved and longed for my father so desperately, and he gave the precious spare time he had to a complete stranger rather than to me. He didn't just cheat on his wife and my mom; he cheated on me—and I did not take this offense lightly at the time. I was a scorned daughter and I understood why my mom, in her uncontained rage in the mid-seventies, ripped most of their wedding pictures in half and tore his face out of our family albums. I knew why she referred to my father as a piece of crap and desecrated his name; while I tried, in vain, to deify the dead man. My dad was a fool in love—more fool than love in actuality. He had no shame and carried on like he didn't have a family or a care in the world—and he flaunted the evidence in a pictorial diary for all to see.

And what a sight it is—even to this day. He did everything with this broad. She was his "biker chick," his sexual playmate, and his confidant. Throughout the photo album, peppered with their commentary, are color photos of the many trips they went on together with the words "Love Always" everywhere. Clarence is smiling wide and she has her arms wrapped around his entire body. They both wore matching black leather motorcycle vests with the words "Newcomers Motorcycle Club, New York, New York," and they were part of a gang that my mother claims was filled with adulterous couples with clueless wives and children back home.

My poor unsuspecting mother was one of those clueless women at the outset. She joined my dad on a few of these biker runs, but was repulsed by the low-life behavior, which was completely unbecoming to a girl who was raised in a sanctified church. My mother also tells me she was shocked at how her husband so easily wallowed in the mud with these brutes. In a huff, my mother told my father to "Go to hell" and that she wasn't going to leave her five children with a babysitter anymore for this nonsense. My father cursed her right back and entered a fantasyland with Maria, a "sexy mama," as he wrote—whom he believed understood him and his troubles. He accused my long-suffering and faithful mother of "not understanding" him and spending too much of his money without his permission. It was a fair argument, for we must have had the best-dressed apartment in all of Rockaway Beach, with imported Italian furniture, a new piano, custom draperies, and plush wall-to-wall carpeting. When my friends visited our apartment, they always paused at the sight of our exquisitely furnished home. My mother's excessive shopping was the sorry excuse my dad used to bolt for the door.

In a flash, my dad turned his back on everything he knew and loved. He quit singing with the gospel group he cherished, The Thrashing Wonders, and refused to the take the phone calls of Billy Brown or even from his brother Van, who was now lead guitarist for the local act. Instead Clarence spent all of his off-duty time from the fire department with new friends like Dan, Bill, Blanca, Nadia, Maria, Tiny, Karen, Ralph, and some guy known as Rainbow. My dad proudly posed for pictures with his trusty camera in front of their seedy den of iniquity on Avenue B and Seventh Street on Manhattan's Lower East Side, a decaying neighborhood known at the time for drugs and prostitution, an area native New Yorkers refer to as Alphabet City. This was my dad's new home sweet home. Clarence and his girlfriend even got a love shack just down the street from his firehouse and had his mail sent to 38 West 31st street, apartment 908, in Manhattan. My daddy didn't listen to gospel music anymore. All of his new albums were rock, like Jimi Hendrix, a guitarist he had secretly admired even when he was still in the church. He especially loved Hendrix' hit version of Bob Dylan's song, "All Along the Watchtower." The first stanza of the song explains my father's freefall from stability: *"There's got to be some way outta here, said the joker to the thief. There's too much confusion, I can't get no relief."*

Back at his real home, in Rockaway, Queens, there was confusion, to be sure. We needed our father more than ever as all hell broke loose. My sister Crystal started having seizures. At least once a week, I found her foaming at the mouth and shaking uncontrollably in her bed. She was barely four years old. We shared a room and the sudden commotion always jarred me out of my sleep as I made a mad dash down the hall to my mother's bedroom, only to see my mother weep with terror as she frantically lifted her unconscious little daughter out of her bed and screamed for me to call 9-1-1. Little Crystal's eyes rolled back in her head as her Minnie Mouse pajamas were twisted around her tiny body. Clarence was nowhere to be found. He was probably in the bed with Maria in their fool's paradise. Not only was my dad not present, my mom didn't have a number to reach him other than at his firehouse in Manhattan. This frightening episode with my sister Crystal was repeated dozens and dozens of times—as she was rushed to nearby Peninsula General Hospital on Rockaway Beach Boulevard, which was a just block away from our apartment. My mother spent untold hours in a cold emergency room with her daughter wrapped in a blanket as the rest of us looked on. The doctors put her on Phenobarbital—a popular medication used to control seizure activity. It didn't work too well because Crystal continued to wake us all in the middle of the night with grand mal seizures.

Exasperated, my mother finally had Crystal admitted and then faced a crucial decision: the doctors wanted to do a spinal tap, which was fraught with risks for a child her age. My religious grandparents, who did not believe in hospitalization or surgery of any kind, begged my mother not to do the invasive procedure. My father did not even come by to visit Crystal in the hospital and was simply briefed by telephone. The little girl never forgot that it was only her mommy at her bedside and not her daddy. The next time she saw our father, the pre-kindergartener immediately snapped, "You didn't come see me in the hospital, Daddy!"

My father looked down and handed her a present, hoping that would wash her memory clean of his transgression. It didn't back then and, to this day, Crystal has no use for my dad or his memory. She never forgave him.

My brother Big Boy was also in desperate need for a father. His autism seemed to worsen with every birthday. Kids in the neighborhood who couldn't care less about his disability picked on him or beat him up, and my poor mother often ran outside in her robe and slippers to save him. Parents screamed obscenities at her as she shielded her mentally disabled son from the onslaught, and she cursed them right back as she hustled my brother inside. My brother needed a father to teach him how to socialize, but Clarence instead chose to socialize with motorcycle bums who meant him absolutely no good. Those losers knew he was married with five small children at home, and they goaded him on as the life of the party. My dad reveled in their presence.

Rather than being obsessed with his children's milestones, Clarence developed an unhealthy obsession with his motorcycle. He didn't take a picture when his twins, Celestal and Cleavon, took their first steps in 1975; instead he photographed every angle of his brand-spanking-new K2 1000 Kawasaki four-cylinder motorcycle, which he spent hundreds of dollars, perhaps more than a thousand, having his Aries astrological sign, the ram, painted on the tank. He even christened his treasured bike with a name: Jessica. Every accessory that was available for motorcycles in the mid-seventies, he purchased and adorned on his bike, which (I begrudgingly admit) was stunning to all who saw it, especially my little friends in Ocean Village. The colorful picture of a Ram's rounded horns—surrounded by stars and other little embellishments made his motorcycle a real stand-out. It was painted by an artist named Tom Becker, whose business card was in my dad's wallet when he died. My father meticulously cleaned his bike with rags, toothbrushes, and polish after every trip. What I would give, even today, for my father to have shown his children such attention and adoration. I have pictures that my father took of his motorcycle from aerial shots to side views, with the chrome shining like mirrors. He even positioned his bike in front of his fire engine, which he was promoted to being able to operate and drive in a coveted position called a chauffeur. He snapped picture after picture.

It's rather embarrassing to see these hundreds of photographs of motorcycles, biker bums, and a girlfriend, and realize that he took not a single picture of his children after 1974. He emotionally checked out from us in an even worse way than his father had disappointed him.

In my dad's defense, although there really isn't a plausible excuse, Clarence was sticking it more to his father than to his wife and children. We were merely a casualty of his very personal war. In a severely misguided attempt at retribution for a lousy childhood, he was still a little boy throwing an adult-size tantrum at his father's expense. I could almost hear his illogical reasoning: "I'll show you, Dad, what it feels like, you hypocrite!"

My father was reckless, but he was not mentally ill. Clarence knew that he was humiliating his wife, crushing the hearts of his five little children, though I'm sure he reasoned we were too young to fully comprehend what was going on. He certainly knew he was torturing his devout mother—who voiced her displeasure with him quite forcefully in his presence. "Boy, you have five children waiting on you! You'd better get it together and go home!" she'd say to her son, whose recklessness reminded her of her husband. Her chastisement didn't matter because my dad had his mind made up and didn't care what any of us thought—as long as he knew he was hurting his father. Fred said not a word as he watched his son's undoing.

Amazingly, my dad didn't miss a beat professionally—other than losing his official fire department badge and being issued a new one (number 6659) for which he was mildly penalized by the department. He remained a studious part-time student at John Jay College and he successfully passed high-level technical exams to become a motor pump operator with the fire department—getting him one step closer to becoming a fire lieutenant— his immediate goal in 1978. He continued his illustrious military career in the United States Army National Guard where, as a staff sergeant, he made regular trips to Camp Drum and West Point in upstate New York, where he trained other soldiers. I have one beautiful black-and-white photo of Clarence at Camp Drum, where he is holding a military phone receiver to his ear and has an MRE (meal ready to eat) in his right hand with a spoon. On his right shoulder is an "airborne" patch and he has a key ring dangling from his belt. He is dressed in green military fatigues and his sleeves are rolled up above his elbow. He looks so handsome and confident. Underneath the picture is a code that I assume only military personnel would understand: "1/105 FA—Direct Fire," and he added a witty commentary, "They always catch me eating."

Looks are deceiving because from the photograph of this distinguished non-commissioned officer, one would never guess that he had an angry wife, furious mother, heartbroken father, and hordes of puzzled relatives who were shocked at his surly behavior. His calm demeanor bore not a trace of a troubled man. I have photos, and a trophy, of him showing off his motorcycle at an event that crowned him with the "best dressed bike." In his busy life of firefighting, soldiering, and socializing with a motorcycle gang, he gave the ones who needed him the most the mere crumbs of his life. He carved out time for us when he had nothing else to do. Slowly but surely, he was signing his own death warrant, for the winds of fate are always severe when innocent children are neglected.

Cheryl Wills

Clarence came home about every two weeks. Perhaps to assuage
his growing guilt, he never missed our birthdays or Thanksgiving and
Christmas—though he no longer joined us on hallowed Easter Sunday.
When his motorcycle thundered up to our townhouse, we were none the
wiser. He was our black Santa—even though he only weighed about
145 pounds and stood five-feet-eight inches tall. He always had a horde
of presents for all of us. On Crystal's birthday in March, he gave her two
presents and the rest of us one, and he always spent the night for at least
a couple of days. With folded arms, my mother watched as we danced,
giggled, and laughed in his presence. She saved her scornful words for him
when they were behind closed doors. One by one, we sat on his strong back
as he did one-armed push-ups and showed him how our teeth had grown or
fallen out, and our report cards. I especially enjoyed showing him my little
kiddie news reports that I had written in my loose-leaf notebook, and he
always remarked that I had good handwriting and a creative streak.

Hindsight is, naturally, 20/20, and when our daddy wasn't home, we
just thought he was living in his bed at the firehouse. When I neared ten
years of age in 1977, I was no longer naïve and I started to think like a
scorned daughter. I didn't have specifics, but I had a nagging feeling
that my daddy was walking into the fire again. After pleading with my
mom about my father's whereabouts, she gave me the phone number to
the firehouse and told me to call him myself—which I did on multiple
occasions.

"Hello, Can I speak to my daddy?" I would ask the captain who
answered the phone.

"Sure, who is this, honey?" said a gentle male voice on the other of the line.

"Cheryl," I always softly replied. The firemen at Engine 1, Ladder
24, now embraced my father as a full-fledged brother, and they saw his
girlfriend Maria come and go from the firehouse. They knew better than
anyone what was going on but, of course, the man's code of honor is that
you see everything, but say nothing. But my repeated calls to the firehouse
must have shamed my father—at least I hope it shamed him real good.

These were the dark years for our family and, cub reporter that I
was, I incessantly badgered my mother and grandparents for my father's
whereabouts—to the point where I drove everybody crazy. Grandma Opal
was especially sympathetic to my concerns as I cried in her strong Southern
arms and begged her to find my daddy. And time and time again she ordered

her son Van to get in his cab and track down my dad so she could give me a firm answer. Uncle Van, who knew his way around Manhattan like the back of his hand, drove to the West Side of Manhattan and parked his yellow medallion cab in front of the firehouse and asked for his brother. My father always slid down the pole with an attitude (Van later told me), and hastily told his brother that he was fine and to tell "Mother" not to worry.

Clarence and Van were brothers, but not each other's keepers or confidants. When they spoke, they kept it light, but they read each other's body language very well. Clarence usually talked about his job and Van usually talked about his adventures with The Thrashing Wonders. They never tried to guilt trip each other or invade each other's privacy. They were weird that way. More than twenty years later, when I spoke with my Uncle Van about my dad's life, he knew every little detail about the firehouse and the military—and absolutely nothing about what made him tick on a personal level as a husband or a father.

Within a few months, I learned little bits and pieces of what was going on by eavesdropping on the telephone. I learned how to pick up our rotary phone and press my finger on the receiver button and gently release it. I heard my mother, in her bedroom with the door closed, calling my father everything but a child of God. She also cursed his parents for not doing more to help her—she took to call her in-laws "outlaws." I became a terrible snoop on the phone, but it was very important to me at the time that I found out exactly what was happening to my daddy. Before long, my sneaky phone monitoring came to a tragic end.

The first shoe dropped during the oppressive summer of 1977. My dad recorded his first brush with death with such accuracy and detail in his photo diary that it makes me wonder if he somehow knew I would write about it one day. While riding his motorcycle with a pack of bikers alongside him southbound on the Palisades Parkway in Rockland County, New York, Clarence wrote that he lost control of his bike at precisely 8:45 p.m. near exit 14A. In his photo album he devoted an entire eight-by-eleven page to a five-by-seven photo of himself with his leg in a cast. At the top of the page he wrote in bold letters, "FIRST ACCIDENT," and in smaller letters he wrote the date: Aug 9, 1977. He jotted the particulars: Broke leg 3 places—Bike OK—Staff Sergeant Robbie following on his 550 Honda.

By pointing out in such bold print that this was his "first" accident, he appeared to suggest that one: it was inevitable; and two: that, it wouldn't be his last. He was right on both points. Unlike his brush with death in the army when he smoked a laced joint that made him straighten up and fly right, Clarence continued to flirt with danger and thumb his nose at decency. He continued to go on runs with his motorcycle buddies to places like Laconia, New Hampshire, where he must have snapped two hundred pictures. During the trip they stopped at the Pancake House, where they parked their bikes in what appeared to be a sea of chrome and metal—there were more than fifty of them. Standing back about twenty feet, my father took a picture of the bikes in front of the restaurant and wrote, "Breakfast stop at pancake house en route to Laconia, N.H."

Along the way, cops stopped the pack of riders and my dad continued to point and shoot his camera, joking in one photo: "license and registration please!" He took pictures of the bikers inside the pancake house as well—where blacks and whites were breaking bread together with heads bowed over plates of sausage and eggs. In one photo, which I cannot even picture in my mind, my dad is in a crappy motel room and took a picture of a group of brunettes and wrote, "girls trying to get up a party at motel in Laconia during rain."

I am repulsed to this day: my daddy was in a nasty motel with these girls? I can't help but wonder where I was during this time. I was undoubtedly somewhere, missing him terribly. What really disturbs me is that in June of that year, when I was preparing for my first graduation from elementary school, my dad missed it and I was so disheartened. It was the first time I wore high heels and pantyhose instead of tights. I was leaving girlhood and entering junior high school and my daddy missed my special day. I still remember the blue wrap dress that my mother allowed me to pick out, with white shoes that had two-inch heels. I was so naturally bony that it hung off of my lanky body like a sheet, but I still felt as sexy as ten-year-old could.

My father didn't have time to see me graduate from P.S. 225, but he had time to romp with these tramps in a seedy motel room in the middle of nowhere. To say that Clarence's priorities were misplaced during this time would be an understatement; he just didn't give a hoot about anyone but himself. At least my grandfather could say he had a fourth grade education and was demoralized by Jim Crow and so forth. What was my father's excuse? He was a college-educated man and a non-commissioned officer in an integrated army. Though he was unaware of his legacy, he was the ungrateful great-great grandson of a slave who fought in a war, just so he could have the opportunities that he relished. He was a deacon and a mason and he understood, to an advanced degree, the mysteries of God and spirituality. He looked upon his wife and five children, turned his back, and deliberately ran into the devil's playground. And to boot, he didn't play his guitar anymore, depriving us all of some of the most beautiful melodies to ever come from the instrument. By 1978, my dad was headed down a slippery slope that he probably thought he could safely veer from at any time. But he was the fool—everyone knows there's only one way to get off a slippery slope—and that's to crash land.

By this time, my mother had enough. Ruth went to Family Court in Queens and spilled the beans. After she finished explaining to a sympathetic judge how her firefighter husband was spending most of his time, energy, and money with a girl who probably hadn't graduated from high school, the judge slammed his gavel down and graciously asked my mother, "How much do you want, Mrs. Wills?"

With that, my mother reported his social security number and my dad's paycheck was garnished—cut by more than half—barely leaving him enough to live on with little Miss Maria. This young lady was fully aware that my dad was married and had five children. She had even written on the back of the few photographs my dad had of us, "Clarence's children, "Cheryl age 10 and Crystal age 4." I am guessing that he somehow assured the young naïve girl that he would divorce my mother and marry her, and we would be her step children.

She is lucky that their marriage never happened, because she would have met the full brunt of our wrath. Even as kids, we would have chewed her up and spit her out—just like we did most of my mother's boyfriends when they dared to step foot in our house. We were tough city kids, a mobilized force, and we didn't mess around with intruders of our personal space.

When my father opened his paycheck, without warning, he saw that it was less than one hundred dollars and called my mother in a fit of rage. He violently cursed her and called her the worst names imaginable. She matched him obscenity for obscenity. Thankfully, I wasn't on the phone to hear the tense exchange, but I strongly sensed that my mother was stressed out in 1977 and 1978. She didn't smile much anymore and had a very short fuse with her five needy kids. I was the biggest pain in the butt, because I always demanded to play with my friends before cleaning my room and I had a smart mouth—just like her.

No one asked if I was hurting at the time, but I was almost as stressed out as my mother because I felt like a fatherless child—even though my father was still very much alive. I also felt as though I had been robbed of my childhood and forced to face mature issues that I was not prepared to deal with, like adultery and hypocrisy. As much as I tried to jump double Dutch, play paddleball, and my beloved Hot Peas and Butter, I couldn't rest peacefully at night for thinking about my parent's troubles. I had a sister with epilepsy, a brother with autism, another baby brother whose legs were so bowed that he had to be fitted with braces, and his twin sister who cried over every real and imagined infraction, and always spilled her juice at the dining room table. I had to do the dishes, vacuum the rugs, clean my room, do my homework, and keep my brother, Big Boy, from hurting our younger siblings. In a blind frenzy, he once slammed his bedroom door and the tip of little Cleavon's finger got caught in the door and snapped cleanly off. My mother put his fingertip on ice and once again rushed yet another child of hers to the emergency room. All this as my daddy pretended he was a swinging bachelor—living the high life with his stupid friends. I was a basket case and I hadn't yet hit puberty.

With his paycheck slashed and my guilt-tripping calls to the firehouse, Clarence somehow broke the news to Maria that they would have to give up their tiny one-bedroom love shack in midtown. I'm guessing that she issued an ultimatum and demanded that my dad divorce my mom. I think he told her to go to hell, too, because there was no further mention of the so-called "sexy mama" when my dad reluctantly moved in with his parents, for the first time in more than a decade.

My grandparents' upstairs living quarters were dilapidated, but huge—with a half-dozen uninhabitable rooms on the second and third floors. My dad moved his belongings into the back room of the living room—where we usually played after church. With my grandparents just upstairs and Van living part-time in the bedroom off the kitchen, when he wasn't with his girlfriend Mazie, the little family from Haywood County, Tennessee, had come full circle and were all living together again. My father refused to go downstairs to church despite his mother's pleading. He laid in his bed many Sunday mornings as the sound of his mother's beautiful voice belted out the gospel songs he had heard his entire life, just one floor below.

My grandmother sang songs like: *"Down at the Cross where my savior died, Down where for cleansing from sin, I cried, There to my heart was the blood applied—singing Glory to his name."*

Clarence heard his father's familiar licks on the guitar, the same rhythms he once played in sync with his dad. Sticking to his stubborn principle, he refused to budge. He was going to make his father "pay"— unaware that his five children were the ones who were actually paying the dearest price of all, and soon Clarence would pay the ultimate price.

Clarence heard a new member, named Deacon Brown, read Psalms 20 as he lifted the offering with the same gold-toned plate that my dad purchased years ago with great pride. After church was over, Fred had to walk past my father's motorcycle, which Clarence had parked just inside the front parlor of the building near where the baptism pool was located. He refused to park his precious bike on the street in Astoria because he feared it would be stolen or damaged. Whenever my father and grandfather crossed paths, they gently tiptoed around the other like two black panthers, each eyeing the other, and poised to pounce upon the other with criticism, but cautiously waiting for the other to make the first move. My father, the inactive deacon, who was a sight to behold in a leather motorcycle jacket, waited with baited breath for his holier-than-thou father to say one word to him. That would have given him an excuse to unleash and say, "You have some nerve saying anything to me!"

But Grandpa Fred knew that's what my father wanted and he flatly refused to give in to his son's tantrums. Fred knew that little Clarence was still crying out for attention—even though the boy was thirty-seven years old.

These were also dark times for Light House Church. The glory years had quickly come and gone. Offended members left as my grandfather insisted that true believers of Christ believed in faith healing and did not rely on doctors for anything. He always criticized women for wearing earrings, bracelets, or anything fancy. African-American women were coming into their own during the mid-1970s and my grandfather singlehanded thought he could stop it—in Jesus' name. Times were changing and my grandfather believed that anyone who didn't believe the way he did was doomed to face God's wrath...and to a lesser degree Elder Wills' dogmatic wrath. As female preachers started to gain traction in some churches, my grandfather dug in his heels and vowed that this was the worst thing that could possibly happen in the world. His membership that had swelled to seventy-five people had dwindled down to about a dozen and he didn't seem to care. Elder Wills felt the truth was on his side and his mind was closed. Every Sunday, he strapped on his guitar and played with his wife, who repeated "Amen" to everything he said.

My grandmother was not nearly as cool, because my dad's behavior humiliated her on a numerous levels. Although Opal was not a braggadocio in any way shape or form, she was viewed as lucky because she had a husband who was a pastor, which was rare among her congregation of single mothers. She had an extra feather in her cap in that her sons were not jailbirds, alcoholics, or drugs addicts, as some of the mothers in Light House Church suffered with as they watched their beautiful children disintegrate into the mean city streets. Church members openly praised Sister Wills and her two articulate and handsome sons—one of whom, Clarence, was a deacon and poised to become a minister. How blessed she was to have her flesh-and-blood sons play the guitar as she sang and danced in the spirit so blissfully to their music. As an added bonus, her son was a big-time firefighter in Manhattan, just over the nearby 59th Street Bridge, and boldly worked side by side with white men—a feat many of the domestic workers and janitors in the congregation thought unimaginable for themselves. The members were not envious but happy to see that one of their own had cracked the glass ceiling. But when my father turned wild and disgraced himself and his family, and they caught sight of a surly looking man on a motorcycle wearing an intimidating leather vest with gang symbols, more than a few figured Sister Wills' luck was too good to be true and had run out. No one openly insulted her or dared to even ask her about her suddenly wayward son, but their looks said it all. "That's what happens when you get too high" some of their smirks hinted. Others quietly assumed, "I guess Clarence is just like the rest of our kids; the devil took him, too."

It was bad enough that Sister Wills dragged her husband out of the gutter and dealt with his adultery and abuse for years on end. Now her oldest boy, whom she loved dearly, was following in his footsteps. Disgusted and full of rage and embarrassment, she stood from her piano during morning worship and publicly gave her testimony that in essence cursed her firstborn: "The devil is trying to take my son, but I know God is able, Saints. And I prayed to the Lord, 'Save him or slay him.'" She was essentially asking God to either return him to church as he was or send him to an early grave. I'm not sure what possessed my grandmother to make such a bold assertion as a hush came over the crowd every time she said it—which she did on more than one occasion. But I know she only meant the first part—but not the second. She didn't want her son to die—but she had eerily and unwittingly cast a spell over his life.

And then came the fire. A small electrical blaze broke out in a corner of the hulking building that housed Light House Church in 1978, but it was bad enough to wipe out half of the tiny storefront sanctuary. My father, a firefighter of course, was not there when it happened but when he later inspected the area and realized what he had long suspected—that (after about nine years in that building) the whole place had become a fire trap and time was running out. My dad knew he had to get his parents out of the more than 100-year-old structure before it was too late.

Surprisingly, I think it was the fire that moved my father to straighten out his life more than anything else. He now saw that his parents were in trouble in more ways than one. The church, which was now partitioned off from the fire damage, was on its last legs. Membership was down to about one dozen people. Many had left in disgust when ugly rumors started to re-surface about my grandfather. Even the candy store was in trouble, because every time Fred opened it, violent gunmen that my grandfather recognized from Astoria Housing Projects, pointed a gun in his face and demanded cash—and candy. Bandits consistently stole his church van, his station wagon, and broke into the house. It's amazing they never held up Sunday service for the little cash offering he collected. The only new member was a friendly and jubilant Jamaican man that everyone called Deacon Lyttle. A tall man who played the harmonica, he taught all of us about Jamaican church culture and introduced the West Indian Beat into the worship services, along with his wife and five children. Deacon Lyttle, a jack of all trades construction worker, helped my grandfather keep the old building from imploding in its final years.

Clarence and his father started talking again. I supposed my father felt he had proved his point and saw firsthand how Fred had again been brought to his knees. It was once more up to the firefighter to rescue his parents. Van remained passive as usual and didn't get involved with anything except music. The same building Clarence helped them move into on 30th Avenue in Astoria, he now had to help them move out of—and the clock was ticking.

Although he didn't immediately sever ties with the motorcycle club, he started to make amends with my mom, and Ruth dropped the court order that garnished his fire department salary, with her husband's promise that he would never put his dummy friends before his children again. Grandpa Fred got word that a stretch of buildings around the corner on Astoria Boulevard were for sale and he took his Clarence to see it. My dad was instantly impressed with the potential for growth. If they purchased three one-story walk-up buildings, Fred could again build a storefront church and live on top and Clarence planned to open a Laundromat to generate income as well as with the rental units on the upper levels. With money he earned from the National Guard, Clarence and his father helped put down a deposit on the buildings, and Fred held fundraisers at the church. Little by little, they were all raising enough money for the big move—in a race against time as the building slowly crumbled in on them.

But Clarence was still sorting out the mess he made of his personal life. One Sunday in 1979, my mom decided to bring us to our grandparents' church at the last minute. When I saw my daddy's motorcycle, I dashed up the stairs with my four sisters and brothers behind me. My startled father hustled a black woman into a side room in the house and my mother saw her shadow. I asked him, "Daddy, will you come downstairs and go to church with us?"

Clarence didn't have a chance to respond when he looked at his wife's face. My mother cursed everybody out in her path, put all of us back into the car and she took us back home to Rockaway Beach. As she slammed the car door, she exclaimed, "I hope he drops dead!"

I cried the entire car ride back on the Grand Central Parkway to the Van Wyck Expressway to the side roads leading to our apartment complex in Rockaway Beach. I hated my mother for that moment because I didn't understand why we had to leave.

Days later, my mother told my father it was time to separate and file for divorce, and she got a lawyer. My grandmother pleaded with my father to go home, warning him that another man would inevitably be raising his children and that he was hurting his wife and children in ways that would surely come back and haunt him someday. And finally my ballsy grandmother said just what she thought: "You're acting *worse* than your father, now!"

The flash of anger that accompanied her statement finally shamed the soldier. If there was one person he didn't want to make angry, it was Opal. He painfully remembered the hell that his mother went through during his own childhood with his father, and Clarence was finally embarrassed to know that he had exceeded that misery. He witnessed their bouts of domestic violence and he saw his mother scream and cry with humiliation. And just like the Bible predicted, the sins of the father were visited upon this son. So many of us were paying a dear price—and, I thought, none worse that I. I didn't know where my daddy was most of the time and he no longer read stories to me at night. I saw him...whenever.

When I finally turned thirteen, I was hip to his game. When I heard his motorcycle rumble up to our parking lot, I stayed put. I didn't run downstairs to greet him anymore and my sisters and brothers and I remained glued to the television, usually watching Bill Cosby's *Fat Albert and the Cosby Kids*.

After holding my peace, I finally had my say. As he walked into our apartment, I was walking out. He expressed shock at my departure as he made his entrance. "Hey, where are *you* going, don't you see I'm home?" he asked me, as he wondered where the little happy girl went.

I snapped back, "Oh, so you decide to come home and I'm supposed to drop what I'm doing? I don't think so." I left and slammed the door behind me and joined in my favorite childhood game of Hot Peas and Butter. After I slammed the door, I feared for a split second that he might open the door and snatch me back inside and punish me for being fresh. But I caught his downcast eyes. He must have realized he had won the battle in sticking it to his father, but lost his daughter. He knew that I fully realized what was going on and I was losing respect for him as a direct result; the jig was up.

I stopped calling the firehouse and I didn't really care when my dad came home or where he went anymore. The loss of my adoring eyes must have stung him heart and soul. The next day, after spending the night, he left his motorcycle at our apartment and drove my mom's car, which he never ever did, to Astoria to bring all of his personal belongings back home to us. He brought most of his books, all of his mason stuff, his awards from the fire department, his Teac reel-to-reel recorder, giant speakers with red covers, almost everything. He still left a few things at his parents' home like his record player; for the times he had a short turnaround—their home in Astoria, Queens, was only eight minutes—by motorcycle—from his firehouse. He kept a small stash there for when he needed to study in absolute peace and quiet—which a house with five children could never guarantee unless it was bedtime.

It was nice to have my daddy back home that summer of 1980. We were back to eating dinner at the table and Daddy sat at the head like he used to—with his dinner plate always framed by a glass of milk and water—a habit he held onto from his military days. He asked us questions at the table like, "Do you know who is the president of the United States?"

I was always the first to shout, "Jimmy Carter," but he always had me stumped on the senators. He asked me if I still wanted to be a reporter and I replied, "Of course, Daddy. I still read the *Daily News* every day and I watch Channel 7 News!" I proceeded to show him my news loose-leaf notebook and tell him what Mayor Ed Koch did at City Hall and what Yankees superstar Reggie Jackson did to tick off Yankees boss George Steinbrenner. He thought that I was smart, and cute, and he told me so. The only time he made me cry during this period was when I sneaked into the living room long after I should have been in bed and watched him study for the fire lieutenant's exam. I was stunned to see my father smoking like a chimney. He looked very different from the sweet Daddy I knew when he sucked his Marlboro cigarette and squinted his eyes as he blew white smoke toward our white piano.

I stood frozen in my pink elephant pajamas and trembled with tears running down my face because I had never seen my daddy smoke before, and smoking, as I was taught, was bad. I went to bed and cried myself to sleep because I had finally seen with my own eyes that my daddy had lost his way. In my view, he was still the nice deacon who read the 20th chapter of Psalms in Grandpa's church while raising the offering. *Who on earth had this man become while he was gone?* I wondered. I was deeply disturbed by the sight of him smoking, but I was still glad daddy was home. I felt safe and secure again.

In the late 1970s rap music had exploded in our neighborhood, created by the homeboys in the Bronx and Queens. We dropped disco like a bad habit and started listening to early rap pioneers like Curtis Blow and The Sugar Hill Gang. Community organizers turned our basketball courts into a club and DJs scratched records, and we shouted "Hooooo!" to the beat. My young male friends stopped doing their homework regularly and instead wrote their own rap lyrics in their loose-leaf notebooks. Every boy and girl had a hip hop name: I had the name "Cheryl Chell" printed on my favorite sweatshirt and my best friend Simone had the name "Nyasian Queen." If something was nice, we said, "That's the joint!" or "Shock it on!" Our updated urban slang was as colorful as it ever was in New York City.

I was also learning the art of relationships. Lonnie was the first boy who really really liked me and I kinda liked him, too, even though he was a little rough around the edges. We were just twelve years old, but he and many boys his age were already drinking heavy duty stuff like Old English Malt Liquor that Lonnie called "O.E." Before I kissed him in the hallway of his building, he chewed Doublemint gum to try to hide the taste; it didn't work.

None of us girls drank alcohol, but almost all of the boys did and, in retrospect, it was so tragic. They were sweet young men full of hope but, in an effort to be cool or "down," as we used to say, they were guzzling beer that had a notoriously high alcohol content. We weren't even in high school yet! They were destroying their minds and their bodies at such a young age; they didn't realize the long-term impact of their deeds. By the time they were all in high school, most of them paid a dear price, usually entering the penal system or worse.

How were these young black male minors able to get alcohol? I don't know the answer to that, but I do know that this was one of the many ways young black men became disillusioned with life before they even had a chance to dream. I weep for all of my young friends who ended up dead or in jail—because I saw the seeds that were planted before them—and I didn't even know at that time that it was a seed of destruction. And I assure you—neither did they.

The terrible seeds that my father had planted were also beginning to bloom, and his life was about to wither away. There's one picture of him that I call, "the last photo," though I don't know if it actually was. My father in seated on a rickety chair in front of the Newcomers Club in Alphabet City, holding a bottle of beer in a brown paper bag. He's wearing dark wraparound sunglasses. He has on his motorcycle vest and his airborne patch is sewed on the front of the right side. No one would ever guess that he was a father of five children—a distinguished mason who mastered and once honored the ancient secrets of the sect. Who would have imagined that this thuggish-looking black dude had a brilliant mind, was a college student and a non-commissioned officer in the United States Army who was respected across the country? My dad—who in the past had always dressed neat as a pin in custom-made suits from a Hong Kong tailor—resembled a bum in blue jeans who had nothing to do all day but sit on the gritty streets of New York and drink his life away in front of a rathole of a club.

From the photograph, however, he didn't even look like he had a job or that he had children. Who would have imagined that this intimidating-looking biker had recently been honored by the New York National Guard with a commendation that saluted this staff sergeant with the 42nd Infantry Division for "outstanding service" during a state emergency in the spring of 1979. Placing this sad photo side by side with other pictures of my father when he acted responsibly—one might assume they were looking at two different people. In a way, they were. I will never know why my dad kept pushing the envelope—but everything was about to come to a head.

Right around Labor Day in 1980, we, as a family, had the whole day planned out to the letter. On September 4th, my dad was supposed to give me money to go school shopping. I was entering the senior class at Junior High School 180 in Rockaway Park, and my classmates and I were poised to dress to impress as we entered ninth grade. The first day of school was just a few days away. My mother's mom, Grandma Sallie, had moved into a building in our complex and was going to babysit my youngster sisters and brothers. My mom and I were going to go to the mall to pick out my new clothes and shoes for the new school year. My dad promised he would be at my apartment by eleven in the morning so we could catch the Labor Day sales. All was forgiven and I had waited in the window for the thunder of my dad's motorcycle starting at eleven o'clock on the nose. Then noon. Then three o'clock. By five p.m., the phone rang. I overheard my mother say, "That girl's been sitting in the window waiting for you all day, now you tell her!"

I left my window seat and snatched the receiver of the Mickey Mouse phone. Mickey looked happy with his white glove extended as I seethed with rage. My father lowered the boom for the last time. "Cheryl, listen, I'll be there tomorrow. I have to work. I'll be there tomorrow, okay?"

I was so disappointed, all I could say was, "Alright, Daddy. Bye." As I slammed the phone back on Mickey's gloved hand I said, "I hope he drops dead."

I didn't really mean what I had said, but enough was enough. This man had hurt me, my mother, my grandmother, my sisters and brothers, too much. And now he missed Big Boy's birthday, which was the day before on September 3rd. This was a new low for the prodigal father who had never missed his children's birthdays. He had moved all of his stuff back home and he still didn't keep his word. I had become a surrogate parent for my younger siblings and I was only thirteen. It wasn't the money or the back-to-school clothing; it was the principle. I still remembered that he missed my sixth grade graduation. I remembered how mad he made my mom, so much so that she lost her joy with us as she served us our breakfast, lunch, and dinner. We were just little kids, but we were hurting like adults.

I went into my room and smacked the last present my dad gave me: a beautiful black doll with a ruby-red Victorian-style gown. She had chiseled features and I kept her right next to my bed. My dad had dropped the ball with me so many times, now I was broken in places that couldn't be fixed. If Clarence had only had one more tomorrow, he probably would have made good on his promise, but as we all know: don't count on tomorrow, because it may never come.

When the phone rang around midnight September 5th, naturally, I went back to my eavesdropping ways; I wondered who would be calling a mother with five small children at such an ungodly hour. I heard a man we knew named Deacon Edward Brown on the other end of the phone say, "I'm so sorry, Ruth."

My mother asked, "Sorry for what?"

He was startled by her response and abruptly hung up. My mother quickly called and woke up her mother, Sallie, and warned her that something bad happened but she didn't yet know to whom.

My mother tried to call my grandparents house in Astoria but there was no answer. Then the phone rang again. It was closer to one a.m. and it was my Grandfather Fred. "Ruth, Clarence got into some kind of accident," he said, knowing Clarence was already dead, but afraid to confirm it. They had already gotten a call from the police department that my dad had been taken to Kings County Morgue.

Van took his parents in a car to the seedy Brooklyn death house, hoping that there had been some kind of mistake. Before she left her house, my Grandmother Opal put a bottle of olive oil in her purse. It was the same oil that my grandfather used to anoint the heads of sinners during prayer in church. My grandmother firmly believed that if she and her husband could touch their son, they could bring him back to life. They believed it because it happened in the Bible when Jesus raised Lazarus from the dead. Van, Opal, and Fred went inside the city-owned morgue and asked to see Clarence Wills. The hospital official asked where the "deceased" man's wife was, and they said she was home in Rockaway. They were dismissed and told that the wife had to identify his remains first before anyone else.

So with that, my grandfather went to a payphone and called us back. When the phone rang, I picked it up almost before my mother did. "The boy is dead."

As long as I live, I will never forget the tone or inflection of my grandfather's voice. I was so shocked by his words I didn't hear my mother's response other than "Oh, no" in her soft voice.

I hung up the phone, the very same Mickey Mouse phone I had wished my father dead on, the same phone my father had lied to me on for the last time, and I went in my bedroom and cried my heart out. Hearing my awful wail, my mother came in the room, realizing she didn't even have to tell me what happened. All of my sisters and brothers woke up except Big Boy. My autistic brother's disorder shielded him from the trauma of this awful night. He heard his big sister cry and he apparently rolled over and finished his slumber. When my mom explained to Crystal, Celestal, and Cleavon that our daddy was dead, they collapsed on my bed and cried, too. My mother, in a state of utter shock, just rubbed my back and tried to tell us to calm down, as the phone began to ring off the hook in the wee hours of the morning.

None of us slept that night. We just watched television and tried to imagine what life would be like without a daddy. My daddy was dead. He was so strong and young and full of life. We were so young we couldn't even comprehend what his death meant or how he died. Perhaps, we wondered, it wasn't even true. All we knew was that our daddy was in a motorcycle accident. The same bike that we took turns riding shotgun on in our parking lot—and the same motorcycle that Daddy sometimes popped a wheelie on to our sheer delight. Thank God, nobody gave us the specifics at the time.

According to my grandmother, it was supposed to be his last run with the Newcomers Motorcycle Club. Shortly before eleven p.m. Clarence was at the club on Avenue B and 7th Street and they headed south on the nearby Williamsburg Bridge, which would have deposited them into Brooklyn. My dad had an unidentified woman on the back of his bike. His old girlfriend Maria was long gone by then. Clarence had just had his motorcycle repaired and, when he found himself behind a very slow driver, he and his fellow bikers—at least one dozen of them, surrounded the slow-moving vehicle, which was probably very intimidating to the driver, especially in the dark on a bridge. Not to mention the deafening roar of motorcyclists angrily and arrogantly revving their engines. They must have sounded like a bomb going off on the bridge. For reasons that my father took with him to the grave, he suddenly sped up and came perilously close to the driver's side of the car. The driver abruptly veered left, probably to get out of the biker's way, and hit my dad with such force that Clarence flew off his bike and slammed face first into a steel beam on the bridge. Not only was he nearly decapitated, his brains partially exploded from his skull and his eyes became dislodged. The entire left side of his body was crushed. My poor daddy never knew what hit him, his eyes blinked behind his green-tinted sunglasses and then he was gone.

The bikers made sure the driver did not leave the scene and they all cursed and held him as they waited for police to arrive. For about twenty minutes, my dad's bloody corpse stopped traffic on the bridge known as the "Willie B," with his shattered and broken remains wrapped inside his black leather jacket, and the bike that he loved more than anything laid flat on its side right next to him. These long-haired trashy men and women had the privilege of seeing my precious father alive for the last time. As my father's blood dripped into the East River underneath the bridge, the people who really loved him all laid in their beds. It was more than a damn shame. My dad was trying to cross a very personal bridge and reclaim his status as a family man. My grandmother believes he was going to hang out with his crew just one more time. But he would never cross either bridge—not the one that had brought him back home or the one that was taking him into Brooklyn with his hooligan friends.

I wonder if a spirit came and took my dad to the "big area" that he woefully described to his mother in that 1964 letter he wrote about to his mother after he smoked a laced joint in the military. Did that same person he once hallucinated about come to "take him into the sky" and later a "big area" where he was floating around in space. Did he see our souls up there, too? This time, my dad had no Bible to press against his heart and he would never live to tell his beloved mother what happened next. It was over; Clarence D. Wills was no more. That brilliant young man, who passed his college-level science and math tests with ease, left his brains on the asphalt of a bridge that is arguably the least known of all of the city's bridges. It's not majestic like the mighty George Washington to its north, nor is it sexy like the Brooklyn Bridge to its immediate south. My shining prince of a father—memorable in all his deeds both good and bad—died on a span that most people in the country have never even heard of in a city known for its famous bridges.

Police immediately ruled it an accident and never conducted a further investigation, to my knowledge. But Opal did. After they left the morgue, without seeing their son and brother, my grandparents and Van went to the motorcycle club about two hours after the accident. These grieved church people, walking slowly into this sleazy filthy club, must have been a sight to behold. Opal, a distraught mother whose son's body was still warm in a morgue less than twenty miles away, spoke first. "Which one of you killed my son?" my grandmother boldly asked.

She had believed right from the outset that her son was sort-of hijacked by these thugs, had joined them against his will and they finally killed him—which was their goal all along. She never could fully accept that her son's floundering was his fault and his fault alone. As was the case with her husband, Opal did not hold the men in her life responsible for their sins—she always pointed the finger elsewhere. But my dad had no one else to blame but himself for this catastrophic ending. Inside my dad's wallet, I found his payment stubs for the dues he paid to the Newcomers Club—whose motto was "brotherhood, a way of life"—which should have read "brotherhood—let us hasten your death." Twenty dollars a month is what my daddy paid these goons for the privilege of throwing his bright future away. And they gave him a receipt for good measure. Twenty dollars a month my daddy paid to have the gravediggers at Calverton National Cemetery open his plot in the ground many years too soon. Unreal.

The dispassionate bikers stood before the somber trio, stunned at Opal's brazen accusation, and tried to assure her that it was an accident and that they in no way shape or form murdered her son. But one disrespectful biker confirmed her conspiracy theory and condescendingly deadpanned, "I didn't like the guy, but I didn't kill him."

That was all the confirmation that my distraught grandmother needed and she soon left with her head bowed. Thirty years later she believes none of the bikers liked him and plotted all along to kill her outstanding son that fateful night on the Williamsburg Bridge. The very fact that this degenerate would say to a mother in mourning whose son had just died that he "didn't like him" was insulting to say the least.

In the end, I blame my father for this appalling exchange, because he should have never been associating with characters like this in the first place. I am deeply embarrassed that my grandparents, who tried their best to live decently as upstanding Christians, had to ever step foot in such a disgusting place. I believe that my father's death was an accident and I do not believe that anyone plotted to kill him. Clarence Wills had become his own executioner and cut his own throat to spite his father. It's as tragic and simple as that.

At my dad's funeral, I had no idea how badly mangled his body was until three funeral directors carefully positioned their bodies in front of the head of his casket before they opened it. I watched their every move as they slowly opened it and all six hands gracefully yet carefully did something to his head. I didn't know then what I know now. They were putting his head back on his neck and adjusting the shiny stainless steel pins that they used to put it in place. And when they stepped away, and I got a full view from my seat, I almost fainted at the ghastly sight.

My beautiful mocha-colored daddy was completely and utterly unrecognizable. He was autopsied and his hairline was at the top of his skull, his eyes were sewn shut, his nose was crooked, his color was two shades blacker and I saw stitches all over his head. And that's just what I saw from the front seat of the church, about ten feet away. It was a grisly sight and I initially wondered why anyone permitted his body to be viewed, because I didn't believe it was him at first. I kept inching up from my seat to get a good look because I thought they brought the wrong body in. I guess I had become a distraction because my grandfather tapped me on the shoulder and shook his head for me to stop.

As people started to work their way around to see my daddy for the last time, I intently watched every person who walked by us. Every single person looked at the five of us children with such sadness in their eyes as they handed my mother envelopes filled with cash. I remember there was one black guy in particular who stood in the long line to see my father in the casket three times; I wondered to myself how he knew my dad. He looked down each and every time and shook his head in disbelief, walked around the length of the church and stood on line again.

Unlike the caricature Hollywood likes to make of black funerals, there were no outbursts, shrieks, or loud crying. I guess everyone expected my Grandmother Opal to break down at the sight of her dead son; she did not. Only one person wept—my Grandfather Fred. At first I heard a steady sniffling, and then I was stunned to turnaround to find his head between his legs. It was an unbelievable sight to me because I had spent my entire life seeing my grandfather perfectly composed and in the pulpit. I had never seen him cry or even come anywhere close to being emotional ever; never ever. My Grandmother Opal just rubbed his arched back as he quietly drowned in his tears.

In hindsight, I understand perfectly why my grandfather cried; he knew that he was partly responsible for my father's present state. He had disappointed my father one too many times as a child and he knew full well that his son worshiped the ground he walked on yet he repeated his reckless behavior. It was a vicious cycle that my grandfather set in motion that was so powerful and magnetic, that my father, despite his intelligence and accomplishments, was destined—and worse—determined to repeat. One might argue that it's nobody's fault but my father's—and there's truth to that, of course; however, there's no denying that my dad was hell-bent on retribution due to his father's hypocrisy through the years. My father was too passionate to let Fred off the hook and, yes, it was my father who paid the ultimate price on that stepchild of a city bridge. But my grandfather's hands were not clean. Had my grandfather considered the powerful influence he had over his sons, September 11, 1980, would have been just another day.

After everyone left the church, it was just the immediate family left to say goodbye. My poor devastated grandmother—who had once mustered the strength to sing at her own mother's funeral—was so grief-stricken that her lips were tightly sealed. Van and Fred calmly walked with her to get one last look at the bright son and brother who had become the leader of the family while yet a teenager—he was the one who had come closest to fulfilling the family's dream. I heard my grandmother talking to my dad as if she were having a conversation with him. It was painful to watch because this time he couldn't respond to his mother, whom he loved dearly. It was difficult to discern exactly what she was saying, but it was a horrible sight to see my jovial, piano-playing grandma bid her beloved son farewell. When my grieving grandparents walked away, the funeral directors motioned for my mother and all of her children to step forward and view our daddy up close. As the oldest, I made a quick judgment call: in one swift motion with my head, I looked at my sisters and brothers and softly said, "We're not going up there." We sat quietly as my mother and her brother David walked slowly up to his casket to see my dad in the deepest of sleep one final time. I knew that the gruesome sight of our father's body would be stuck in our hearts and minds forever, and the view from ten feet back was bad enough.

All of my siblings obeyed me except one: Crystal. She was eight years old and felt badly that my mother stood there without her children and ran to her side. As Crystal bolted from her seat for the casket I said, "You'll be sorry."

The rest of us sat stone-faced as we watched our mother regrettably look at the end of what could have been—what should have been—a beautiful marriage that should have continued to this day.

There are no words to accurately explain what a horror show this was for me, from the moment I heard my grandfather report my dad's death on the phone until his flag-draped casket was saluted by a military honor guard at Calverton National Cemetery in Suffolk County, New York. I was two weeks shy of my fourteenth birthday. I had missed the first week of school and now I had to live the rest of my life as a fatherless child. What had I done to deserve this purgatory at such a young age? When I finally returned to school, all of my friends asked where I had been: "My father died," I had to explain about a hundred times, at least, to my fellow students and teachers. And every response was the same, "Ooh."

When I graduated from junior high school in June of 1981, there were more upheavals. Shortly after my dad died, some thugs broke into our apartment in Ocean Village and stole everything they could, including my mother's wedding ring and almost all of my father's stereo equipment. They even took a two-dollar bill that my uncle David gave me for good luck that I had taped to my bedroom wall. Soon after, my mother called a real estate agent and purchased a house in Hempstead, Long Island—a suburb of New York City. Almost simultaneously, my grandparents moved out of the big house that I had loved, to the new property on Astoria Boulevard. I was uprooted so much that my head was spinning. The old Light House Church was gone and I had to say goodbye to all of my friends from Ocean Village—with my father's dead body still fresh in my mind. It was too much change in a matter of a year.

Cheryl Wills

I hated Long Island at first. When I got on the yellow school bus to go to Uniondale High School, I didn't know anybody and ate in the cafeteria by myself on the first day—next to chatty groups of students who had all grown up together through junior high school. But I quickly made friends like Gabriella Phelps, Debra Porter, and Kim West. I was shocked a few months later to see some of my old friends from the Rockaways, like Eddie Torres and Kelda Savage, had left the beachfront hood and moved to the suburbs as well.

My mother, still a scorned woman, tried to go on with her life and date men but to no avail. I gave each of them holy hell—and my siblings helped run each and every one of them away. I felt it was my daughterly duty to protect my daddy's turf and memory, and no man was going to take his place. My mother tried to control us, but she was outnumbered and we were all too grief stricken to be ignored.

My grandfather became a picture-perfect husband, grandfather, and surrogate father to us all. He purchased a new van and took us everywhere in it—to church conventions in other states, to my grandmother's relatives in Ohio, and up and down the eastern seaboard, including Disney World in Orlando, Florida. He had built a new storefront church called Light House and he picked us up every Sunday and returned us to Long Island. After church we ate pizza or hamburgers and played games, and he gave all five of us an allowance of a few dollars each. He was such an upstanding man that even Van joined to church and played his guitar alongside his father and mother. It was a bittersweet though, because our father's absence was very noticeable. We sang in the church's chorus called The Little Faith Choir and enjoyed hearing our grandmother sing, and watching our grandfather preach and baptize people in a hole in the floor that he dug into a baptism pool.

His grandchildren never saw Fred drink, smoke, curse, or even lie. During Christmastime when he joined us in our new board games, he flatly refused to even pick up the dice—he was a new man in every way. We didn't understand why at the time, but now I understand. He wasn't going to be a hypocrite ever again. He still embraced the same extreme beliefs, but he didn't impose them on people anymore. After experiencing the ultimate letdown of our father's death, our grandfather never ever let us down; if he promised something he did it and we became happy kids again. I guess my dad died so his father could finally live up to his own creed. We lost a father, but gained a phenomenal grandfather in return.

After I graduated from Uniondale High School where I wrote in my yearbook that I wanted to be a journalist or a secretary (my back-up plan), I decided to attend nearby Nassau Community College because it would have been too traumatic to go away to college and leave my younger siblings just a few short years after my father's death. After graduation from the junior college, I transferred to Syracuse University where I majored in Broadcast Journalism at the famed S. I. Newhouse School for Public Communications. Every summer my grandfather packed his church van to the roof and hauled all of my stuff to my dorm in September and back home every May. And when I graduated inside the famous Carrier Dome in 1989, my grandfather was as proud as any man could be. Most people mistakenly thought he was my father—and in reality, he was. My father's spirit was enveloped inside him, body and soul, and he took care of his grandchildren as if he had fathered us himself. I could not have asked for a better grandfather.

I was devastated when he was diagnosed with lung cancer in 1997. My grandfather had a cough that wouldn't quit but he refused to see a doctor and believed Jesus would heal his body, just as he had always preached. But one day Grandpa Fred said to me, "I can't keep any food down—everything I put in my mouth tastes like cotton."

I had become frustrated with him because I begged him to see a doctor and he refused. I finally told him, "Well, Grandpa, if you can't eat, you will surely die. So if you still don't understand why you should see a doctor now, then Grandma will find you dead of starvation in the bed!"

For the first time in his life, he didn't have the strength to go downstairs and preach on Sunday mornings and he had become skin and bones. After pleading with him for hours one day, I finally convinced him to let me take him to Astoria General Hospital where an x-ray revealed a tumor had spread from his lungs to his throat and was literally choking him to death. It was inoperable. They wanted to admit him, but he refused. I helped him back to his bed, where I saw dozens of cough drops on his nightstand. Poor thing had been using the throat lozenges to relieve a deadly cancer—all in the name of religion. When we returned from the hospital, my grandfather sat down on the couch and said, "I guess we weren't meant to have nothin'."

I was stunned by his remark because I didn't know that my grandfather actually wanted anything more than what he had. Turns out, he never stopped dreaming after his inaugural bus ride to New York City where he hoped to find a field of dreams. I was also saddened by his statement because he had apparently concluded that his life had been a failure. "I guess we weren't meant to have nothin'"—his final testament still rings in my ears and breaks my heart. Over his nearly seventy-five years, he had gained little but lost much—the worst of which was his firstborn son. My grandpa really wanted to be a big-time preacher with a real church, but he never made it out of the storefront. I tried to bring as much sunshine into his life as I could—I organized a fiftieth wedding anniversary celebration for him. He and my grandmother were feted with their favorite music and church friends. My grandpa wore a white tuxedo with a top hat and was so happy that he didn't take it off—even in the church.

When I graduated from junior college at the Nassau Coliseum, he made sure that he sat in an empty section where I could see him and he could wave at me and I could wave back, which we did to each other about one dozen times. When I got married in 1994, he proudly walked me down the aisle in the place of my father—the first and last time he was ever given such an honor—and during the elegant reception he looked into the video camera and said, "This is the greatest day in our family! God bless you, Cheryl."

So, even after the tragedy of my father's death, we managed to have some good times together as a family. But in my grandfather's final analysis, I suppose it wasn't what he had expected. His poignant words revealed to me that he died a disappointed and unfulfilled man. I was very sorry that I didn't have the power to change it, because he deserved more. Sure, he had made mistakes, but who doesn't? Maybe he beat himself up over my dad's death and never got over it. He tried to educate and better himself by reading dictionaries, encyclopedias, and Bible concordances. He wrote his sermons on the back of utility company envelopes and other assorted bills. He constantly struggled to be a better man—the best way he knew how. Sometimes he failed miserably, but he never stopped reaching and, in my view, he succeeded.

When he died on March 17, 1997, I was devastated—even though, unlike my father's sudden death, I had plenty of warning. My Grandmother Opal was mortified by his passing and, despite her fervent prayers and anointing his head with oil, he drifted away in her arms on a hospital bed. Van's reaction was the most hurtful to witness; he tried to act like he wasn't hurt and, at one point during the planning of the funeral, Van remarked,

"Mother will be worse," indicating that the passing of his mother would be the ultimate blow. Ultimately, Van would never see his mother buried, because he died of cancer, too, in December of 2006—just a couple of weeks before Christmas. He had colon cancer surgery and flatly refused to get chemotherapy treatment as required, afterwards. He ignored calls from nurses, doctors, his wife, and even me. He didn't believe in faith healing like his parents, and used common sense, so I called him to ask why he ignored doctors' orders.

He said, "I don't care if I never step foot in a hospital again." And he didn't until it was too late. When a doctor told him point blank that he had weeks to live, Van was stunned and so was his wife Viola, who he married when he was about fifty years old.

Van had never been affectionate to us and didn't really embrace us as his dead brother's children, the way he should have. He was cool and distant and dropped the ball with us, too, but in some awkward way we understood his emotional dysfunction. By the time he died, he became one of the best gospel guitarists in the country and everyone who heard him was amazed by his musical prowess and interpretation. When he collapsed in a Connecticut hospital while signing in to get a useless chemotherapy treatment, he didn't know what hit him, either. Seconds after he hit the floor his last words were, "Where's my hat?" He had become extremely self-conscious about his loss of hair during chemo.

The last thing Van said to me was, "Thanks for taking care of Mother." And indeed, I will happily take care of her for the rest of her life. When I looked into Grandma Opal's eyes and told her that her only surviving child was dead, she frowned and stared into my eyes, and said nothing. My brother Cleavon was there along with a minister from the church, James Adams. We feared this would be the blow that finally caused her to lose her composure. But, ever the rock, she refused to give the cruel winds of fate satisfaction. Shocked and stunned once again, she intently listened to me explain how Van walked into the hospital and suffered a massive heart attack right in the hospital's reception area.

"They killed him," she said. "Those doctors, they killed him. I told him not to go back there."

I knew the drill; it was my grandmother's protective conspiracy theory again. She couldn't accept that her son refused to follow doctors' orders. My Uncle Van would be alive today had he gotten chemotherapy immediately after the surgery but, in the end, he proved he was as stubborn as his father and brother.

Once again, I was so sad for my dear grandmother. This day she never saw coming—because she couldn't imagine burying her baby boy. Van had remained with her through all of the storms of life—even when his father and his brother acted like fools. He was always the steady one who stayed by her side—even when they became homeless for a while. Van was the most careful of all four of them and learned from most of their mistakes. He was not ambitious but he was consistent, and my grandmother adored the way he played the guitar, although she didn't have the strength to dance to his music anymore. His death marked the end of the beautiful music that the Wills family created. My brother Cleavon and I were deeply saddened that we would never hear the sounds of our grandfather and our father through Van's fingertips ever again. It was surreal. One of the last times we heard him play was at a gospel program he organized in Harlem a couple of years before his death. He sang a solo, which was a signature song of my grandmother's called "This Old Soul of Mine." When Van reached the lyrics, *"by and by, when the morning comes,"* I almost fell over as Van got choked up and tears spilled from his eyes. Van did not cry, ever. I could almost see my father and grandfather flash across his mind, as he became so immobilized with grief in front of the microphone that he couldn't even pluck a string on his guitar. Stunned by his own burst of emotion, he shook his head and wisecracked to the audience, "It's hard to sing and cry at the same time."

The audience roared with a mellow laughter and the drummer couldn't take his eyes off the steely guitarist that had finally melted his icy demeanor. My brother Cleavon and I looked at each other in complete shock and mouthed, "OMG—Van is crying?!"

Poor Van had been through an awful lot, yet he always wore a cool veil over his face—until that moment. As he sang the songs he once sang with my dad and his mother, he just couldn't pretend that he didn't miss Clarence anymore and, judging from his brief flash of emotion, he apparently missed him more than any of us could possibly imagine. I was thankful to have captured the moment on videotape.

After we buried Van at Calverton National Cemetery in Long Island, just yards away from his brother, we were afraid to leave my grandmother home alone, but we had no choice. Her sister Laura stayed with her for a few weeks through the holidays, but after that, Opal was the last one standing—and had to go it alone. Even in her mid-eighties, my grandmother still refuses medical care, though cataracts are slowly robbing her of her sight. At this writing, I am trying to persuade her to have cataract surgery so she can see clearly. But she, like her husband Fred, flatly refuses. Every Sunday she still goes downstairs to the Light House Church, which burns with memories for her, and takes her seat at the piano and belts out gospel songs in the same manner she did sixty years ago when she joined the little Christian church in Indiana. I am too big, of course, to sit next to her on her piano stool, but I still sit in the seat directly across from her, and I am amazed how she still remembers the words to all of her songs and tickles the ivories the very same way without ever going off key.

Opal's body is getting smaller, her strides are shorter and she has to hold on to something or somebody when she walks, but she's still sharp as a tack and remembers everything about her life with her two fine boys and her dashing husband. Even when I was a kid, I thought they had all lived such fascinating and sometimes tragic lives and, when I told my grandmother I was writing a book about "Grandpa, Daddy, and Van," she was very excited. I tried to warn her and said, "Grandma, I'm gonna tell the good and the bad, okay?"

She said, "Tell it; just get it right." And she helped me get it right, by recalling incidents that I had never even heard about like when soldiers broke my dad's guitar in the army because they were sick of him playing gospel music. I sat on the edge of her couch and hung on her every word— she remembered events as though they happened yesterday.

I was also thrilled to tell my grandmother about Sandy and Emma Wills—the field and house slaves who changed the destinies of their future grandchildren. I explained to her how I learned about Grandpa's great grandfather by logging onto a computer and searching a website called ancestry dot com. When I showed her some of the documents detailing Sandy and Emma's transition from slavery to freedom, she was amazed. "Can you imagine how brave Sandy was, Grandma, to walk in the shadow of death from his plantation to join the military to fight for his freedom?" I asked my grandmother.

Her small eyes opened wide as she said, "Isn't that something? I'm not surprised, your father, grandfather, and uncle were great—I knew they had to come from great people."

I nodded my head in agreement and gazed at my elderly grandmother with empathy for what she had experienced. Fred, Clarence, and Van were her everything, and one by one she said goodbye to them, too soon—she also buried two other babies—one pretty little caramel-colored baby girl who died shortly after childbirth that Opal hastily named "Freddie Opal" as her desperate breaths quickly stopped shortly after entering the world. She also buried her son Harry James, who died at about eight months of age due to sudden illness. Opal remembers that my father took his baby brother's death especially hard—considering he was a toddler himself. Opal tried her best to pray her way through all of this misery, and it worked—it kept her from losing her mind and it stabilized her battered soul.

My grandma says she's very proud that I'm a television newscaster—she was one of the first that I shared my dreams with, and she was also my first interview. As a kid I always asked about her childhood in Haywood County, Tennessee, and wrote down stories like the one where she fell off the rocking chair into a roaring fireplace when she was about nine years old and marveled at the scars on her hands that bore witness to the harrowing accident. She went through the fire, too, and remarkably she can still sing and play the piano as if her life had been one beautiful song. And indeed it was—a song of strength in the face of storms and, Mother Wills, as the church folks now call her, still stands the test.

So does my mother. Ruth raised five children singlehandedly and never dropped the ball with us. She proved to have dignity in the face of humiliation and fortitude in the wake of chaos. Other mothers have walked away from their children for much less. The five of us were a handful, to be sure, but my mom never once abandoned us, berated us, or stopped believing in our futures. Ruth was there for every track meet, every graduation, every school play, and every parent-teacher's conference. After my dad's funeral, all five of us slept in her queen-sized bed for weeks—we were like little weaning puppies scarred by the horrifying experience we had just witnessed but didn't yet fully comprehend. She never kicked us out of her bed as we all jockeyed for the best position—praying that our mommy never died the way our daddy did—she was all we had left. Ruth was a force of nature during this time and did her very best to be a mother and a father to us. She was, and still is, our modern-day Emma.

My autistic brother, Big Boy, is in his early forties and is doing just fine. His disability shielded him from the agony of our father's death. My mother says about eight years after our dad died, he looked at my mother and said, "Daddy's dead and he's never coming back, huh?"

We were shocked to learn that he may have considered our father's passing a temporary condition. It was certainly the first funeral that any of us had been to—and it turns out nobody ever fully explained the permanence of death to Big Boy.

Undeterred, my brother graduated from Uniondale High School in 1989 with a special diploma issued by the Committee of Special Education and approved by the Board of Education. My mother demanded that all five of her children graduate—including Big Boy. Now, he wants to be a professional cartoonist some day and has thousands of original characters that he's created like SuperStretch and Lardball. Every time one of us has a birthday, he draws us a custom-made birthday card with one his special characters on a piece of plain white paper that he folds in half. He and my mom live together in a house on Long Island, just a couple of miles away from me and the rest of my siblings in the New York City suburb.

While Big Boy is still not entirely sociable, he does enjoy music and special programs offered through the county. But he stunned us all when he became then-Senator Barack Obama's biggest fan. We were all shocked because we thought he knew nothing about politics, but somehow this charismatic politician from Chicago awakened something in my forty-year-old autistic brother. During the campaign, Big Boy drew Obama campaign posters and posted them all over town. I kept one he designed where one of his cartoon characters, colored green and blue, says with outstretched arms, "He's my kind of President!!!" The smaller character replies, "The most greatest ever!! And at the bottom of his self-made poster, he wrote, "He's one man in a million without a doubt. Please vote for it!!" I wanted to correct his grammar to "Please vote for him," but he had already plastered them around town and I figured, it was perfect just the way it was because it came from his heart. And this was the first time anyone of us had seen Big Boy really come fully alive and take interest in something outside of his private world.

It was a needle-on-the-record moment. Startled by my brother's sudden interest, I purchased every Obama T-shirt, sweatshirt, hat, and button I could find for his extra-large size. Big Boy wore these every day for the entire campaign and still does. Some people with autism tend to be repetitive in their actions, so my brother doesn't fully realize that

215

the campaigning has come to an end, but I'm okay with that, too. This incredible enthusiasm comes from a kid who spent his entire life watching cartoons, eating Skippy peanut sandwiches and little else. People called him "Cheryl's retarded brother," but oh, did we get the last laugh. Big Boy is doing A-OK, even better than most of those insensitive clods that disparaged my baby brother and made all of us cry. When I had the honor of attending President Obama's inauguration, I was seated on the lawn of the United States capitol, in the VIP orange section, and thought of my little brother, Big Boy. I called him every step of the way and said, "Big Boy, I'm here—I'm freezing to death—but I'm here—I'm watching him being sworn in!" and my brother replied in his very unique speaking voice, "Whoo hoo! Way to go, Sis!"

On top of that, Big Boy proved to be remarkably similar to my father, his namesake, by framing every award and citation he has ever received from the many special education programs that he has attended over the years. He has dozens of bowling trophies on a shelf and plaques on his wall. He has certificates of achievement for his artistry from the county executives in Long Island. And his biggest award is when he entered a contest and won first prize for creating the winning logo for VESID—the Vocational and Educational Services for Individuals with Disabilities. During the awards ceremony, he was congratulated by government officials, including the First Lady of New York State at the time, Matilda Cuomo.

As I stood in my brother's bedroom, where he makes his bed and keeps all of his books and papers in perfect order, I asked, "Big Boy, do you remember Daddy? Do you have a picture of Daddy?"

He opened a drawer and opened a small album that was in his nightstand and handed me a picture. With tears in my eyes, I saw a photo of my dad when he was at his finest, a church deacon with a Sunday school book in his hand, dressed to the nines in a tailored dark suit, holding his little namesake's hand—who could not have been more than two years old. "Of course, I remember Daddy, Sis," he said in his familiar tone.

I was so choked up that I had to sit down on his bed and weep. Who knew?!

My other siblings, Crystal, Celestal, and Cleavon all attended college and are working professionally. Fortunately, Crystal outgrew her epilepsy and no longer takes medication. We are all still very close and, if someone offends one of us, they had offended us all. Together we share each other's birthdays and all of the holidays, especially Christmas—where we try to replicate the fun we had as kids for our own children—who have never had the privilege to play Hot Peas and Butter and they lose vital human interaction while burying their faces in video games and other stupid technology that robs them of interpersonal relations. I let all of them know that, as the oldest, I expect all of them to be prepared to carry the torch of Sandy and Emma Wills and the grandfather they never knew who died on his motorcycle.

The Bible says, "By ye fruits, ye shall know them"—and we all reflect our late father in a variety of ways. My brother Cleavon and I are our dad's fiercest defenders—and usually turn every family gathering into a debate about my father's legacy. My sister Crystal has his athletic ability and coaches track and mentors young stars. And my sister Celestial is a teacher and is pursuing her master's degree and eventually wants to obtain her PhD, something my dad would have been extremely proud of and would have done himself—had he lived.

In the foyer of my home is a beautiful framed portrait of my father, right next to the front door, which visitors cannot help but notice when they walk out. I always have my prepared answer ready when they inevitably ask, "Who's the guy with the guitar?"

"That's my dad, Clarence. He was a fireman, a paratrooper, and a non-commissioned officer in the army, who was killed on his motorcycle when we were kids. He integrated Engine 1 in Manhattan right across from Madison Square Garden."

The usual response is a simple "Wow." They're also shocked when they learn that my husband John was born on September 4th—the same day that my daddy died. It's like my father's fingerprints are everywhere around me.

I love telling people about my Grandpa Fred, too. I am really impressed with how my grandpa made his own storefront church out of discarded items salvaged from a junkyard. He consecrated the place and polished it as though it were New York's most famous church, Saint Patrick's Cathedral. When I first started reporting on New York 1, I made a conscious decision to keep my maiden name: Wills. I'm certainly glad I did with the discovery of Sandy Wills. But back in the early 1990s, I kept the Wills surname because I wanted my grandpa to see his last name on television. I'd call him just minutes before I appeared on television and I'd say, "Turn on Channel One, Grandpa! I'm coming on—you'll see our name." After my two-minute segment was over, I always called back and said, "Did you see, Grandpa? Did you see?"

He always spoke to me as though I were eight years old and said, "That's just great! I saw you! I stay somebody messin' with Cheryl!" It's a country term and I wasn't raised in Haywood County, Tennessee, so I don't know exactly what "I stay" means in that context, but he said it to every one of his grandchildren until the day he died. We always took it to mean I love you—and I know he did love us to death. If I could see him now, I'd tell him, "See, Grandpa, you were wrong, we *were* meant to be something after all."

I've had some incredible assignments as a reporter and anchor at *New York 1 News*. When the events of September 11th, 2001, happened, I broke down with word of the deaths of hundreds of firefighters and police officers. I know my father, who would have probably been retired had he lived, would have rushed to the scene along with many of the other retirees, and done his best to pitch in. He was that kind of man, and he learned from the best. I will never forget how the fire department supported my family after my father's death. Some firemen came and took us to the circus at Madison Square Garden; other's just sat with my mother in our living room after handing her envelopes of cash. Whenever I see them in Midtown, I want to go up to them and say, "Hey, you'll never believe who my father is!" but I don't want to appear arrogant or stupid—so I just smile and wave at them with great enthusiasm.

I've interviewed a lot of famous people, such as Bill Cosby, Harry Belafonte, and Ruby Dee; and I've met presidents, senators, heads of state, and some of the most famous fashion designers in the country, like Betsey Johnson and Carmen Marc Valvo, who tell me they like my work on television. The coolest assignment I've ever had was when I rode the Intrepid on a rare journey that probably won't happen for another one hundred years—from a port on Staten Island—back to its base on Manhattan's West Side—where the former carrier is a popular museum and source of pride for veterans. I have also met and interviewed veterans from World War II and I hung on their every word as they shared incredible combat and honor. It was the trip of a lifetime as I watched New Yorkers lined along the shores of Manhattan's Hudson River salute the Intrepid as it slowly cruised by.

I have had my share of ups and downs but, all things considered, I am having the time of my life as a newscaster. I get to host swank events at places like the famed Apollo Theater in Harlem and the ritzy Plaza Hotel. I bring young students from the inner city to my newsroom and teach them about the business—most importantly exposing them to a world they often wrongly believe they don't belong in or deserve. I always make a point to tell them: "You are worthy, you are smart, and you can have this, and so much more."

I've traveled all over the world and I always buy an extra ticket and hotel room for my mom. As a family we have visited Hong Kong, London, and many other places in between. It is my honor to treat my mother like a queen—I will never forget how she didn't give up on her children when the going got tough. I'm far more proud of her than she could ever be of me.

When McDonald's honored me and a handful of my colleagues as a broadcasting legend at the Waldorf Astoria Hotel in February of 2010, in my speech I proudly thanked my mom, Ruth, for standing by her children when her firefighter husband was killed. The crowd interrupted me and applauded her. The look on her face was priceless. I also thanked my dad, who set the stage for my success—despite his tragic end. Yes, he is my hero and, yes, I forgive him for his discretions. I know he regrets hurting his family and we still miss his presence some thirty years later. His absence is a hole in our hearts that can never be filled and, no matter how many times I smile on television, deep inside I'm still the little girl who is crying in her tambourine because I can't hear my daddy's music anymore.

I have a few friends who despise their fathers and I'm always taken aback but I understand their pain. As they go on their tirades about how "rotten" their dads are, I usually respond with: I would trade everything I own, for one just moment with my dead father, and I'd happily start my entire life over from scratch. It always gives them pause—a few were even moved to make amends with their fathers. You never know how much you love a person, until they're locked away forever in a cold grave. Better to never forget and forgive—than to die a slow death of anger and resentment. You don't win a prize for successfully holding a grudge— everyone loses in the end.

One of my best friends from Syracuse University is Quentin Stith, a brilliant writer and activist, who categorically rejected his family's slave master's surname and changed his name to Agyei Tyehimba. His distinguished father also stumbled in the final years of his life and we often chat for hours on end about our respective father's troubles. I'm always moved when he explains how his father tearfully and sincerely apologized to him in the final months of his life for dropping the ball as a dad. I always explain to my dear friend how blessed he is that he had those precious moments with his father—painful and emotional as it was. My dad, Clarence, was snatched from me like a thief in the night and I never had such an opportunity. The last thing my father said to me was a lie— he claimed he had to work and left me waiting for him, when he actually preferred to be with his friends rather than his children. The last time I heard my father's precious voice I slammed the phone down and wished him dead. What a way for a father and daughter to say their final goodbyes, huh?

I know so deeply in my heart that my father's spirit is remorseful and sorry for his last words and actions. How I wish I had a moment to hear my father apologize; not until I wrote about his life some thirty years after his death did I realize his actions were not personal against me and my siblings. He just lost his way, that's all. It was the end of his world—but it was not the end of ours. We have the opportunity to go on living and knowing that our daddy loved us, no matter what.

If I've learned anything in my forty-plus years—it's that great people sometimes make great mistakes. What I'm most proud about my daddy is that he wasn't afraid to live and he damn sure wasn't afraid to die. He faced the fires of life and took pictures every step along the way as if to say, "Don't forget me."

Here's one thing I know for sure—my dad is not the first or last to throw his blessed life away because a parent let him down as a kid. It's a curious force of nature that clouds all reason and logic. Why do children want to hurt themselves as retribution for their parent's transgressions? American children, in particular, have a knack for quietly putting their parents on trial and then meting out punishment on themselves. It almost always ends ugly. I've seen it time and time again in my friends, family, celebrities I've never met, and even myself. The first and last time I smoked a cigarette was two weeks after my father died when one my thirteen-year-old friends stole her father's cigarettes. I vividly remember saying, "What the hell, I ain't got nothing to live for now!" And with that I puffed and passed the cancer stick to my gal pals.

I had no qualms revealing my father's full story but I was hesitant to air my grandpa's dirty laundry because he ran in circles with proud preachers—some of whom also did things in the dark with a wink and a nod to each other. I know they are probably horrified by this biography, and I don't care. They will undoubtedly think I should have allowed my grandfather to rest in peace and let sleeping dogs lie. They will say, "How dare you talk about a Holiness preacher like this—shame on you, Cheryl!"

Well, let me answer these self-righteous holier-than-thou critics directly—and there will be many, I am sure. All of these dark secrets and hypocrisies in the church cost me my daddy's life. Nobody alive today, with the sole exception of my Grandma Opal, loved and honored my father and grandfather more than I, and I regret that none of these "preachers" had the influence to stop and counsel my grandfather as he unwittingly trampled the innocent souls of his two sons. Being a minister of God is much more than a title or a calling, or an opportunity for you to "preach" to somebody. It's a hefty responsibility, and people, young and old alike, closely watch men of the cloth. I personally know dozens of boys and girls who grew up watching their spiritually anointed fathers—and when they realized their dads were not all they cracked up to be—it was a devastation that miserably colored their entire lives. Some became paralyzed with grief, depression, and disappointment; others emotionally shut down and never trusted anybody, like my Uncle Van—and more than a few—some famously—became reckless with their lives, like my dad, in a misguided effort to right their parent's wrongs and repeat their secret hypocrisy with open hypocrisy. And because many black church folks do not advocate therapy—these wounded children became adults whose inner wounds festered and ballooned into an emotional inferno. All of this crap is why I had to stare at my beloved daddy's mangled corpse many years too early on September 11, 1980.

About one week after my father's funeral, I went to my grandparent's house and saw what my father left behind. It was the last place he laid his head before he smashed face first into the beam on the Williamsburg Bridge. Although he had moved most of his belongings back to our home in the Rockaways, I was deeply moved to witness the last things he touched. There were his many notebooks, textbooks, pens of different colors, and highlighters. A half cup of seven-day-old coffee was on his bed table next to cufflinks and blue fire shirts that needed to be laundered.

The only piece of stereo equipment left was a record player and one speaker. All of his other state-of-the-art Teac stereo equipment was at our home in Rockaway. On the record player was an old 45 rpm record by Motown pioneer, Smokey Robinson: "Sweet Harmony," which was a very personal song that Smokey wrote in 1973 as a farewell to his former singing group, The Miracles, Motown's first chart-topping group, which he formed in 1955 with buddies from his high school in Detroit. Smokey's decision to go solo was obviously a tough decision for the stunning green-eyed soul singer who had made himself a household name with his longtime friends. "Sweet Harmony" was the last favorite song that my music-loving daddy would ever have.

Every morning as my dad readied for work in 1979 and 1980, he played the song over and over. As he studied for the fire lieutenant's exam, which legend has that he passed posthumously, he looped it on his reel to reel so he wouldn't have to keep getting up and changing the needle back to the beginning of the record.

Two days before my fourteenth birthday during that unforgettable September of 1980, I put the needle on the record and I was instantly struck by the beauty of the song and how it reflected my dad's miracle of life.

It starts with a rare spoken word from Smokey, which could easily be re-interpreted as a cryptic message from my dad to me and my family and his many friends and colleagues that he left behind. With the sounds of a single guitar playing behind him, Smokey says:

> "This song is dedicated to some people with whom I had the pleasure of spending over half the years I've lived till now when we've come to our fork in the road. And though our feet may travel a different path from now on, I want them to know how I feel about them and that I wish them well."

Smokey's world-famous falsetto then croons, "*Sweet Harmony, go on and blow on—stay in perfect tune...with your own familiar song, make the world aware, that you're still going strong, spread your joy around the world.*"

The next stanza of the poem is especially touching: *"I believe in miracles, if you can dream it can be done. Though a task is made for two, it can be done well by one. Spread your joy around the world."*

My dad believed in miracles and one by one he made miracles happen. But every miracle has a dark side and that's the part of life's song that my daddy sang a little off key. But with broken wings, he managed to spread joy around the world. Whether he was jumping out of airplanes or leading a hastily formed band in France, my beautiful daddy's sweet harmony sprung from his sonorous tenor voice and reverberated through his fingers as he made sweet-sounding music on his favorite guitar.

Pardon the simplistic analogy but, in each of our lives, it appears as though we are all repeatedly presented with two buttons of opportunity where we can either punch a ticket to "Play" or "Pass." The most joyful and daring among us hit Play most of the time, and the most cautious and fearful hit Pass. I'm not suggesting that one is better than the other, but it seems to me, reflecting upon my father and even Sandy's life, the more you hit Play, the more you learn, and the more you hit Pass, you sometimes miss a critical learning opportunity. Every time Clarence Wills came to that proverbial fork in the road—he hit Play. U.S. Military—Play! New York City Fire Department: Play! College: Play! His younger brother Van often passed.

One might argue that that's why my dad lived only to age thirty-eight and my uncle lived to be almost twice his age. But what's age but a number if you haven't fully lived? Even Sandy, downtrodden as society forced him to be, hit "Play" when presented with the historic opportunity to fight for his freedom, and no one on earth at that time was more indoctrinated to be fearful than an African slave in the United States of America in 1863. His actions set a hurricane of grace in motion for all of his future descendants. My dad, caught up in that fanciful whirlwind, ran, jumped, sang, danced, and sped his way through life for all of his precious thirty-eight years. Had he lived, I guess he would have been swimming with great white sharks by now. He never stopped reaching for the gold and he was a student of life until he drew his last breath.

When my Uncle Van was dying of cancer in 2006, I spoke to him one afternoon for about four hours about my dad's life and he told me things that neither I, nor anyone else in the family, knew about him, all of which are contained in this book. It was easily the longest we had ever spoken to each other by phone. Most of our conversations lasted less than five minutes because he wasn't much of a talker. At the end of our discussion, Van summed up my dad's life with a tinge of regret by referring to his brother as a "shooting star." But, aren't the shooting stars the ones we all remember the most?

My beloved father, who I am confident I will see again when I make my eternal transition, had many highs and a few crushing lows, but I will always revere him for his courage and his long joyride of a life. Clarence Douglas Wills wasn't afraid to live, and he wasn't afraid to make mistakes and stumble and fall flat on his face. Paratrooper to the bitter end, he always jumped and said, "Follow me."

He died free, just like his Great-great grandfather Sandy would have wanted.

Acknowledgments

In Loving Memory

Fred Wills (1922–97), Clarence Wills (1942–80), and Van Wills
(1945–2006)
All three of you were such colorful, talented, and courageous men who
played your guitars in a way that will forever ring in my head. Should I
ever get the opportunity to dance into heaven—I hope the three of you will
be playing my song.

My maternal grandparents, Hardy and Sallie Ford
I miss you so much and will always remember your strength, decency,
and dignity.

Special Thanks...

To my mom, Ruth: How do I thank the woman who singlehandedly
kept the ship afloat after the captain died? Always a steady hand, you kept
the family's vision alive, even when dark clouds hovered above us. I love
you, Mommy, and all that I have is because of you.

To my grandma, Opal: Thank you for being the best grandmother
in the world! A Bible-toting, piano-playing, soulful-singing, strong-armed
Tennessee gal who takes no prisoners when it comes to the truth. I love you
with all of my heart.

To my husband John: Thanks for putting up with my drama (!) while I
wracked my brains trying to write this book and waking up in the middle of
the night in a cold sweat with bursts of inspiration. Love you much.

To my only son, Johnny-boy, I'm counting on you, kiddo! I'm passing the baton to you next—get ready and stay ready. You're my favorite son of all time.

Very special thanks to my siblings: Big Boy—you are the best cartoonist in the world, brother dear. I hope you're ready for Prime Time because it's coming! Crystal-Ball—what would I ever do without you? Celestial—what would I ever do without you, too? LOL. Cleavon, my fellow defender of our father's legacy, we finally done did it, huh!

To the next generation of Wills', my niece Tina-Baby, Maggie, and Eli the Spy: as you grow older, this book should hold great meaning for you. I regret that you never met your Grandfather Clarence. You would have loved him.

To my classy mother-in-law, Mary: thank you for being such an independent and strong-willed woman. I admire you in every way and thank you for your unyielding support. And my brother-in-law Briven Jackson, you are a joy to our family.

To Uncle Clinton and Aunt Annie, Aunt Elaine, Aunt LaPearl, Aunt Laura (special thanks for your wonderful pictures), Aunt MaryRuth, Uncle Squire, Uncle Harry, Aunt Doll, Aunt Polly, Aunt Anna Louise, Aunt Viola, Aunt Mazie, and my zillions of cousins: Christopher, Diane, Tiger, Leisha, Lisa, Lawrence, George, Kimberly, Ronald, Alby, Javonna, Tracey, Lauren, Brenda, Annette, Gloria, Bilal, Butch, Nanda, LaShawn, Gwen, Kathy, Willie Jr., Rafael, Ruthie, Daniel, Eric, Debra, Wesley, Karen, Tim, Priscilla, Marilyn, Carl, Valerie, Lanora, Felicia, Christopher, Harriet West Moore, and so many more cuzzos who are regrettably too numerous to mention—thank you for your support and love throughout the years.

To John Myers, Helen Johnson, Cheryl Thomas, and Minnie Myers—and all of your children, Valerie, Neicy, Vivian, Junior, Joycelyn and Jeannine, and your many grandchildren—thank you for being terrific in-laws.

To my editor, Marly. Thank you for making my manuscript really sing. You shared my vision and walked back in time with me word for word. Writing a biography is so dramatically different from writing the news and you helped me navigate my way through these choppy literary waters. I really appreciate your enthusiasm and creativity! You were heaven sent!

To my colleagues at *New York 1 News*, particularly vice president and general manager, Steve Paulus, who gave me the opportunity of a lifetime in 1992 and allowed me to sit at the anchor desk even when I had no idea what I was doing. Thanks for believing in me, Steve. I will never forget.

A debt of gratitude also goes out to NY1 news director, Bernadine Han. Thanks, Bernie, for everything, and keep poking holes in that glass ceiling in the news business.

A huge shout out to NY1 assistant news director, Dan Jacobson, who always "keeps it real" and is an excellent force of nature in the newsroom. It is an absolute honor and privilege to work with you.

Peter Landis, the managing editor par excellence: thank you for teaching me the mechanics of news writing. You are the best in the business.

To all of my hardworking colleagues at NY1 who have voiced their support as I wrote this book night and day: Lewis Dodley (my mentor), Robin Sanders, Vivian Lee, Eric Gonon, Ruschell Boone, Nikki Polite, Nikia Redhead, Frank DiLella, Jessica Prater, Kim Winston, Allison Cheng, Melissa Maguire, Alex Gonzalez, Hector Reyes, Stephanie Simon, Shazia Khan, Ty Milburn, Carlos Hernandez and Olumide Earth. Your words of encouragement energized me all along the way.

Walter Emanuel Robinson, my friend of more than thirty years: thank you for being my right hand, my eyes and ears, and my chief organizer. You are the best! Thanks also to Tahiesha Hunter, Tarika Joshua, and Melinda Jennings for helping Walter with this enormous undertaking.

Terrie Williams: Thank you doesn't begin to cut it. I don't know how to thank you, my mentor, for years and years of support and guidance. You are—as you say in your own book—"a woman on fire." I'm deeply honored to call you my friend.

Rev. Al Sharpton and Rachel Noerdlinger: thank you for your encouragement and support through this process. I am very grateful.

To the finest television writer in the business, Richard Huff, of the *New York Daily News*. I deeply thank you for everything. You are the man! Period.

Nayaba Arinde and Elinor Tatum of the **Amsterdam News**: thank you for writing such a thoughtful article about my book in your historic newspaper! I will always cherish it.

My friend the "Marvelous" Marva Allen of the legendary HueMan Bookstore in Harlem: you are a class act and I am very proud of your accomplishments in business and beyond. Thank you for your unyielding support and friendship.

Warrington Hudlin, the president of the Black Filmmaker Foundation (BFF), thank you for your support and words of wisdom during the development of this book. You are one of the greatest story-tellers of my generation and it's truly an honor to know you.

To my peeps who are my "sister friends" for life, no matter what: Simone (my oldest friend in the entire world) and Vanessa Courtlandt, Sheril Brown, Patricia and Pamela Davis, Gabriella Phelps, Kim West, Debra Porter, Doris Ramseur, Abbe Abboa-Offei, Jessica Fragoso, Molly Rokasy, Lisa Papada, Ruschell Boone, Debbie Modeste-Humes, Harriet Brown, Lorna Graham, Jean Woody, Karen McNeil, Sandi Holland, Billie Braithwaite, Dina Abrams, Donna Smith, Rene Brinkley, Tara Riley-Patrick, Chotsani Williams, Maureen Greene, Valerie Sims, Linda, Carol and Judy Lomax, Carole and Raquel Younger, Alvina Alston, Angela, Darianne and Tonya Hawkins, and Danielle Frierson.

DIE FREE

To the lovely young ladies and gentlemen I mentor: Shumaya Hassan, Taquana Stanford, Tenyse Williams, Darian Guzman, Elizabeth Koraca, Na'Tasha Simmons, Tatiana Antoine, Tamani Wooley, Elizabeth Saab, and Alicia Alford.

A major shout out to folks who have inspired and mentored me throughout my career: Delores Ledbetter, Bill McCreary, John Roland, Hazel Dukes, Dr. Marcella Maxwell, The Honorable Judge Tanya Kennedy, Denise Courtlandt, Pat Haynes, Jean Woody, Henry Chu, Dabney and Amelia Montgomery, Yvonne Singleton-Davis, Rev. Melvin E. Wilson, Jean Fuentes, Sheila Stainback, Wilma Tootle, Philip and Sandy Hawkins, Gerry and Teresa Luke, Cecelia Good, Michael Robinson, Mavis Brooks, Carole Younger, Jean Claude Baker, and especially Philip O'Brien—who opened doors for me in the news business. I will always be grateful for your guidance and advice.

To all of my fellow thespians of The Inner Circle of City Hall Journalists including The fabulous Shelly Strickler, Larry Sutton, Mark Lieberman, Jane Tillman Irving, and the inimitable Jim Harney.

Much love goes to the esteemed members of the United African Congress, especially President Sidique Wai and Chairman Dr. Mohammed Nurhussein. Thank you for your ongoing support and love.

My heart belongs to the staff and students at The Children's Storefront Independent School in Harlem, including Kathy Egmont, Michael Williams, Daniel Brewer, Caryn Campbell, and the outstanding board of trustees, led by Michael Stubbs and Chris LaSala, that keeps the school open year after year, and especially Gail Freeman, president of Freeman Philanthropic Services who gives her heart and soul to the school.

To my best buds from Syracuse University, Agyei Tyehimba and Sam "the man" Reynolds, I love you both. You are my brothers for life.

Rockaway Beach is like the blood in my veins—and O.V. is in the house always: Eddie Torres, "Louie Louie" Troche, Kenny Davis, Gregg, Vicki and Steve Bassett, Tina and Flo, Beatrice and Michael, Lonnie, Robbie and Sharon Riles, Robert, Shawn, Carlene, and Gweek Gweek

Turpin, Angela, Darianne, Tony, and Tanya Hawkins, Yvette, Stephanie and Crystal Martin, Wendi Lucas, Puddin Bilbo, Kenny Haynes, Tyrone "Thumper" Forte, Vance Courtlandt, Gilbert Boyd, David Houston, Marcia Torres, and Martin Owens. What I would give to play just one more game of Hot Peas and Butter! I'm hiding the belt y'all!

I'm also grateful to Lou Szucs, Craig Rice, and all the folks at Ancestry. com. Were it not for this website, I would have never discovered Sandy and Emma Wills. Thanks also go to Chaddra Moore from the Tennessee State Library and Archives, Director Frank Martin and Martin Pratt: Thanks for spreading the word. Rashida Hodge and Derrick Adkins—you will always be part of our family and I appreciate your endless support. Danette Wills, you are a phenomenal woman—I wish we were related. Joe and Serita Davis, Blaine Robinson, Dr. Brenda Greene, Whitney Kyles, Tom Joyner, Barbara Boone, Philip Cooke, Derek Gibbs, Rev. Benjamin Freeman, Mark Noble, Tuesday Brooks, Chris Humes, and especially Max Robinson of the Harlem Book Fair—Thank you for everything.

My personal photographer, Alonzo Boldin, and my webmaster extraordinaire, Christopher DiLella, you guys rock!

Carmen Marc Valvo and Frank Pulice: you bring all the bells and whistles to New York's Fashion Week and I hold you both in the highest regard. Thank you for vthe honor of wearing your couture dresses for the *Die Free* photo shoot! It was a dream come true!

My colleagues of the New York Press Club and The National Association of Black Journalists: Keep fighting to protect the rights of the free press!

The Light House Church Family: Thank you for being there for my grandmother. Many thanks to Elder James Adams and wife Jackie, Deacon Lomax, Deacon Middleton, Deacon Green, Deacon Lyttle, Sis. Lomax, Sis. Brown, Sis. Long, Mother Gilmore, Sis. Jackson, Sis. McCleese, Bro. Luther Allen, Sis. Brenda, and everyone who has visited Light House Church through the last forty-plus years.

And finally—the cover shoot shout out:

Hair: Sabrina of Salon Innovations Queens, New York; Makeup: Tiffany Stout and Noelle Hyman; Dress: Carmen Marc Valvo; and cover photo by the phenomenally talented photographer: Tony Gale. And I'd like to thank my daddy for the use of his original fire hat and boots. Now that's what I call a prop! :D

Resources

Websites and tips that can help you trace your family legacy:

www.ancestry.com – by far the world's largest family history resource with more than four billion records.

www.africanancestry.com – helps people of African descent discover their roots using DNA.

www.onegreatfamily.com – bills itself as the world's largest online family tree and uses the latest technology to find ancestors.

www.dnatribes.com – tests your autosomal DNA inherited from both maternal and paternal ancestors and compares it to the largest global database of more than 1,000 ethnic populations and 39 world regions.

www.myheritage.com – uses free genealogy software to create and organize your family tree.

www.archives.com – boasts more than one billion records.

www.apgen.org – Association of Professional Genealogists. If you have money to spare, you can hire a genealogist to do the legwork for you.

TIPS

✓ Talk to your family members. Parents, grandparents, aunts, uncles, and cousins are your starting point. Ask everyone how far back they can go in their family tree. Even rumors can be useful.

✓ If you have a relative that served in the military, you can order their records from the government. (Be forewarned: it may cost you, depending on your relationship). The military keeps detailed records of all soldiers who served in the United States Armed Forces.

✓ Collect family records, including marriage and death certificates, diplomas, photographs, Bibles, and even postcards. Preserve the writings of your grandparents and parents.

✓ Search and focus on one surname at a time. Doing too many surnames can get confusing and lead to frustration. Pick the family that was the most stable and lived in the same place for a long time. I chose the Wills family because they lived in Haywood County, Tennessee, for more than a century, and were easy to trace with census records.

✓ Visit the community where your family lived. Check the local cemeteries and libraries for further information about local newspapers and archives.

✓ If and when you believe you've found a historical figure in your family, hire a professional genealogist to confirm the discovery *before* you tell the world.